MW00812073

FACILITATOR'S MANUAL FOR

REBUILDING

SECOND EDITION

When Your Relationship Ends

BRUCE FISHER, Ed.D.

WITH JERE BIERHAUS

Copyright © 1984, 1994, 2004
by Estate of Bruce Fisher
Fifth Printing, January 2012

All rights reserved under International and Pan-American Copyrights Conventions. No part of this book may be reproduced, stored in a retrieval system, or transmitted in any form or by any means, electronic, mechanical, photocopying, recording or otherwise, without express written permission of the author or publisher, except for brief quotations in critical reviews.

Publisher's Note
This publication is designed to provide accurate and authoritative information in regard to the subject matter covered. It is sold with the understanding that the publisher is not engaged in rendering psychological, medical, or other professional services. If expert assistance or counseling is needed, the services of a competent professional should be sought.

Acknowledgements:
Much of the material and content of this Facilitator's Manual was provided by Jere Bierhaus, who began teaching the Ten-Week Rebuilding Seminar in 1991. Special contributions from Jere are the Lesson Plans for each of the ten sessions. We acknowledge him for sharing this valuable information which he has found to be helpful for participants taking this educational seminar.

Acknowledgement is also given to Robert Stewart for creating and developing the "Rebuilding for Kids Seminar" which is explained more fully in Appendix A of this manual.

Printed in the United States of America on acid-free paper.

Published by:
Hart-Fisher Publishing Company/Hart Light Center
6461 Baseline Road
Boulder, Colorado 80303

Distributed by:
Impact ✿ Publishers®
POST OFFICE BOX 6016
ATASCADERO, CALIFORNIA 93423-6016
www.impactpublishers.com

Contents

Note to the Reader

During Bruce's last months, before cancer stole him from us in the spring of 1998, he and I often discussed the future of his books, and the changes and updates he wanted for them. He remained committed to the nineteen-step "rebuilding blocks" model, and wanted changes only when they were warranted by the evidence. And for Bruce, *evidence* came directly from the thousands of clients who participated in the divorce seminars he taught — and trained others to teach — for a quarter century. I tried very hard to make the third edition of Bruce's *Rebuilding: When Your Relationship Ends* the book he wanted it to be. As it turned out, the changes from the second edition were often subtle, but I can assure you they come straight out of the real world of women and men who've put their lives back together after divorce.

This edition of the *Facilitator's Manual for Rebuilding* has been revised to reflect the third edition of *Rebuilding*. Minor edits have also been made to update the text. However, Bruce's original style and substance have been retained. As a result, this *Manual* sounds more like the work of a caring counselor than that of a professional writer.

And so it is.

— Robert E. Alberti, Ph.D.
Impact Publishers, Inc.

Preface
About the Educational Model
— Bruce Fisher, Ed.D.

There is a new paradigm of personal growth becoming more prevalent in our society today. It is part of the expanding consciousness that is taking place. People are wanting information, guidance, and support so they can make loving choices about how to live their lives. This means having healthy relationships, being better parents, having more meaning in their lives and taking responsibility for the life they are creating. This Rebuilding Seminar is part of this movement.

I have had feedback of various kinds about the educational model. It has been labeled pop psychology. It has been insinuated that it is a superficial method of intervention. It has been misunderstood by many professionals because it does not fit into the ethical guidelines defined by traditional theorists. It has been criticized because it is not easy to define what is education and what is therapy. It has created fear among some because it appears to be more effective and less expensive than traditional therapy. Professional organizations such as the American Association of Marriage and Family Therapists do not have ethical guidelines for educational models. There is no legal case law concerning the educational model in the legal profession.

I will share some of the antecedents of the Educational Model and outline its strengths in order to help the model become more widely known and accepted. I will share some of the antecedents of it and outline the strengths of the model in order to help the concept become more widely known and accepted.

Let me use an analogy to make my point. Here in Boulder, Colorado we have a facility that is used in the summer for concerts, programs and entertainment. It is called the Chautauqua Auditorium. It was built around 1898. A book titled *The Grand Assembly* explains the history of the Chautauqua movement which began in 1830 with the organization of Lyceums. These were organizations named for ancient Greek self-education groups. Eventually the movement consisted largely of meetings with famous teachers and speakers presiding.

The word Chautauqua comes from the lake in the state of New York where the movement began. The Chautauqua movement had roots which drew deeply from America's underlying character. People all over America demonstrated their need to express themselves through self-improvement.

Unfortunately, the movement suddenly died out in 1928 with the coming of radio and the automobile.

Socrates stated the famous maxim, "Know Thyself." Eric Fromm's writings emphasize the need for us to do our personal work in order to build a better relationship with oneself. I believe that a healthy relationship with oneself provides a seedbed from which healthy relationships with others can grow. World peace begins with finding peace within ourselves. The Rebuilding Educational Model is based upon beliefs such as these. We need to build and create a healthy relationship with ourselves before we can have healthy relationships with others.

What are some of the special and unique aspects of the educational model? Here are some cogent ways of defining this new paradigm.

- There is an underlying philosophical belief in education that we are capable of taking charge of our lives. With information, guidance, and support, we can learn to make loving choices in our lives. We can become responsible for the life we are creating.

- There is a textbook with reading assignments and concepts to be learned.

- There are homework assignments designed to help integrate and internalize the concepts learned in the reading assignments.

- There are class presentations and group discussions that help participants to understand the concepts relevant to developing life skills.

- Many of the behavior changes that take place in this seminar are outside of the class setting. The homework provides specific methods to learn the chosen behavior.

- The seminar meets for three hours, one night a week for ten weeks making a total of thirty contact hours. The length of the program is specific and agreed upon by the participant before enrolling.

- There are specific behavioral objectives or concepts to be learned each week. The class is structured with specific topics to be covered.

- There are no third party payments from insurance companies or an accompanying psychological diagnosis.

- There is no encouragement to self-disclose or to share anything of a personal nature. The emphasis is upon learning skills and applying them to daily life.

- Continuing college credit has been granted for this seminar in the past. It is possible to apply for and receive credit if people are interested and will take the responsibility to do it.

- The facilitator does not always have graduate degrees. What is important is to be a good group leader. The leader needs to implement and set up the class and then allow the participants and the group process to take over. The leader role emphasizes teaching and leading the group discussions. One does not necessarily need to be a therapist in order to teach people life skills. Therapists are for helping people with emotional, mental, and psychological problems.

- By comparison, participation in Alcoholics Anonymous and other self-help groups is more like therapy than attending this education model.

- Participants of this educational model are encouraged to write and keep a journal outside of class.

- In our Relationships Seminar participants learn communication skills. The facilitator is not aware of the content of these communication exercises. We teach the skills and the participants use the skills to make and create a better life for themselves.

- This model has been offered as a Community College class.

Another movement taking place in our society today is the emphasis upon volunteerism. People are volunteering to learn new job and career skills. These people are often volunteering in an area they find more interesting than their current career. Many are wanting to do something to help make the world a better place. Being a volunteer brings a new and fresh dimension to their lives.

This educational model provides an experience in volunteering that is healing, growing, expanding, fulfilling and satisfying. People are spending up to ten hours a week just to have the experience. There are always enough people to volunteer without pay and we often have a waiting list of interested people. Volunteerism and educational models go together hand in glove.

The educational model provides a much needed service. It is a partial answer to the health care crisis facing our society today. It is part of the movement whereby people are learning to take charge of their lives instead of following the dictates of an authority figure. Education is better than ignorance. Love is better than fear. The Truth can set you free.

It is my goal and purpose to expand the awareness and use of the educational model. My vision includes the development of specific ethical guidelines by State Licensing Agencies and Professional Organizations. It includes the development of case law in the legal system to more clearly define the educational model. It includes having the model taught in Graduate Schools so that future graduates and teachers are familiar with how to offer educational seminars. It includes having research, such as the Research Data in this Manual, which will indicate the value and benefits of the educational model. It includes proving the financial cost of the educational model to be much less than for more traditional intervention programs. It includes showing that "people helping people" with the Volunteer Helper Program can be a way for people to become more self-actualized and empowered. It includes providing ways for families to become stronger through education in order to deal with the tremendous challenges facing them today. It includes giving people the information they are desperately seeking through self-help books, community college classes, and lectures all in a packaged program to make their search for knowledge on how to lead a responsible life full of personal satisfaction much easier to obtain.

– Bruce Fisher
Boulder, Colorado
Winter 1994

How To Use this Facilitator's Manual

This Manual is designed to be used with the *Rebuilding: When Your Relationship Ends* textbook, and the *Rebuilding Workbook* in the "Fisher Rebuilding Ten-Week Educational Seminar." This Manual includes everything that is in the *Rebuilding Workbook* plus other material such as the How To Facilitate sections and the Fisher Divorce Adjustment Scale Scoring and Research Data. It is written to answer any question you might have in facilitating the Seminar.

The Ten Selected Chapters in *Rebuilding*

We have identified what we believe to be the most important and difficult to understand chapters in the *Rebuilding* Textbook to study during the ten weeks of the Rebuilding Seminar. The lesson plans suggest reading the rest of the chapters in *Rebuilding* if participants have time. Some of your participants will want to read the complete book before the Seminar and then spend extra time each week reading the chapter that will be emphasized in the next session of the Seminar. You may find the "How Are You Doing?" checklist at the end of each chapter good discussion questions. We suggest after the Ten Week Seminar is completed that participants go back and complete any homework they were not able to do during the Seminar. They may find it helpful to do some of the homework exercises again.

Copying Pages from This Book

This Facilitator's Manual is copyrighted but you may need to copy some of the pages from this book so they can be completed and turned in. I would like to make a suggestion. Some of you may want to print up forms that make carbonless copies leaving a completed copy for both the participant and the facilitator of the Personal Information Sheet, the Participants Registration Agreement, and the Volunteer Helpers Agreement Form. Other sheets such as the Final Course Evaluation Sheet, the Fisher Divorce Adjustment Scale Answer Sheet, and the Class Attendance Form may need to be photocopied.

We hereby give you permission to copy page 106 ("diploma") and those pages which include the following copyright notice: "Reprinted with permission from *Facilitator's Manual for Rebuilding When Your Relationship Ends*, by Bruce Fisher and Jere Bierhaus."

Volunteer Helpers

We have included a section in this Workbook on the Volunteer Helper Program. Volunteer helpers are graduates of the Ten-Week Seminar who are invited to come back and be active listeners and helpers to the present class participants. Using the volunteer helpers will make the Seminar experience more powerful and meaningful for the participants. I strongly urge you to implement the Volunteer Helper Program.

Widows and Widowers

Even though the majority of people reading Rebuilding and participating in the Rebuilding Seminar are ending a relationship through divorce, some of the participants may be widows or widowers. This Manual includes a modified version of the first Chapter in Rebuilding, and a modified version of the Fisher Divorce Adjustment Scale for widowed people. We hope these two additions will make the seminar more helpful for widowed people.

Quality Control of the Model

I have spent a great deal of time and energy thinking about how to maintain quality control of this educational model. We have been facilitating this model since 1974 and have learned a great deal about what works and what doesn't. I have decided to not do any licensing or franchising of the Model because I want to keep my life as simple as I can. I suggest in the Training Workshop that you teach the Model the first time as it was designed. As you continue to teach, you may find you have special strengths as a facilitator that you want to use, or you may find that your participants have special needs that could be met by changing certain procedures in the Model. You may choose to make some modifications. However, using the Workbook and this Manual will help maintain quality control of the Model and help you facilitate the Model in what we think is the most effective way to facilitate this Model.

We hope you will find this Facilitator's Manual helpful. You will find it fun and enjoyable to teach this Seminar. You will also be impressed, and maybe amazed, at the growth of the participants.

Lovingly,

Bruce

Session One
The Rebuilding Blocks

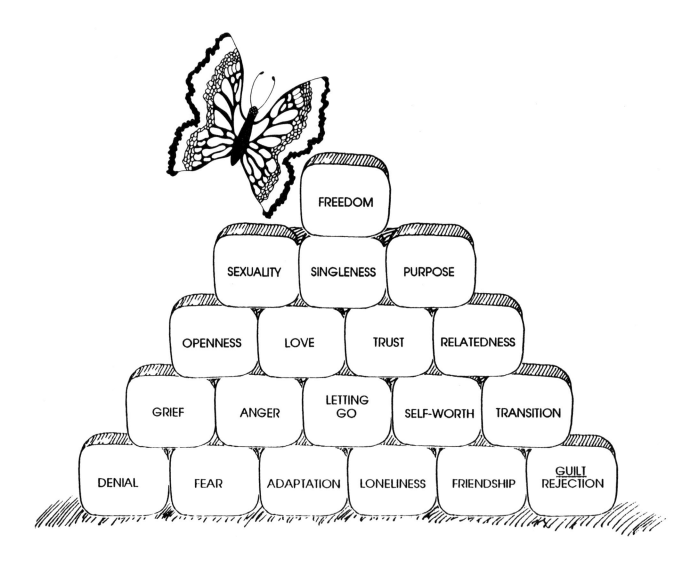

You are probably experiencing the painful feelings that come when a love relationship ends. There is a proven 19-step process of adjustment to the loss of a love. This session provides an overview and an introduction to the Rebuilding Blocks which form that process.

Lesson Plan for Session One
The Rebuilding Blocks

Goals for Session One:
1. To recognize that rebuilding your life when a love relationship ends is a process that takes time.
2. To understand how the Rebuilding process — as pictured by the Rebuilding Blocks — will help.
3. To get to know the other seminar participants, the volunteer(s), and the leader(s).
4. To commit to confidentiality: anything personal shared here, stays here.
5. To understand the importance of three key tools for your learning and growth process: homework; a journal; affirmations.

Agenda for Session One (assumes an evening meeting time):
6:30 to 7:00 p.m. Sign in at the door, put on a name tag, help yourself to something to drink, get acquainted with other participants and volunteer helpers, and make yourself comfortable.

7:00 to 8:30 p.m. Presentation about Dr. Bruce Fisher's "Rebuilding Blocks" by the facilitator(s). **(This presentation is open to the public.)**

8:30 to 9:00 p.m. Break
1. Register for the seminar by filling out a registration agreement and turning it in with a check to a facilitator.
2. Pick up copies of *Rebuilding: When Your Relationship Ends*, and the *Rebuilding Workbook*.
3. Sign your name to the "Class Attendance Sheet." Mark H on the week you would like the class to meet in your home and G on the week you would like to bring goodies.

(Registered participants *only* after break)
9:00 to 9:10 p.m. Pass out class lists. Discuss the homework assignments, journaling, affirmations.

9:10 to 9:50 p.m. Small groups, led by volunteer helpers. Sample questions:
- Which "Rebuilding Blocks" appear to be the most challenging for you?
- What is your present relationship situation?
- Tell us something about yourself so we can get to know you better.
- What do you hope to get out of this seminar?

9:50 to 10:00 p.m. Big group time and closure.

Homework For Next Week's Seminar: (* Indicates Most Important Homework)
*1. Take the "Fisher Divorce Adjustment Scale" and bring back the completed answer sheet next week.
*2. Read Chapter 4, "Adaptation" in *Rebuilding: When Your Relationship Ends*.
*3. Call three people in the class in order to start building a support system. Use the small group sample questions on tonight's lesson plan as a guideline for something to talk about.
*4. Fill out the personal information sheet and turn it in to a facilitator next week.
 5. Read Chapter 1, "The Rebuilding Blocks" in the book to review the presentation of Session One.
 6. Start keeping a journal. Write as many "I feel _____" messages as possible. You may wish to start by writing your reactions to opening night after class tonight.
 7. If possible, read chapters 2 and 3 in the book.
 8. If you can't make it to the seminar one night, please call your facilitator. Thanks!

Facilitating Session One

The Rebuilding Blocks

Importance of Opening Night

Opening night is very important! There are many reasons for this. Normally about half of the participants are early in the process and still in deep emotional pain. Not only are they in deep pain but they have never been in a growth group situation before. It takes a great deal of courage for many of them to show up opening night. It is very important that they feel welcome and accepted.

When I first started teaching the Rebuilding Seminar I attempted to cover more material than the people were able to hear on opening night. Gradually I learned to accomplish only two things. 1) Present the rebuilding blocks so people could understand the adjustment process. The blocks are visual and the concept of climbing the mountain is easily understood. Participants will remember the presentation using the rebuilding blocks. 2) The other goal for opening night is to help people feel welcome and part of the group. The volunteer helpers play an important role in this endeavor. This is usually done after the break.

The rebuilding blocks presentation helps people understand the rebuilding process. It also gives them hope and a belief that they can climb the mountain. One participant stated that the facilitator symbolically gathers the people at the bottom of the mountain and carries them to the top. When I travel to another community, I always ask that a rebuilding block presentation be set up for the people to experience. Listening to the rebuilding blocks lecture can make a significant impact upon people and their adjustment process.

I like to ask each volunteer helper to share with the group the rebuilding block that was the most significant for them. While I am presenting, I have the volunteer helper stand up and share with the group how they dealt with that particular block. It provides variety to the presentation and also helps

the volunteer to connect with the group. The participants easily identify with what the recent participant (volunteer) is sharing.

I suggest you make a set of rebuilding blocks from colored construction paper with each block having a color that represents the feeling. For example, a red sheet for anger, a blue sheet for loneliness. Make the writing on the blocks large and dark enough to be read from across the room. After you have completed writing and possibly putting some graphics on each block, cover each side with a sheet of clear contact paper to protect the construction paper.

A variation with the presentation is to place the blocks in a pile on the floor to symbolize the participants' life being in shambles. Then one by one place the blocks on the wall to symbolize the participants' putting their lives in order. It makes an effective presentation.

I also suggest using the page in the workbook showing the rebuilding blocks so that each observer to the presentation can make notes for the individual blocks. This will enable them to refer to important aspects of the blocks throughout the seminar.

My experience dictates that opening night can be presented free and open to the general public rather than limiting it to participants who have registered for the ten week seminar. Former participants oftentimes bring a guest who ends up taking the class. Listening to the building block presentation helps people work through the process even though they may not be enrolling in the class. It is also a way for those who are not sure they want to take the class to make a better decision about enrolling. I also encourage former class members to come back and hear the presentation. They often are surprised at how differently they perceive the rebuilding blocks since the first time they heard the presentation.

I can guarantee you will hear feedback from people stating, "I thought I had worked through the whole process, but listening to this presentation helps me to understand I still have some more areas to work through." This presentation is an efficient and effective method of setting the stage for the ten week class.

Role of Volunteer Helpers

Opening night is also the most important night for volunteer helpers. As an overview of the ten week process, opening night is when the volunteers: invest the most of themselves in the group process. Each week the volunteers become less predominant until by the tenth night it may be hard to distinguish the volunteers from the participants.

Realistically, the volunteer duties start before opening night with the calling of any participants who have registered in advance. There may be some that need support and encouragement from a call before opening night in order to find the courage to make it to the first meeting. Also, some may need a ride to opening night and it may be possible for a volunteer to provide a ride. Calls from volunteer helpers will increase the number who attend and have a positive experience on opening night. I have heard many participants state how much it meant to them to receive these calls.

In the interim between seminars I have attempted to implement a support group for those recently separated so they can attend as soon as they separate. This is a worthwhile project and I encourage you to do it in your community. Many who advance register for the class are in the divorce pits and need support before the next session begins.

Volunteers need to be at the meeting thirty minutes ahead of time. It is important to have a volunteer (possibly male) stationed in the parking lot, at the front door of the building, and in the doorway to the meeting room. Many volunteers are surprised that they are able to spot the people looking for the divorce class. They can identify them from the other people coming from the parking lot. It is indeed a difficult experience to attend opening night for many participants.

The rules for volunteers on opening night are specific. "Do not spend time talking to anyone you know." The expectation is to spend as much time with the new members as possible. Also, we caution the volunteers not make a big display of hugging and talking with former classmates. The new person is fragile and might leave immediately if they see a group of former class members talking, hugging, and laughing in the room

The question of name tags needs to be decided. I like only volunteers having name tags at the beginning of the meeting so they can easily be identified. During break each person that registers completes their own name tag for the rest of the evening. Some facilitator's prefer to have name tags for every person present at the beginning of the meeting. I have found some participants feel more self-conscious with a name tag. They feel a need to hide. Being anonymous helps until they feel welcome and accepted.

When we train volunteers we suggest that during the ten weeks if anyone leaves the meeting room, a volunteer is expected to follow them out to see if they need support or someone to talk to. They may only be going to the rest room. On the other hand, they may really feel good when someone expresses an interest in them. Also, during the break, and any other time, I suggest volunteers keep looking for strays — anyone who is alone and by themselves. Some people need a lot of emotional space opening night and don't want to sit near anyone or have anyone look them in the eye. Each volunteer needs to become sensitive to the signals and body language of the new member and not overwhelm them with too much physical and emotional closeness.

At the beginning of the meeting I like to ask a couple of volunteers to share how they felt on opening night. This again allows the participants to connect and identify with the volunteers. It also helps to diffuse the anxiety the new member is feeling. They don't feel so uncomfortable when they find out the volunteers felt the same things they are experiencing on opening night.

The volunteer needs to think ahead of time about which block they want to talk about. I also like to ask them to share what was their most important and significant learning experience during the ten weeks. Setting up a precedent of having the volunteers be a part of the presentation on opening night sets the stage and prepares the participants to expect volunteer involvement during the remaining ten weeks.

I ask the volunteers to bring refreshments on opening night. Having food and drink makes a difference in the atmosphere of the meeting. After the first night participants are asked to bring refreshments. They tend to bring the same kind of food and drink as was there on opening night.

Registration of participants takes place during break. It is helpful to have volunteers help with registration. Also during break several new members may have questions about the format of the class, doubts if they are ready to take the class, and fears they need to express. It is very important volunteers connect with as many new members as possible during break.

After break the lesson plans indicate small group activities led by volunteers. If the class enrollment is small, this activity might be done in the large group. Volunteers as small group leaders make some important connections and often the members in their small group are the people they will call outside of class the following week. Volunteers are trained to be active listeners. On opening night it is especially important for them to be attentive to the needs of the new participants.

At the end of the evening it is helpful to assign specific people for the volunteers to call. I have learned that I can tell on the second night of class if the volunteers have made their calls. If the volunteers call their assigned class members the participants will be more likely to call others. If this is the case, the beginning of a trust level will be evident during the second night of class. If the volunteers don't call, participants probably won't make calls either. As a result the second night of class will be stiff and uncomfortable.

An indication of whether or not the participants have had their needs met in the class is their attitude at the completion of the ten weeks. If they don't feel the ten weeks were long enough and they want more class meetings, the class has not been as effective as possible. Before I used volunteers I often found people wanting more classes. Now with the use of volunteers there is seldom a class member who does not feel finished with class at the end of the ten weeks.

Registration of Participants
The ideal would be to advance register each person, have them take the FDAS before reading the textbook or hearing the rebuilding block presentation. It would be helpful to have them start reading the textbook before opening night. The only time I have been able to do this was after news media publicity created so much interest that the classes were filled with people who registered before opening night.

Even if you can't advance register the whole class, it is helpful to register as many as possible before opening night. I ask for an advance registration deposit of *$30* to cover the cost of the book and materials. The textbook, work book, personal information sheet, information letter about the class, and the FDAS questions and answer sheet are mailed to them. See the example of a letter (page 6) to be mailed back to a person who advance registered.

Normally registration takes place during the break on opening night. Following is a discussion of the items to be taken care of during registration.

1) The personal information form will be filled out with more thought if they take it home and mail it in or bring it to class the following week. This is especially true concerning the reasons and goals they have for taking the class. People will not remember what they filled out in the personal information sheet if they fill it out during opening night. Some will not remember to complete it during the week and will need to be reminded by the volunteers when they call to mail it back or bring it the second night of class.

Have a copy of the sheet with name, address, and phone number. This is helpful to have each person fill out when they come in the door and before they receive a name tag if you choose to use them.

2) Each person receives a copy of the *Rebuilding* book and a *Rebuilding Workbook*. The workbook has a) a copy of the lesson plans for each session b) a copy of the Registration Agreement Form c) the FDAS questions and answer sheet.

3) Payment of class fee. Included in the Registration Form in the workbook is the fee payment plan. Hopefully each participant will be able to pay the class fee on opening night however, some will need to make financial arrangements.

After Break
Before break, at the end of the rebuilding block presentation, the facilitator invites those who are registered for the class to remain after break in order to become acquainted with the other participants. This is a polite way of sending home any visitors and guests. It is important that only those registered participate after break. This is the beginning of the group process. The group begins to develop a bond and a level of trust.

In the large group the facilitator welcomes everyone. It is important to call attention to the registration agreement form concerning confidentiality and emotional involvement. The participants will appreciate the facilitator taking a *strong stand* in favor of confidentiality and against emotional involvement. Signing the registration agreement provides a commitment from the participants in these two crucial areas.

This is the way I express the rules about emotional and sexual involvement.

"I know you are adults and able to make your own decisions. However let me suggest some ideas for you to think about. (I say the next sentence in a loud voice). I suggest you do not become romantically and sexually involved with the other participants during the next ten weeks. I don't suggest this from a parental viewpoint of telling you what to do. I don't suggest this because of strong moral values. I suggest it from a pragmatic viewpoint.

If you start investing in another relationship while in this class, you will probably invest more in the relationship and less in your own growth and adjustment. The relationship you start in this class will have a foundation of neediness. It will most likely be similar, or opposite, to the relationship you are ending. It probably will not last very long. In fact it may end during the ten weeks and then you will have to decide whether the dumper or the dumpee will finish in the class. Most likely one of you will drop out and miss the growth that could take place if you finished the class.

As a participant you need to be free to be open, honest and willing to share yourself. You need to invest in your own growth and adjustment. Being free of the dating and romantic games will enhance your growth. For these reasons, I suggest you do not become romantically and sexually involved during the next ten weeks. Please think about what I have said."

The first three or four weeks is the time most relationships will start to develop in the class. After a few weeks, if the support system is working, the participants become more like brothers and sisters. At this point in time thoughts of romantic and sexual involvement are less likely to occur.

Facilitator's need to develop an approach to homework that is appropriate to their style of teaching. Some will want to place strong expectations on the participants to complete the homework. Others may say things like: "Just showing up to class will be helpful. Reading the book will increase the benefits of the class. Participating, reading, and doing the homework results in maximum growth during the next ten weeks." Participants early in the process, and especially dumpees, will have difficulty doing much homework until they begin to survive emotionally. On the other hand, those who resist due to laziness or lack of motivation need to be encouraged to do the homework. Participants that do not do the homework will find themselves missing out on much of the growth that is possible.

On opening night I always like to mention that part of the homework is calling another participant before the next meeting takes place. Participants need to identify another person they would like to call outside of class during the sharing.

If the total class size is small, the sharing and getting acquainted can take place with the total class. However it is recommended that you organize small groups because class members will feel more comfortable and share more in small groups. There should be one or two volunteer helpers in each small group. The small groups could be from four to eight members.

Having the lesson plans in the workbook allows the participants to know what the homework for next week is. They can see specific objectives for each session and think about the discussion questions that will be used in small groups. It is also helpful for anyone who misses a session to be able to have a copy of the lesson plans.

I encourage people to keep a journal during the ten weeks. I mention to participants at the end of opening night that many will continue to process the class experience after the class is over. Some will have difficulty sleeping. I encourage people to write in their journal after class in order to process the class experience. Suggesting it the first night may help them to continue to journal each week after class.

After Class

Many participants have not had a listening person who understands what they are feeling and experiencing before opening night. They are needing to talk. If possible it is ideal to be able to continue talking in the meeting room after class. However in many public rooms the participants will have to leave as soon as class is over. Try to arrange a meeting place to gather after class. It might be a public place or the home of one of the volunteers. As a facilitator, my boundaries allowed me to stay for an hour after class before I left. Often there is a volunteer who is willing to stay as long as the person wants to talk. Sometimes the new participant will end up talking to a volunteer until 2:00 or 3:00 AM. Most people continue to process the class long after the meeting is over.

Comments on the Following Pages

Page 8 is for each person attending opening night to sign when they enter the room.

Page 10 is helpful for people to better understand the expectations of the participants. We are also in an age of litigation and having participants sign the copy and turn it in gives you more protection if someone should decide to not follow the expectations.

Page 11 is helpful and I encourage you to have each participant complete it so you can get to know them better.

Page 13 is appropriate if you don't expect each participant to pay the fee in advance. I put this sheet on a data base in my computer. "I am female" or "I am male" are written to help participants feel they are not the only person feeling what they are feeling.

Page 16 is a helpful letter from Bunny to better prepare you for your first opening night. Having the *Rebuilding Workbook* makes opening night easier for the facilitator.

Pages 18 to 21 are information sheets for you.

This is an example of a letter that might e-mailed back to those participants who have advance registered. Feel free to copy or cut and paste this letter.

<Facilitators Letterhead>

Dear Special Person,

<Current Calendar Date>

We have received your deposit for the "Rebuilding When Your Relationship Ends Seminar.'" Welcome to an exciting and growing experience. You will be pleasantly surprised and pleased with the personal growth and adjustment taking place in you and with the other class members in the next few weeks. Opening night is Wednesday September 4th, 7:00 to 10:00 PM at the Quality Inn Motel (formerly. Howard Johnsons) located at I-25 and Hampden Avenue. Enclosed is a map to the Motel.

Enclosed is a copy of the textbook titled: *Rebuilding: When Your Relationship Ends.* Please read as much in the textbook as you have time to do before opening night. Also enclosed is a Personal Information Sheet and the Fisher Divorce Adjustment Scale Questions and Answer Sheet. **Please fill out both of these forms immediately and mail to the above address, or bring them to the opening night of class.**

The opening night Rebuilding Blocks presentation from 7:00 to 8:30 PM is free and open to the public. Please extend a welcome to anyone you know who might be interested in hearing the presentation. Even if your friends can't take the class, they may benefit from hearing the presentation. After the break at 8:30 those of you participating in the ten-week class will be asked to stay and discuss the presentation and to start becoming acquainted with the other participants.

I am enclosing a flyer with information about our "Rebuilding When Your Relationship Ends" and "Rebuilding Relationships Classes for Singles and/or Couples." Please share them with a friend who might benefit from participating in one of these classes.

Start getting yourself psyched up for a exciting and challenging time. Be sure to remember what a special person you are. I'm looking forward to becoming better acquainted with you the next ten weeks.

Lovingly,

Bruce

Outline and Overview of the Ten Sessions
for the
Rebuilding Seminar

The following is an overview of the ten sessions of the seminar and the topics to be discussed in each session. The reading assignments listed are chapters from the book *Rebuilding: When Your Relationship Ends*, third edition, by Dr. Bruce Fisher and Dr. Robert Alberti. Notice that some of the chapters in the book are not covered in these ten sessions. We have identified the topics which are typically the most important and challenging, and we believe you will benefit the most by covering them during the seminar. If you have the time and energy you will find it helpful to read the chapters in the book which are not emphasized in the ten-week seminar. We encourage you to keep meeting as a group, discussing each of the remaining chapters after the ten-week seminar is completed.

Session One: **The Rebuilding Blocks.** Chapter 1, pages 5-28. The rebuilding blocks give you an overview of the adjustment process used in this seminar to help you make your crisis into a creative experience.

Session Two: **Adaptation** - "But it Worked When I Was a Kid." Chapter 4, pages 52-65. You may have learned and developed adaptive behavior during your formative years in order to get your needs met. This adaptive behavior may become maladaptive behavior in your adult relationships. You may find it helpful to develop more authentic behavior.

Session Three: **Grief** - "There's This Terrible Feeling of Loss." Chapter 8, pages 96-109. An important aspect of ending a love relationship is grieving your various losses of love. There is a connection between overcoming denial, grieving, and disentangling from the former love partner.

Session Four: **Anger** - "Damn the S.O.B.!" Chapter 9, pages 110-127. Ending a love relationship results in feelings of anger. Resolving this anger allows you to find forgiveness for yourself and for your former love partner. It is important to deal with your angry feelings because they can last for months and maybe years after the physical separation.

Session Five: **Self-worth** - "Maybe I'm Not So Bad After All." Chapter 11, pages 136-146. The previous sessions have helped you work through your painful feelings. Improving your feelings of self-worth will help you move beyond pain and find the strength to grow.

Session Six: **Transition** - "I'm Waking Up and Putting Away My Leftovers." Chapter 12, pages 148-164. After improving your self-worth, you are emotionally stronger and ready to experience personal growth. You are ready to wake up and begin taking charge of your life.

Session Seven: **Openness** – "I've Been Hiding Behind A Mask." Chapter 13, pages 166-175. You have been using a great deal of emotional energy trying to be someone other than who really you are. You may choose to be free to be you.

Session Eight: **Love** - "Could Somebody Really Care for Me?" Chapter 14, pages 176-187. It is okay to love yourself. The more you love yourself, the more authentically you can love others.

Session Nine: **Relatedness** - "Growing Relationships Help Me Rebuild." Chapter 16, pages 200-215. The relationships that develop following the ending of an important relationship can be an important part of your growing process. You may find the friendships you make in this class help you to grow and adjust.

Session Ten: **Sexuality** - "I'm Interested, but I'm Scared." Chapter 17, pages 216-232. You long for emotional intimacy but you're afraid. Intimacy starts with becoming better acquainted and more intimate with yourself. Understanding your own sexuality, and learning more about the way others feel will be very helpful.

Rebuilding: When Your Relationship Ends
Opening Night Sign-Up Sheet

Name

Address

City   State   Zip

Home Phone   Work Phone   e-mail address

Name

Address

City   State   Zip

Home Phone   Work Phone   e-mail address

Name

Address

City   State   Zip

Home Phone   Work Phone   e-mail address

Name

Address

City   State   Zip

Home Phone   Work Phone   e-mail address

Name

Address

City   State   Zip

Home Phone   Work Phone   e-mail address

The Rebuilding Blocks

			Freedom			
		Sexuality	Singleness	Purpose		
	Openness	Love	Trust	Relatedness		
	Grief	Anger	Letting Go	Self-Worth	Transition	
Denial	Fear	Adaptation	Loneliness	Friendship	Guilt/Rejection	

Please write your reactions to the Rebuilding Block Presentation

1. **Denial**

2. **Fear**

3. **Adaptation**

4. **Loneliness**

5. **Friendship**

6. **Guilt/Rejection**

7. **Grief**

8. **Anger**

9. **Letting Go**

10. **Self-Worth**

11. **Transition**

12. **Openness**

13. **Love**

14. **Trust**

15. **Relatedness**

16. **Sexuality**

17. **Singleness**

18. **Purpose**

19. **Freedom**

Participant's Registration Agreement
for the
Rebuilding Seminar

The Rebuilding Seminar is a ten-week educational program designed to help people adjust to the ending of a love relationship. It is not a therapy group. The seminar meets for three hours, one night a week for ten weeks, a total of thirty contact hours. In order to receive the maximum benefit from this seminar, you are encouraged to attend as many of the ten sessions as possible, and to complete as much of the homework as possible.

The textbook for this seminar is the third edition of the best-selling book *Rebuilding: When Your Relationship Ends*. In addition, each participant will be provided with the *Rebuilding Workbook*. The facilitator may include the cost of these two books in the fee for the seminar, or you may be asked to purchase them separately.

Registration Agreement:

I understand that I will experience more growth during this class if I attend all ten sessions, and do the assigned homework. I agree to do both to the best of my ability.

I agree that information of a personal nature which is shared with me by a participant, volunteer, or facilitator involved in this seminar will be kept strictly confidential by me during and after this seminar.

I understand that I may benefit from the friendship and support of other people involved in this seminar. I acknowledge it could be detrimental to everyone involved if, during this seminar, I enter into romantic or sexual relationships with others. I agree to not become romantically or sexually involved with other seminar participants, volunteers, or facilitator's during this ten week seminar.

I understand that this is a supportive educational seminar and not a therapy group. I specifically release the facilitator's involved in this seminar from any responsibility for my wellness. I unconditionally release them from all liability whatsoever as a result of my interaction with other seminar participants, volunteers, or facilitator's during the duration of this seminar and at any time in the future. I agree to be accountable and responsible for my own behavior.

Fee:

The fee for this ten-week seminar is $_____. A minimum of $ _____ is due by opening night as a non-refundable registration fee. I have paid $_____ before or on opening night. I agree to pay the remainder of the fee no later than the sixth night of the seminar. I will receive a $_____ discount if I previously purchased the textbook. There will be no refund of fees paid under any circumstances unless agreed to in writing by the facilitator.

I have read and completely understand and agree to the terms of this agreement. I further understand that failure to comply with any of the terms of this agreement may result in my being terminated from participation in this educational seminar.

_____

Name

_____

Address   City   Zip

_____   _____

Home Phone   Work Phone

_____   _____   _____

Signature of seminar participant   Signature of seminar facilitator   Date

Both the participant and the facilitator should retain a copy of this sheet.

Personal Information Sheet for the Rebuilding Seminar

Please answer the following questions. (All information will be kept confidential)

Name _____   Home phone _____

Address _____   Work phone _____

City, State _____ Zip _____ Birthday _____

Relationship Situation:
Who ended your last relationship? ____You did   ____Your former love-partner did   ____You both did

____ Single   ____ Separated   ____ Divorced   ____ Married   ____ Widowed

____ Not dating ____ Casual dating ____ Dating one person only   ____ Living together ____ Engaged

Separated ____ months.   Married ____ years.

Employment:
Name of
employer_____Occupation_____

____ Work with others   ____ Work alone   ____ Involved in management

Children:
Ages _____ When do they spend time with you? _____

Family of Origin and Childhood Experiences: _____ Basically happy, normal childhood
____ Parents divorced ____ Parent(s) alcoholic ____ Parent(s) died ____ Parents' marriage unhappy
____ Childhood verbal abuse _____ Childhood physical abuse _____ Childhood sexual abuse
____ Adopted ____ Birth Order _____ # of sisters _____ # of brothers

Therapy Situation:
Are you presently seeing a therapist for individual or marital counseling? __ yes __ no
If yes, have you discussed attending this seminar with your therapist?   __ yes __ no
Therapist's Name _____ Therapist's Phone Number_____

How did you hear about this Seminar?
___ Friend who had taken seminar   ___ Attorney   ___ Clergy person
___ Counselor or therapist   ___ Newspaper   ___ Doctor
___ Read one of Bruce's books   ___ TV or Radio Show   ___ Other-explain:_____

Goals and reasons for taking this seminar.

1.

2.

3.

4.

5.

Facilitator's: We suggest you make a copy of this sheet and retain the copy in your files.

Rebuilding Class Attendance Form

Mark P for present, A for absent, G for goodies, and H for having class in your home

Session Number	1	2	3	4	5	6	7	8	9	10
Date of each session										
Class Members										
1										
2										
3										
4										
5										
6										
7										
8										
9										
10										
11										
12										
13										
14										
15										
16										
17										
18										
19										
20										
21										
22										
23										
24										
25										

Facilitators: Make a copy of this sheet and pass it around each night so that participants can mark it.

Payment of Fees by Participants for The Rebuilding Seminar

Session Number	1	2	3	4	5	6	7	8	9	10
Date of each session										
Class Members										
1										
2										
3										
4										
5										
6										
7										
8										
9										
10										
11										
12										
13										
14										
15										
16										
17										
18										
19										
20										
21										
22										
23										
24										
25										

I Am Female And My Life Is In Shambles!

(To be read by all human beings)

Just as the last few pieces of the picture puzzle of who am I were being put in place,
Someone came along and knocked all of the pieces on the floor.
What do I do?—my life is in shambles.

I have never felt so confused and crazy.
How can I go on?
Who am I?
If I don't know who I am, how can I continue to work? to parent? to face my friends? to convince my parents they aren't a failure because of my divorce?

I am the one who is responsible for the members of my family.
I took on that job at some time—I don't know when.
But I do know I failed at what a woman is supposed to be—the one who holds the family together.

The pieces of me seem to be so chaotic that I will never be able to sort them out,
I thought I knew the colors and shapes of the various parts of me.
Now I question how I could have been so dumb, so naive, so false and inauthentic.
I want to hide and not let anyone know what a mess I am.

Wow! I got the courage to come to opening night of the Rebuilding class,
Thank you Jane for talking me into coming.
I wanted to be here but be invisible so no one can see my pain.
I was surprised to find others who appeared to be in as much pain as me.
I decided I was not so all alone.

I watched the Rebuilding blocks fit together,
I even climbed some of the mountain internally and began to feel some hope.
Can I trust the Rebuilding blocks?
Will the process work for me?
It has worked for thousands of others
What have I got to lose?
There is nothing deeper and more frightening than the abyss I have been in since I separated.
I might as well give it a try. Sign me up for the climb up the mountain.

Embrace my Pain? Are you kidding?
I would much sooner embrace another warm body.
But even that thought is scary.
Anything I think about doing is scary.
"Your pain is the breaking of the shell of your understanding,
It is the bitter potion by which the Physician within you heals your sick self."
I want to heal. I want to become. I want to be happy and free—more than I have ever been.
Embracing my pain is not what I thought I would be doing when I decided to become married.

I want to tell my story. Tell everyone how unfair it is. To feel sorry for myself.
It made sense when I heard that it was okay to talk out whatever I was feeling.
And to say at the end of my story—"But I am working on it" was a new idea.
I do think it is my story and not anyone else's.
Maybe I can create the ending of my story and make it turn out like I want it to.

Thank you Jane for helping me be here tonight.
I am committed to climb to the top of the mountain and find freedom.
I will put the pieces together and find my identity.
I will take charge of my life and become the person I am capable of being.
I am committed to grow. I am committed to be me.

I Am Male And I Am Totally Alone

(To be read by all human beings)

I was sitting by the warm fire of married love,
Suddenly I am alone and out in the cold.
It's not so bad. I can adjust to anything because I am a strong and self sufficient male.
Why do I feel so cold?

I provided like my father did.
My family never went hungry.
I want someone to hug me—but my father never did.
The most warmth I have ever known is when she loved me.
And now I don't feel her love anymore.

I kept busy—maybe too busy to feel.
It is so cold out here. I want to find warm love again.
I didn't know I could be so lonely.
The emptiness inside of me is absolute.
I think I have been vacuum packed inside of a shell that it impermeable.

John told me about this class.
Said there would be other males here who were just as lonely as I.
I told him I was the only person on the North Pole and there was no one else like me.
I am beginning to discover I was wrong.
I never thought I could be wrong. Males are always right. My father taught me that.

Wow! The Rebuilding blocks make so much sense.
Climbing the mountain looks like an adventure—a problem I can solve.
It is scary to have to climb alone. She used to hold my hand when I felt afraid.
Maybe the textbook will be a trail guide for me to help me find my way alone.
It seems to be the only friend I have right now.
The book helps me to understand what I am experiencing.
No one ever helped me to understand myself before.
This climb is scary because I have to feel instead of keeping busy.
Where is my mommy?

Embrace my pain? Grieve? Us males don't grieve. That's only for females.
But I am cold. What can I do to feel warmer? How can I keep from freezing to death?
I become uncomfortable when I feel. Surprise! I'm not as cold when I am uncomfortable.
Maybe the coldness I feel is within me.
Maybe it is not because she is gone but because I am gone. Gone from myself.
Maybe I can create a warm fire of love within me. Something that will keep the cold away.

I've decided I need to climb the mountain.
It is a new and different journey—not like what I learned about life from father.
What did I learn about life from him? I never knew him.
Maybe I learned loneliness from him. I never thought about him being lonely till now.
Sign me up. I need this class. Maybe I need to learn that males grieve also.

I see myself as hard with her providing softness to my life.
I see myself needing her in order to feel for me when I couldn't feel for me.
I want to find softness within me to balance out my hardness.
I want to become whole, more balanced, warm inside.

I don't want to say "But I'm working on it."
I just want to learn how to tell my story like my female friends do so easily.
I want my life to unfold gently like a flower blooming,
Instead of my life being the solution to a math problem.
I am committed to grow. I am committed to be me.

This is a copy of a wonderful better that I think you will find interesting and helpful in preparing for opening night. Thank you Bunny for sharing with us.

Dear Bruce, Jere and Joanne,

You've probably seen those bumper stickers that read "I SURVIVED THE BOULDER MALL AT HALLOWEEN." Well, I'm tempted to have one made up that says "I SURVIVED THE FIRST NIGHT OF MY REBUILDING SEMINAR."

Since you were all "rooting" for me, you'll be happy to know that my first class went as scheduled on May 18 with one volunteer and 12 participants (and two more who have since enrolled). Because the date of the second meeting was over Memorial Day, we voted not to hold an official class, but to have an informal gathering. Nine people showed up for that and we had a good time getting acquainted. My second class will be tonight. The youngest class member is 24 and married 3 years. The oldest is 69 and married 47 years. We are five men and nine women, plus a male volunteer.

Already I have experienced two rewarding incidents: one woman was still wearing her rings though her divorce was final seven months ago. She took them off after our first class thanks to the denial rebuilding block. Another woman called to say our lecture about the pitfalls of getting prematurely involved helped give her the courage to move out on a live-in relationship who was pressuring her to "cheer up or get out."

I would like to share my startup experiences in hopes they will help other new facilitator's get started: First of all, I suggest you do not let people know this is your first time conducting a workshop. Adhere to the old saying '"Fake it 'til you make it." There is nothing to be gained by advertising that you're a newbie. In fact, you may lose some potential participants who won't have confidence in a "new" person. Don't try to be something you aren't, but don't attribute your lack of knowledge or nervousness to your newness either. Prepare well, don't complicate things, be calm, breathe deeply, tell people you'll get back to them with an answer.

a) **Credibility.** I found that being associated with a large local church helped lend a certain credibility to the workshop, especially since I am new in the city and people are not familiar with Dr. Fisher's seminars. Having a central meeting location for the ten weeks also avoided moving around the city to various homes.

b) **Brochure.** Before publicizing your seminar, I feel it is important to have a brochure or flier ready to mail out to people who want to know about the workshop.

c) **Advertising.** 95% of all my inquiries came from an ad in the Personal column of our large metro newspaper. It read: "Divorce recovery workshop with friends and support. Classes begin May 18. 272- 6907." I ran the ad daily, including Sunday, beginning 3 weeks prior to the class. Since I am willing to take people up until the second class, I also ran the ad a fourth week, between Class One and Class Two (which produced two more participants). At $50 per week, the ad seemed expensive, but more than paid for itself. It produced considerably better than did my ads in suburban newspapers, mailings to churches, postings in the public libraries, mailings to therapists and announcements over public service radio.

d) **Follow-Up.** Out of 46 responses to the ad, I received one crank call, one looking for a social club, and 44 who were genuinely seeking help. I mailed all of them a brochure. It's important to keep a record of their name, address, phone number and a few notes about their personal situation as shared on the phone. The reason it's important is because only ONE person voluntarily mailed me their registration… others signed up only after I made a follow-up call to talk with them about the workshop.

e) **Payment Plan.** The workshop fee (including materials) was $150. I found that lack of money was the main reason people can't and don't register. Because I was eager to have at least 10 people in the group, I was willing to make "arrangements," through either a payment plan or "financial grants" courtesy of the sponsoring church.

f) **Advance registration/Deposit.** A paid-in-advance deposit virtually guarantees the person will attend the first night. On the flip side, I found that those with no deposit did not show up opening night. What worked for me was to tell people that we want them to take the FDAS prior to reading the book and prior to seeing the video, and that I would send them the FDAS and their textbook as soon as I received their deposit.

g) **Volunteers.** This was difficult for me, since there were no previous workshops from which to recruit. Also, I am new to the city and do not have a network of friends who might want to help. I happened to receive a call from a man who had worked through his divorce quite well and therefore concluded he did not need our class. However, the idea of being a volunteer appealed to him, and he was willing to donate 30 hours to classes, plus telephoning time on the outside. (Bunny discovered he wasn't as adjusted as he thought he was.)

h) **Opening night.** I gave each participant a folder containing:

1. Class Roster
2. Payment Plan
3. Personal Information Sheet
4. Information about the Seminar
5. Copy of Rocky Mountain News article
6. Blank sheet of paper for note taking

Items 2-5 gave people something to read or to do while they were waiting for the session to start. Be sure to label the inside of the folder (and their textbook) with your name/address/phone number for their quick and easy reference.

Other items I took to Opening Night included:

1. Name Tags and a couple of pens
2. Brochures
3. Extra textbooks and folders
4. Box of tissues
5. Refreshments
6. Dr. Fisher's Video
7. "Boom Box" and cassette tape with relaxation music

Thanks again for your thoughts and support! Yours toward a healthy and happy future,

Bunny

Description of the Educational Seminar
for the
Rebuilding When Your Relationship Ends Seminar

We want to extend some words of welcome to you. We want to acknowledge you for finding the courage to come to opening night and to enroll in the ten week seminar. The seminar has been offered all over the planet. By the end of 1994 there will have been approximately a quarter of a million people who have participated in this seminar.

This is an educational seminar, including a textbook, homework assignments, a structured format for each session described in the lesson plans and specific behavioral objectives. This is in contrast to a group therapy experience which is much less structured and has different objectives and goals. We believe this educational model is the most effective method available to help you adjust to the ending of a love relationship.

The seminar is designed to help people make a crisis into a creative experience. A crisis usually includes emotional and psychological pain. If this pain can be embraced and used as motivation to grow and adjust it will help people make the crisis a creative experience. The goal of the seminar is to not only help people adjust, but also to help them transform and learn to take charge of their lives. Most graduates of this seminar are better able to adjust to the ending of their love relationship, and they are also more capable of building and creating more lasting and healthy relationships.
The following is a list and description of the components of this Rebuilding Seminar:

Rebuilding: When Your Relationship Ends, **Third Edition (2000)**
The textbook uses the Rebuilding Blocks concept to help people understand the rebuilding after a crisis adjustment process. There are twenty chapters in the textbook. Ten of them will be assigned during the seminar. Appendix A includes, "A Workshop for Children of Divorce" and introduces the concept of "The Healing Separation" — an alternative to divorce.

Rebuilding Workbook
This workbook is to be used in conjunction with the textbook for those attending the Rebuilding Seminar. It has been designed to guide participants through the ten sessions of the seminar. It also provides space to take notes and write feelings and reactions to the seminar experience and reading assignments. It includes supplemental information not found in the textbook. It is an essential part of the seminar.

Facilitator's Manual
The Facilitator's Manual provides information on how to facilitate the seminar. Part 1 includes the Lesson Plans which describe and discuss the format for each of the ten sessions. Part 2 is designed to answer questions the facilitator might have while teaching the seminar. Part 3 describes the use of the Fisher Divorce Adjustment Scale. Part 4 describes the Volunteer Helper Program.

Fisher Divorce Adjustment Scale (FDAS)
This is a 100-item personality scale designed to give the person feedback about their adjustment to the ending of a love relationship. It is used as a pre-test in the seminar to help the person understand the areas they need to work on. It is also given as a post-test to give feedback to the participant about the growth they experienced during the ten weeks of the seminar.

Volunteer Helpers Support Program
Upon completing the ten week seminar, certain graduates are selected and asked to be volunteer helpers in a later seminar. There is a training session to prepare them to be better volunteers. They take part in the seminar each week by leading small group discussions, giving support to others, and assisting the facilitator in various ways. They also arrange and attend various social gatherings outside the seminar. Their most important function is to give support to the participants, especially by calling them in between the sessions of the seminar.

How to Create the "Rebuilding Seminar" in Your Community

The "Fisher Rebuilding Seminar" has had over 100,000 participants in United States, Canada, Australia, and Great Britain. It has proven to be an inexpensive way to effectively meet the needs of people who are ending a love relationship. Here are some ways you can create and implement the Seminar in your community:

1. Book Discussion Group.

Many communities have organized a weekly discussion group. They discuss a chapter each week from the book titled, *Rebuilding: When Your Relationship Ends* by Dr. Bruce Fisher and Dr. Robert E. Alberti. There is a check list at the end of each Chapter which people can use as discussion questions. The discussion group typically meets continuously throughout the year. **Cost:** $14.95 for the book.

2. "Rebuilding Ten-Week Seminar." (For more personal growth)

This ten-week Seminar is a psycho-educational model using the textbook *Rebuilding: When Your Relationship Ends*. It has a facilitator(s), structured class format, homework, and uses the *volunteer helpers support system*. The facilitator(s) can purchase the *Facilitator's Manual* which explains how to implement the Seminar. The facilitator(s) should be proficient at working with people and preferably have a degree in a helping profession. This model greatly increases the personal growth of the participants over the book discussion program. **Cost:** $50.00 for the *Facilitator's Manual*. (Plus Textbooks for each participant.)

3. Establish an "Expanded Program." (For maximum personal growth)

In addition to the "Rebuilding Seminar" the following seminars are offered:

"Children of Divorce" workshop for graduates of the Rebuilding Seminar and their children. Information on this Workshop is in Appendix A.

"Rebuilding Relationships for Singles" ten-week follow up seminar to the "Rebuilding Seminar" for those wanting to build a better relationship with themselves and with others. Textbook is *Loving Choices* by Dr. Bruce Fisher and Nina Hart.

"Rebuilding Relationships for Couples" ten-week seminar for any two people who want to build and create a more healthy relationship than what they have known in the past. For some couples this is a divorce prevention seminar. Textbook is *Loving Choices* by Dr. Bruce Fisher and Nina Hart.

Social Support Group and newsletter organized and run by the group members. Other group activities and seminars offered according to the needs of the people.

4. An Alternative: Establish a "Beginning Experience" Team in your Community.

This group is sponsored by a Christian Church and offers A Weekend Experience plus a wide variety of growth groups and social support. The expanded program includes offering the "Rebuilding Seminar." Contact:

Beginning Experience International Ministry Center
1657 Commerce Drive, Ste. 2B
South Bend, IN 46628
phone (866) 810-8877 or (574) 283-0279

Comments on the Order of Topics for the Ten Sessions

I want to share some of my thinking concerning the order of the ten topics in the sessions. There is an adjustment process that is time related. People experience different feelings early in the process than they do later on. There is more pain early in the process and the painful blocks need to be experienced before climbing the mountain to the more introspective and transformation blocks. The blocks are arranged in an order that resembles the way a person experiences them during the rebuilding after a crisis process.

I suggest when you first start teaching this seminar you teach the topics in the order they have been arranged in the book and in this facilitator's manual. After you have some experience, you may find a need to change the order of topics to utilize your strengths as a facilitator, and to better meet the needs of participants in your community.

Session one is the Rebuilding Blocks. This provides an overview of the rebuilding after a crisis process. Participants and readers relate to the symbolic mountain. It provides a way of organizing a complex process into an easily understood model.

The second session on adaptive behavior is a wake-up call. Learning that I married to balance out my unbalanced parts is a concept that is new to many participants. One of the most powerful items on the FDAS states, "I blame my former love partner for the failure of our relationship." People early in the process do project the blame, but after working through the process people take more responsibility for their contribution to the problems and difficulties. This chapter helps people to become aware of how they contributed to the ending of their relationship.

This chapter also helps people to realize why they need to climb the mountain of adjustment. It helps them overcome denial. It helps them perform an autopsy on why the relationship died or ended. Statements like, "I married someone under responsible. And if they weren't under responsible enough, I trained them to be more under responsible" encourage people to own their behavior. People begin to understand how they chose their partner. It was more than just "falling in love." And they begin to see the need for the remaining eight sessions to help them improve their relationship with themselves.

Denial, fear, loneliness, loss of friends, guilt, rejection, grief, anger, and disentanglement are what might be called the "divorce pits." They are painful feelings that people experience early in the process. These blocks are universal in that almost everyone experiences all of them more or less. We need to experience the pain so we can work through it and begin taking charge of our life. Until we let go of these painful feelings, we will have difficulty reaching our potential and to be as loving as we are capable of being. We need to take advantage of the adjustment process to not only adjust to the ending of a love relationship but also to learn to take charge of our lives. If the class were simply about divorce recovery, we could do the seminar in five or six sessions.

I have chosen grief and anger as the two divorce pit blocks discussed in class because people usually have difficulty with these two blocks. Many of the other blocks, such as fear, are definitely important and need to dealt with. Many will work through these other blocks indirectly while taking the class. I don't know how easy it will be for them to work through these blocks without the class experience. I hope reading the other chapters in the book will be helpful in working through the other blocks.

There is a possible variation concerning grief and anger. Some people need to grieve before they can express anger. Some people need to express anger before they can grieve. When you view the FDAS class average scores, you may find some classes more angry and some classes more grieving. For some classes you may want to reverse the order and have anger before grief.

Self-worth gives people the emotional strength to climb out of the divorce pits. There is a high correlation between feelings of self-worth and working through the painful blocks. The better you feel about yourself, the easier it will be for you to overcome the painful feelings early in the adjustment process.

I estimate in the past five percent of the graduates of this seminar have decided to go back and work on their past marriage after completing the ten week seminar: (They often are successful at doing this.) I think this five percent can be increased two or three times by participants having more awareness of the problems in relationships. The transition chapter is designed to help people wake up on an emotional level and become aware of the many influences upon their primary love relationship. Realizing they married someone like one of their parents is often part of this waking up. It takes emotional strength to look at oneself and participants will need to work through the divorce pits and improve self-worth before taking this journey into self.

Sessions seven through nine are the chapters where people do transformation work which will help them build and create healthier love relationships in the future. This happens when they start building healthier relationships with themselves. Learning the masks they have been using to emotionally distance people, understanding the need for self-love, and using growing relationships as a way to enhance their individual growth process, all lead to healthier relationships.

Sexuality and intimacy can present a problem in class. It is an emotionally laden topic and many have an emotional charge around the topic. It is frightening for many after divorce. Many are not ready to talk about sexuality during the ten week class. Participants need to realize this chapter on sexuality is really about intimacy. And the reason it is on the last night of class is that true intimacy is not possible until participants have climbed to the top of the mountain and worked through many of the stumbling blocks from the first nine sessions of the seminar.

Other topics might be used the last night of class instead of sexuality. For example, talking about goals for the future and looking at lifelines is a good topic for the last session. Using the last night for closure and experiential activities that will help people adjust to the ending of the ten week class works well. (They may need to grieve the loss of the class) A follow up session three months later on sexuality would allow participants more adjustment time before dealing with this difficult subject. Whenever it is offered, sexuality is an important topic and needs to be included in this Rebuilding Seminar.

Here is an important variation in the order of topics. We do four ten week classes a year. It works out on the calendar that you need to start a class just after Thanksgiving in order to do this. This allows for four sessions before Christmas. This is a very important (but difficult) time to start the class because it provides the people with a support system to help them over the Christmas Holidays. I found it helpful to do the self-worth session before Christmas to give people the emotional strength to face and deal with their families over Christmas. Then have the anger session after Christmas to help them work through the anger that usually results from the stress of Christmas and being with the family of origin.

Let me summarize the order of topics. The rebuilding blocks model provides a trail guide to climb the mountain. Looking at adaptive behaviors provides motivation to climb the mountain. Working through grief and anger unloads some of our burdens so we can climb more easily. Self-worth gives us the strength to make the rest of the climb.

Transition takes advantage of the improved view we gain as we climb. We reach a point in the climb where we can take off the masks we have been hiding behind. We take time to stop and rest in the climb while we nurture ourselves with self-love. We realize the friendships we have made with other participants in the seminar are healthy and a model of how relationships can help us grow towards health. We learn that intimacy is more important than sexuality. We discover the ten week class is not just divorce recovery, but is more about learning to take charge of our lives by learning to make loving choices. We leave the chrysalis and find the freedom to become a butterfly.

Session Two
Adaptation
"But It Worked When I Was a Kid!"

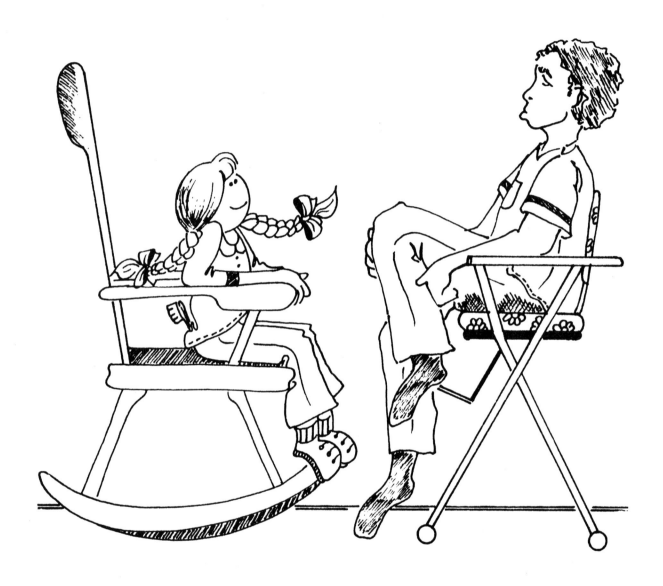

Growing up, we all learned a variety of ways to adapt when our needs for love and attention were unfulfilled. Some of those strategies may have helped us get by as children, but they are excess baggage for grown-ups. An over- or under-responsible style, for example, is not effective in adult relationships. The process of rebuilding offers many opportunities to change your unhealthy parts into authentic, relationship-enhancing behaviors.

Lesson Plan for Session Two

Adaptation: But It Worked When I Was a Kid!

Goals for Session Two:
1. To learn more about your adaptive behavior, healthy and unhealthy.
2. To identify, accept, embrace, and nurture your adaptive behavior parts, which are ways of being that have helped you survive.
3. To better understand how your unhealthy adaptive behaviors have contributed to the difficulties in your relationships.
4. To get to know yourself and others in the class better by sharing openly in small groups.
5. To begin to understand the value of building a support network both inside and outside the class
6. To learn and use affirmations that will help your process.

Agenda for Session Two:
6:45 to 7:00 p.m. Arrive, greet new friends, get a hug, and a cup of tea or coffee.

7:00 to 7:10 p.m. Relaxation Exercise - "Breathing through our fears."

7:10 to 7:45 p.m. Small groups led by volunteer helpers. Suggested questions:
- How did your week go?
- Were you able to do the homework of calling three other people? How did it feel to make
- calls? How did it feel to receive calls?
- What was your reaction to taking the *Fisher Divorce Adjustment Scale*?
- What did you learn from the "Adaptation" chapter?

7:45 to 8:30 p.m. Presentation on "Adaptive Behavior."

8:30 to 8:45 p.m. Break.

8:45 to 9:00 p.m. Talk about homework assignments and meeting place for next week. Turn in *Fisher Divorce Adjustment Scale* answer sheets, Personal Information Sheets, and Registration Agreements (if not done last week).

9:00 to 9:50 p.m. Small group discussion of the "Adaptive Behavior" presentation, and the "Adaptation" chapter in *Rebuilding: When Your Relationship Ends.* Sample questions:
- What kinds of adaptive behaviors did you learn as a child?
- What kind of adaptive behaviors did you use in your last love relationship? What kind of adaptive behaviors did your former love partner do?
- How did your unhealthy adaptive behavior cause you difficulty in your last relationship?
- What feelings have kept you stuck in rigid adaptive behavior?
- What can you do to nurture and take care of yourself this week?

9:50 to 10:00 p.m. Big group time and closure. Time for "I feel ____" messages.

Homework For Next Week's Seminar: (* Indicates most important homework)
*1. Read Chapter 8 "Grief" in *Rebuilding*.
*2. Call at least three people on the class list to get to know each other and create your support network.
*3. Do the homework suggested on the Adaptive Behavior Homework Sheet (p. 26).
 4. Read Chapter 5 on "Loneliness," Chapter 6 on "Friendship," and Chapter 7 on "Guilt/Rejection" if you have time.

Facilitating Session Two

Adaptation:
But It Worked When I Was a Kid!

This session helps participants discover their need to climb the mountain of adjustment so they won't repeat the same patterns of interaction in their future relationships. It helps them perform an autopsy upon their last relationship and why it ended or died. Having this chapter and session early in the ten weeks gives participants time to start changing behavior while they have the support of other class members to make these changes.

7:10 to 7:45 PM. Small or large group discussion?
The second session of this ten week class is usually when the group feeling emerges. This is especially true if the volunteer helpers have been calling participants which then results in participants calling each other. Is there anything in the class experience that can help improve this feeling of belonging to the group?

When I have smaller classes of fifteen or less, I usually do the opening sharing in the large group. It takes a long time to complete the exercise but the participants feel a part of the group after the sharing. With larger classes it is difficult to take enough time to share as a large group so I suggest the small group in order to have more time for other activities. The smaller group is more intimate and allows the participants to get to know a few people better. Participating in the large group allows them to know more people but not as intimately. Which plan you use will depend upon the size of your class, and your decision as to which size group will enhance the feeling and sense of belonging the most.

Should the small groups have the same or different participants each week?
Participants have a strong desire to get to know as many people in the class as possible. I once separated a class of twenty-eight into two groups and never allowed people to be in the other group. They complained frequently about not getting to know all of the people in the group. I suggest you

mix the participants in the group each week. Start the first week or two by counting off with as many groups as you have volunteer helpers. After a couple of weeks I suggest participants go with a small group leader they have not been with before. This usually mixes the groups enough.

On the other hand if you are having a class of maybe fifty or more, I would suggest you set it up to have a small group with a consistent membership each week. This allows them to have a home and a safe place in the large group. It is hard to have a group feeling in a group of fifty or more people.

Response to Homework Assignments
As a teacher, I believe any homework assigned needs to have the facilitator respond to the completed homework. In the small groups, the leader needs to ask each participant if they were able to call another person. This helps make the homework more meaningful and allows the participants to process what doing the homework meant to them.

There will most likely be at least one or more that did not make any calls. I "massage" their lack of doing the homework. I ask them what was the difficulty in calling. They often state they didn't want to bother another person. I then ask them if they received any calls. They will say yes if the volunteers have done their job. I ask how it felt to receive a call. They usually state happy, joyful, or positive feelings.

I then point out the inconsistency of their answers. They didn't want to bother another but when they received the call, they felt positive feelings. "Is it possible the person you call might feel the same feelings you felt instead of feeling bothered?" And then I encourage them to complete the calling before the next class because the homework sort of builds each week. If you don't do the homework for this week, it will be more difficult to do the homework for the next

24

week. Usually by the third week, every participant is completing the homework.

7:45 to 8:45 PM Suggested Large Group Presentation on Adaptive Behavior

This presentation follows the outline listed on the adaptive homework sheet on the next page. Participants sometimes have trouble thinking of adaptive and survivor behavior in the same context. I believe it is a continuum with one end just a few of your needs not getting met which leads to adaptive behavior. The other end of the continuum, with a lot of your needs not getting met, leads to the need for survivor behavior.

It is interesting to see the reaction of the participants when they are asked about healthy personality or relationship traits. Many have not thought about that before. After filling the blackboard or flip chart with a list of healthy traits, I ask them which of those traits were affirmed, supported, and encouraged in their childhood. They typically can find one or two. No wonder when we have the choice to choose between a healthy relationship and an unhealthy relationship, we choose the unhealthy one. It is more familiar to most of us.

After the group has ascertained that not many healthy traits were encouraged in their childhood years, I suggest when they didn't get their needs met, they called in an adaptive-survivor part. A partial list of those is on the homework sheet. This starts people thinking about their adaptive behavior.

This exercise is helpful to people in taking ownership for their contribution to the problems in their past relationship. It is easy to blame the other for their adaptive behavior without realizing that you have an equal and opposite adaptive behavior in your personality. You choose your partner to balance out your disowned or disused parts.

The next step is to identify what some of the your unmet needs are that lead you to choose your adaptive behavior. The list on the homework page is pretty inclusive but there are no doubt others not listed. It will be difficult for you to eliminate your adaptive behavior until you meet some of those unmet needs.

The homework is helpful for people to determine some of your adaptive behaviors. The important part is to do the homework which should help you to discover what your unmet needs were or are. If you say no to someone who asks you to do something, what do you feel? If the homework is difficult for you to do, then you know you have the right homework for your adaptive part.

The solutions are an important part of this exercise. I have asked participants since the beginning of doing this Seminar in 1974 to do something nice for themselves this week. Doing some self-care is an important solution to diminishing your somewhat compulsive need to do adaptive behavior .

It can be argued that this session is too difficult for those who have recently separated. There are some that are overwhelmed by looking at their adaptive parts. The old adage of planting seeds is appropriate in this situation. Not everyone is ready to assimilate this concept. For some it will take some time to germinate before they can benefit from learning the lessons we are trying to teach. For most participants this will be an important wake up call leading them to greater awareness of what adaptive behavior is all about. We teach it early in the class so the participants have time to work on change and transformation by practicing new behavior with other members of the class.

Huggle Time

The huggle is sort of a trademark of the Fisher classes. It is a great way to bring closure to the evening. It provides some touching which is very healing to those adjusting to a crisis. It is simply standing in a circle like a football huddle and touching each other in a way that is comfortable for everyone. Instead of football this is about the game of life. The comfortable touching may be only joining the little pinkie finger with the people next to them. It may be holding hands. Or it may be putting an arm around the shoulder of the person next to them.

It may be uncomfortable for some people to do a huggle. They may have come from a non-touching family of origin. They may be the introvert described in the Myers Briggs Personality Test who needs to be alone. They may have such a big love wound that they are afraid of touching of any sort.

I suggest "try it — you may like it." I support those who are having difficulty to talk about it while standing in the circle. I accept them because they are doing what is appropriate for them. If the person doesn't huggle this night of class, they may have trouble hugging for the rest of the ten weeks.

If you don't feel the group has enough closeness and trust to huggle, it may be appropriate to wait until the third session to huggle.

Looking Forward to Next Class

Introduce and talk about the topic of grief for next week's class. It is a good teaching technique to create continuity to the upcoming class, and to review the past week's class.

Adaptive Behavior Homework Sheet

Make a list of healthy, natural, and authentic behaviors.
Here are some examples mentioned in the Rebuilding Seminar "Adaptation" session. Examples: (1) Expressing feelings (2) Nurturing yourself (3) Asking for what you want and need (4) Being vulnerable with people around you (5) Asking questions (6) Having fun. Continue your own list and start thinking about what are healthy and healing behaviors.

Identify which of the above healthy traits (from your own list) were affirmed, encouraged, and supported at home or by your family of origin.
This is a difficult question helping you to look more closely at your childhood. When you didn't get your needs met in natural, authentic ways, you likely developed adaptive ("survivor") behaviors. The behaviors you chose were probably the best ones for your situation.

Identify some common adaptive behaviors and suggested homework for each:
1. If you identified yourself as **perfectionist** in your past relationship(s), your homework is to do less compulsive behavior. Examples: leave your bed unmade; let the dishes stack up a little.
2. If you identified yourself as an **over-responsible** person in your past relationship(s), your homework is to ask someone to do something for you and to say "no" when someone asks you to do something for them.
3. If you identified yourself as a **logical, rational** adult person in your past relationship(s), your homework is to say "I feel" messages every day and list as many feelings as you can each time.
4. If you identified yourself as a **people pleaser** in your past relationship(s), your homework is to figure out some homework to do on your own which will please *you* and help you build an identity of your own by tuning in to your own wants and needs.
5. If you identified yourself as having **other adaptive behaviors,** determine appropriate homework designed to help you experiment with becoming more authentic or balanced.
6. **If you don't know which adaptive-survivor behavior you have been doing,** your homework is to do all five of these homework assignments to see which are the most difficult for you. Those are the ones you need to work on the most.

Identify the underlying feelings or unmet needs from your childhood.
When you do this homework, pay attention to which one of the following six feelings seem to motivate your adaptive behavior. These six are guilt, rejection, fear, low self-worth, anger, or learned behavior (the urge to automatically behave in ways you learned as a child). Realize that you will have difficulty being authentic until you work through these six feelings. You can minimize these feelings by learning to give to yourself the love, nurturing and support you may not have received as a child. These are some suggestions of things to do to minimize these feelings:
1. **Guilt:** Put up a sign that says, "I'm Not Responsible" and read it daily.
2. **Rejection:** Have a friend or loved one write a list of ten or more things they like about you. Read the list until you believe it.
3. **Fear:** Write out a list of your fears. Share this list with a trusted person.
4. **Low self-worth:** Make a list of ten things you like about yourself. Read the list until you start to believe that the things you wrote are true.
5. **Anger:** Write "I am angry at you because..." as many times as possible. Then rewrite the list with "I am angry at myself because...."
6. **Learned behavior:** Make a list of the "shoulds" you learned as a child. Read each one and if you don't agree with it, rewrite it into something you do believe. Example: "Always eat everything on your plate" might be changed to, "I don't have to eat everything on my plate when I am on a diet," or "It's OK to stop eating when I'm full."

Solutions to Overcome Unhealthy Adaptive/Survivor Behaviors
Give to yourself the things you didn't get when you were young. Nurture and take care of yourself in as many ways as possible. Do something nice for yourself such as eating an ice cream cone, taking a bubble bath, exercising, taking a walk, reading a good book, getting a sun tan, and giving yourself a pat on the back as you progress. Try some new ways of behaving. Be as authentic and honest as you can with people. Be gentle with yourself; criticizing yourself usually won't help! Change takes time and is usually gradual. Give yourself lots of encouragement! Read and practice saying to yourself the statements on the handout sheet entitled "101 Ways to Praise a Child."

List of Adaptive Behaviors

Here is a partial list of adaptive behaviors — there are many more. You may have chosen one or more of these behaviors to help you survive, adapt, or to make the most of your childhood situation. Of all the possible behaviors you could have chosen, you probably chose the best one for you, considering the environment you grew up in. The behavior usually worked well in your childhood but it doesn't work as well in your adult relationships.

Adults tend to become more balanced, often by attracting people with different behaviors. If you chose one of the behaviors from the list below, you probably chose a person to be in relationship with that has a behavior from the opposite list. You thought you chose a love partner because you fell in love. Maybe you fell in love with a behavior in another that you have not yet developed in yourself. After the honeymoon period in your love relationship, you may dislike a behavior in another that you have not learned to develop or accept in yourself.

These adaptive behaviors aren't necessarily bad. It's only when they are rigid or extreme that they become a problem. Many of these behaviors protected you. If you felt pain, anger, fear, or hurt as a child, you needed to find ways to protect yourself. The process of taking charge of your life begins with your awareness of your behavior. Because this behavior often started when you were feeling pain, you may feel pain when you start recognizing and owning these parts of yourself. Healing usually occurs when you embrace your pain and decide to learn from it.

Because you developed these behaviors to compensate for unmet needs, you can continue your healing by learning to meet these unmet needs. Over-responsible people have learned to be good givers but usually have trouble taking. Start giving to yourself in the same manner you have been giving to others. When you start attempting to become responsible for yourself instead of being over-responsible for everyone else you usually will perceive yourself as being selfish. We suggest you look at this as *self-care* rather than selfish. Learning to nurture yourself will diminish your need for adaptive behavior.

To summarize, awareness will help you identify your adaptive behaviors, which will lead toward more authentic behavior. So, pay attention! Notice how you behave in your relationships with others. Be honest with yourself. Embracing any pain you may feel will help the pain become your teacher and help you discover your need for nurturing. You'll develop more self-respect and you may find it takes less effort to be authentic. The end result is that you will enjoy your life instead of adapting in order to survive.

Aggressive	vs.	Passive	Let's be logical	vs.	Off the wall
Over responsible	vs.	Under responsible	Fighter	vs.	Runner
Perfectionist	vs.	People pleaser	Blamer	vs.	I'm to blame
Controller	vs.	Rebellious	Clown	vs.	Invisible
Good Shepherd	vs.	Black sheep	Judge	vs.	Chameleon
Urge to help	vs.	I need help	Do it myself	vs.	Help me
Loves too much	vs.	Play it cool	Over-doer	vs.	Procrastinator
Smother mother	vs.	Wounded child	Work-aholic	vs.	Laid back
Superman	vs.	Lois Lane	Treadmill	vs.	Let's have fun
Superwoman	vs.	Casper Milquetoast	Complainer	vs.	Checks out
Intimidate	vs.	Martyr	It's your fault	vs.	It's my fault
Competitor	vs.	I can't	Gambler	vs.	Don't rock the boat
Caretaker	vs.	Victim	Whiner	vs.	Suffer in silence
Know it all	vs.	I don't know	Organizer	vs.	Disorganized
Criticizes others	vs.	Takes in criticism	Life of the party	vs.	Shy
Flame thrower	vs.	Asbestos suit	Center of attention	vs.	Withdrawn
Optimist	vs.	Pessimist	Confronter	vs.	Avoider
Righteous	vs.	I'm not okay	Enabler	vs.	Drug abuser

Authentic and Adaptive / Survivor Behaviors

This chart shows a continuum of five adaptive/survivor contrasted with more authentic behaviors. The goal is to grow from adaptive/survivor behavior towards authentic behavior.

Adaptive / Survivor Behavior	Authentic Behavior
Perfectionist Expects perfection in others Provides rigid limits to others Wants to look good Strives for perfection Hooks defensive response in others Makes others feel not OK Wants to change another Never enough	**Strives for Excellence** Gives constructive feedback to others Provides healthy limits to others Not concerned with appearances Strives for excellence Hooks appropriate response in others Helps others to feel OK Accepts others Satisfied with accomplishments
Over-responsible Smother-mother Gives another a fish Giving is self serving Hooks adaptive response in others Makes others feel not OK Controlling Caretaker Enabler Feels selfish when taking care of self	**Responsible to Self** Empathetic nurturing Teaches another to fish Giving is unselfish Hooks natural response in others Helps others to feel OK A catalyst to another's growth Caregiver Tough love Is able to do self-care
Rational-Logical Rigid Unable to access feelings Uses only facts and interpretations Dictator Makes others feel not OK Uses learned survival strategies Concerned with doing it the right way Expresses opinions, tries to convince others	**Thoughts and Feelings Balanced** Flexible Able to access feelings Uses all sub-personality parts Chairman of the board Makes others feel OK Makes loving choices Concerned about others Expresses beliefs and listens to others
Rebel Wants own way, rebellious Upsets system Behavior results in more chaos Concerned with rebelling Selfish manipulation Hooks criticism in others	**Healthy Identity** Able to bring about change Helps system work better Behavior results in efficiency and effectiveness Adjusts to situation Positive manipulation Hooks support in others
Needy and Hurt Child Mimics others Pretends to have a good time Expresses what others feel and express Concerned about fitting in Follower Hooks rescuing in others	**Natural and Creative Child** Creative and spontaneous Fun loving Expresses feelings easily Inner directed Leader Hooks spontaneity in others

It is Never My Responsibility to:

Give what I really don't want to give
Sacrifice my integrity to anyone
Do more than I have time to do
Drain my strength for others
Listen to unwise counsel
Retain an unfair relationship
Be anyone but exactly who I am
Conform to unreasonable demands
Be one-hundred percent perfect
Follow the crowd
Submit to overbearing conditions
Meekly let life pass me by
It is never my responsibility to give up who I am to anyone
for fear of abandonment.

— Author Unknown

When I Feel Responsible ...

FOR Others	TO Others
I fix	I show empathy
I protect	I encourage
I rescue	I share
I control	I confront
I carry their feelings	I level with them
I don't listen	I listen
I am insensitive	I am sensitive
***	***
I feel tired	I feel relaxed
I feel anxious	I feel free
I feel fearful	I feel aware
I feel liable	I feel high self-esteem
***	***
I am concerned with:	*I am concerned with:*
the solution	relating person to person
answers	feelings
circumstance	the person
being right	discovering truth
details	the big picture
performance	relating
***	***
I am a manipulator.	I am a helper guide.
I expect the person to	I expect the person to be
live up to my expectations.	responsible for self.
I feel fearful and hang on.	I can trust and let go.

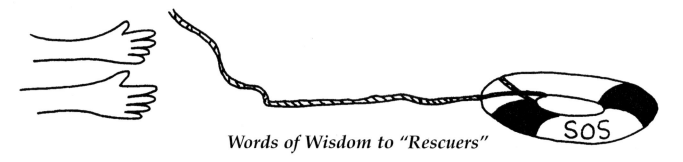

Words of Wisdom to "Rescuers"

A *rescuer* is a person who creates relationships with someone who *needs* rescuing. It feels so good for the rescuer to find someone to rescue, and it feels so good for the person needing rescuing, that often the two people end up being in a committed relationship with each other; an *over-responsible person* in relationship with an *under-responsible* person. I taught about 2,000 people ending a relationship in the Rebuilding class and the majority of them described their last relationship as an over- and under-responsible relationship.

You rescuers can easily believe you are "superior" to those who need rescuing. You believe you are doing all of these wonderful things that will get you brownie points in Heaven. It's true the things you get done are impressive. You are doing many kind deeds to, and for, others. Many times you provided an environment that allowed the other person to make tremendous personal growth. However, it is helpful to realize that your *rescuing* is often *controlling* others, keeping them smaller, weaker, dependent, and unable to do things for themselves. Your need to rescue someone means you will have to keep them in need of rescuing.

How did you become a rescuer? During your formative years, your emotional development became stunted. You stopped getting all of your needs met. You compensated by finding another little child in someone else who had also stopped growing. You began to give to them the things you were wishing someone would give to you. It made you feel better but it set up a dangerous precedent. You began being so involved in helping another that you were able to avoid looking at how much you needed to take care of yourself. You began the development of an adaptive-survivor part in order to feel better and get more of your needs met.

There are a wide variety of situations that could have encouraged you to develop a rescuer pattern of behavior. Sometimes you felt frustrated because you weren't getting enough attention or love. Sometimes you learned you could manipulate your environment by developing adaptive behaviors. Sometimes you felt very criticized and became adaptive to feel better instead of feeling not okay. Sometimes you suffered from a lack of parenting because your parents were not around or were especially weak in parenting skills. Sometimes everyone around you were under-responsible, perhaps even in an altered state due to drugs of some sort. You learned to be an over-responsible rescuer in order to keep your family functioning.

If you were to make a list of the many adaptive/survivor behaviors you could have chosen, being a rescuer was probably the best choice you could have made. It helped you make the most of your situation. It not only helped you to get more needs met, it often was very helpful to the people around you. It worked well in your formative years. It doesn't work as well in your adult relationships.

Relationships that are over/under often become stressful and sometimes end. Rescuers often become emotionally drained. The last stage of the relationship usually includes anger because you have given so much and received so little. You aren't able to see your contribution to the problem. You have difficulty taking so even if they tried to give to you, you would have trouble receiving. For you, it is easier to give than receive.

The system of interaction between the two people can become upset. Here are some examples. The couple have a baby and the rescuer is too busy with the baby to continue rescuing the partner. The rescuer finds a stronger identity by doing self-care. (This always feels selfish to rescuers when they start becoming responsible to self instead of over-responsible.) The person who is under-responsible becomes tired of being controlled and either leaves the relationship or becomes more responsible for self in the relationship. Any one of these "upsetting-the-system behaviors" can contribute to the ending of the relationship. If asked, you can usually identify when the system began to change. This can be the beginning of the end of your relationship. It is possible to change within the relationship without it ending, but both parties have to have awareness plus good communication to do this.

Leaving the relationship will not help rescuers to change. Instead you will probably find another person needing rescuing and create another over/under relationship. The challenge is to change the relationship with yourself by learning to become responsible for self instead of being either over- or under-responsible. It usually includes learning to take emotionally, instead of always emotionally giving to another. It means giving to yourself the things that you didn't get enough of in your formative years.

Think of the wonderful things that could happen if you transformed your well-developed "giving to others part" into a "giving to yourself part." You might find the happiness, contentment, and inner peace that you deserve. Good luck on your journey.

— Bruce

101 Ways To Praise A Child

These comments are good to share with your children, but they are also healing for you to say to yourself.

A big hug.
A-1 job.
A big kiss.
Awesome.
Beautiful.
Beautiful work.
Beautiful sharing.
Bingo.
Bravo.
Creative job.
Dynamite.
Excellent.
Exceptional performance.
Fantastic.
Fantastic job.
Good for you.
Great discovery.
Good.
Good job.
Great.
Hot dog.
How smart.
Hooray for you.
How nice.
Hip, hip, hooray.
I like you.
I trust you.
I respect you.
I knew you could do it.
I'm proud of you.
Looking good
Magnificent.
Marvelous.

My buddy.
Now you're flying.
Neat.
Nice work.
Now you've got it.
Nothing can stop you now.
Outstanding
Outstanding performance.
Phenomenal.
Remarkable.
Say, I love you.
Spectacular.
Super.
Super star.
Super job.
Super work.
Terrific.
That's correct.
That's incredible.
That's the best.
Way to go.
Wow.
What an imagination.
What a good listener.
Well done.
You are fun.
You are exciting.
You are responsible.
You believe.
You figured it out.
You mean a lot to me.
You make me happy.
You tried hard.

You made my day.
You make me laugh.
You mean the world to me.
You brighten my day.
You learned it right.
You care.
You're a winner.
You're growing up.
You're special.
You're important.
You're on target.
You're on your way.
You've got a friend.
You're wonderful.
You're spectacular.
You're perfect.
You're darling.
You're precious.
You're a joy.
You're a treasure.
You're catching on.
You're beautiful.
You're unique.
You've discovered the secret.
You're on top of it.
You're incredible.
You're a real Trouper.
You're important.
You're sensational.
You're a good friend.
You're A-OK.
You're fantastic.

PS: Remember, a smile is worth a thousand words.

© The Bureau for At-Risk Youth, 135 Dupont Street, Plainview, NY 11803

Risks

To laugh is to risk appearing the fool.

To weep is to risk appearing sentimental.

To reach out to another is to risk involvement.

To expose feelings is to risk exposing your true self.

To place your ideas, your dreams before a crowd is to risk their loss.

To love is to risk not being loved in return.

To live is to risk dying.

To hope is to risk despair.

To try is to risk failure.

But risks must be taken, because the greatest hazard in life is to risk nothing.

The person who risks nothing, does nothing, has nothing and is nothing.

They may avoid suffering and sorrow but they cannot learn, feel, change, grow, love, live.

Chained by their certitude's they are a slave, they have forfeited their freedom.

Only a person who risks is free.

– Author Unknown

A hug is a great gift.
One size fits all,
and it's easy to exchange.

Affirmations

Writing and saying affirmations out loud can be a powerful experience. Here are some examples of affirmations. We invite you to write one or more affirmations that are important for you in your own personal growth and self-actualization. Post them in a prominent place and say them out loud at least once a day.

1. I am making this crisis into a creative experience.
2. I am learning new and healthier ways of interacting with others.
3. I am taking charge of my life and creating the happiness I deserve.

My first affirmation is:

My second affirmation is:

My third affirmation is:

My reactions to the reading assignment in *Rebuilding* are:

My reactions to the Adaptation session of the Rebuilding Seminar:

What were some of the important things I learned in Session Two?

What are some of the important changes I am making in my thinking and my actions?

Session Three
Grief

"There's This Terrible Feeling of Loss"

Grief is an important part of your divorce process. You need to work through grief's emotions in order to let go of the dead love relationship. An intellectual grasp of the stages of grief can help you become emotionally aware of grief. Then you can do the grieving that you may have been afraid of before.

Lesson Plan For Session Three

Grief: There's This Terrible Feeling of Loss

Goals for Session Three:
1. To understand the process of grieving your loss(es).
2. To become aware of and understand the symptoms of your grief.
3. To give yourself permission to grieve as much and as long as you need to.
4. To learn the importance of self-care during your grief process.
5. To write a "good-bye letter," letting go of your past relationship(s).
6. To understand how to do "grief management."
7. To make an agreement with other group members to call someone if you're feeling really down or suicidal.
8. To understand the results of your *Fisher Divorce Adjustment Scale.*
9. To learn and use affirmations that will help you work through your grief process.

Agenda for Session Three:

6:45 to 7:00 p.m. Arrive, greet new friends, get a hug, and a cup of tea or coffee.

7:00 to 7:15 p.m. Centering and Connecting Exercise. Discuss lesson plans.

7:15 to 7:45 p.m. Small group discussion. What are the losses you're experiencing right now? What are you afraid you'll lose? How are these losses affecting you in terms of the feelings you're having? What kinds of losses are your children going through? What are some losses you've experienced in the past? How did your week go? What did you learn from the experience of doing the adaptive behavior homework? (see last week's lesson plans) Which of the six underlying feelings of guilt, rejection, fear, anger, low self-concept, or learned behavior are keeping you stuck in rigid, adaptive behavior?

7:45 to 8:00 p.m. Share the results of the *Fisher Divorce Adjustment Scale* scoring.

8:00 to 8:15 p.m. Discuss suicidal feelings and do a "no-suicide pact" with the group.

8:15 to 8:30 p.m. Break.

8:30 to 9:00 p.m. Lecture and presentation on grief and grief symptoms. Talk about writing the good-bye letter. Read a grief good-bye letter. Music.

9:00 to 9:55 p.m. Small group exercise. Spend about 20 minutes writing a good-bye letter. Write it to your former love-partner if possible. Otherwise, write it to the biggest loss you are ready to say good-bye to: pets, home, neighbors, husband or wife role, your old self, an old loss, etc. Read your letter to the other members of your small group, if you're willing, or have someone else read it out loud for you.

9:55 to 10:00 p.m. "Huggle-time" and closure. Time for "I feel ____" messages.

Homework For Next Week's Seminar: (* Indicates Most Important Homework)
*1. Read Chapter 9, "Anger" in *Rebuilding*.
*2. Let yourself grieve as much as you need to. If necessary manage your grief by setting aside some time to really let go and sob uncontrollably.
3. Call one or more group members for support in your grief process.
4. Write more good-bye letters to the biggest losses of love that you're ready to let go of. (We don't recommend that you send these letters, they're designed to help you grieve and heal.)
5. Continue nurturing yourself by doing some things that make you feel good this week.
6. Continue to do the homework on your adaptive behavior. (Example: asking someone to do something for you, or saying no when someone asks you to do something for them.)
7. Read Chapter 7, "Guilt & Rejection" in *Rebuilding* if you have enough time and energy.

Facilitating Session Three

Grief:
There's this Terrible Feeling of Loss

Facilitating Grief Work for the Participants

I have found that many people ending a relationship through separation and divorce do not know and understand that they are grieving. With the death of a spouse there is a funeral service, grief rituals, and many society mores and practices to help everyone understand there is a grieving process. Where is the funeral for divorce? It can be argued the final court hearing is the divorce funeral.

In many communities it is possible to obtain the final divorce decree without a court hearing. Has the couple missed out on having the funeral? Will this inhibit their process of grieving? Some people might need to find another ritual that will help them realize the relationship has ended.

People ending a love relationship don't always know it is necessary to grieve the loss. Some people don't understand what the grieving process is like. They need permission and support to actually do the grieving necessary as a part of the ending of a relationship whether through death or divorce.

A Suggested Breathing and Centering Guided Exercise

Because grieving is stressful and difficult, I teach participants how to deal with this stress through breathing exercises. I suggest they find a comfortable body position, close their eyes, and experience the following breathing exercise. I gently talk them through it.

"Take five deep belly breaths expanding your stomach with as much air as possible. Breathe deeply so that all of your lung capacity is used. Breathe in through your nose but breathe out through out through your mouth, making as much breath noise as possible. Breathing is a way we can cleanse our bodies. Blowing out the air feels cleansing to our bodies.

Next try a different way of breathing. Instead of taking more time to inhale than exhale,

reverse it by exhaling as long as possible. Shape your mouth as though you were going to whistle but blow gently instead for as long as you can blow. It helps to attain an altered state and to go into an alpha brain wave pattern. Do this type of breathing for three times.

Next, go into your body and check for any tightness or tension. We all know you breathe into your lungs but imagine you are breathing into that place in your body which is needing love and attention. Send love energy into the tense places by thanking your body for telling you that you need to relax and let go of some tension. Breathing and sending love to those parts of your body may result in a feeling of profound relaxation and calmness.

Next, go into that place in your solar plexus that is your special place. A place where you carry many of your feelings. A place where the little person inside of you may reside. Breathe into that place. Send love energy by saying to yourself, "I think you are a neat person" "I like you." "I want to make you feel safe and comfortable." "It is okay to feel stressful and weary sometimes while I am grieving a loss of love." Think of some things you can say to that special spot that will make it feel good.

While you are in this state of being inside yourself think of some positive affirmations you can say to yourself. Here are some examples. "I am capable of grieving my loss of love." "It is okay to experience the grief symptoms I am feeling in my body." "I am open to learning ways of healing myself." What affirmation can you give for yourself?

Now check in and determine how you are feeling. Are there any spots in your body that need more attention and love? Do you feel more relaxed? Are you ready to open your eyes? Come back to the room and open your eyes when you are ready."

I like to ask for participants to share their experience with the group. It completes the exercise and allows them to process what the centering exercise was like for themselves and others.

Small Group Discussion

This is a good time to emphasize the importance of the homework assignments by asking each participant to share what it was like to do the homework. Which adaptive behavior have they learned to do? What did they feel when they did the homework? What did they learn about themselves by doing the homework? For those who didn't do the homework, suggest that they do it for the next week. They will have observed how much benefit those that completed the homework received and will be more motivated to do the homework in order to gain the same benefits. Participants need to know they will be asked to talk about the homework and this provides more motivation to complete the homework.

Sharing the Results of the FDAS

It is possible and desirable to encourage the participants to mail in their completed FDAS answer sheets so the results can be shared in the second session. Most likely you will not have all of the answer sheets turned in and scored by the second session. Consequently, you will be sharing FDAS results in the third session.

I like to have both the participant's individual profile and the class average profile on each individual profile sheet. This can be done by tracing a class average profile on a blank sheet of paper as a master and running the individual profile sheets through a copy machine. I teach about the profile sheet by showing a sample profile sheet with the class average on it. If you hand out the individual profile sheets the participants will be interested only in looking at their profiles and not listen to the explanations of the scoring profiles. I suggest you explain the scoring results and then pass out the individual profile sheets.

There is always a concern about the participants who have a profile near the bottom of the graph which indicates they are feeling a lot of emotional pain. These people know they are hurting but the stark reality of seeing it on the sheet is difficult for some. If the class average is on the sheet they are able to see they are not that different from the class average. I publicly state that it is okay and normal for some people in the class to have low scores. This does not mean they are mentally disturbed or sick. It only means they are hurting emotionally about the ending of their love relationship which they already know. I offer some hope by pointing out that the people with the lowest pre-test scores will show the most gain when they take the FDAS at the end of the class.

There is a confidentiality question of how much to share with the volunteer helpers concerning the participants' scores on the FDAS. To play it safe I only share with the volunteers the people with low scores so they can be on the lookout for them. I don't let the volunteers see the individual profile sheets or the actual scores. Most of the people will naturally share their scoring results with others and with the volunteers. It is a good line to keep telling the volunteers, "Keep looking out for the strays."

I encourage participants to ask about any questions they might have concerning their individual FDAS scores. It is good to share these results before the break because people can then ask questions during the break.

Suicide Feelings and the Suicide Pact

Those with a low FDAS score, possibly under a total score of 300, will often be thinking of suicide. I think it is best to mention this. A good approach may be saying, "Some of you may be feeling suicidal. This is normal and okay. On the other hand, it is important that you discuss your feelings with the facilitator or someone you feel safe with." *Do not underestimate the importance of emphasizing this.*

I asked most of the 200 classes that I taught about feelings of suicide. About 75% of class participants admit to having feelings of suicide sometime since their separation. Enrolling in the class will often greatly diminish the feelings of suicide. Some will still feel suicidal even though they are in the seminar. In fact, they may not act on their suicidal feelings until they have progressed far enough to feel stronger. Some participants will have suicidal thoughts during the fourth stage of grief which may come months or even years after the actual separation.

Here is a great motto. "Anything you can talk out, you don't have to act out." It is very helpful to talk about suicide in the class. Give permission for each person to talk about it. The volunteers have had some suicide training as part of the volunteer training day and many of them will be okay to listen to participants talk about suicide. We had about 8,000 participants in the divorce seminars here in Colorado before we had a suicide. That is much below the average probability for suicide in people going through the adjustment process after a love relationship has ended. I want to go after the lost sheep even if it is such a small percent of those taking the class.

We have implemented a suicide pact. After we have talked about suicide in class we form a circle and hold hands. I ask them to repeat after me, "I believe I will feel better by talking to another person. Therefore, I promise to reach out and call or talk to another person if I should be feeling suicidal." I highly recommend this exercise as a way of encouraging people to talk to another when they are feeling suicidal.

Grief Presentation and Letter of Goodbye
The lesson plans explain much of this activity. Basically the presentation needs to reinforce that it is okay to grieve and to give people permission to grieve. Appropriate music will help most people experience feelings of grief. The good-bye letters will also help to facilitate the grieving.

Micro Lab Small Group Activity
The purpose of this group activity is to encourage participants to experience grief. It is an alternative method of helping participants experience their feelings of grief. I believe the letter of good-bye will bring better grieving results for most classes.

Questions are designed to start on a more superficial level and to delve deeper with each question. Expected time to complete the exercise might be from five to ten minutes for each person in the small group. A different person starts each time when answering the next question.

Questions
1. Share with the group a happy or exciting thing that happened to you this past week.
2. Share with the group your first impression of your spouse when you first met him or her.
3. Share with the group how you and your spouse informed each other that you or he/she wanted a divorce.
4. Share with the group your feelings of inadequacy at the time of your separation.
5. Share with the group the saddest feeling or loneliest feeling you've had since the separation or divorce.

The Body Sculpture Handout Sheets
We have found it more appropriate to do the body sculptures on the anger night. The *Rebuilding* book has the body sculptures in the Trust chapter. It is a very powerful exercise and I highly recommend doing it in this session. It usually helps people to get in touch with their feelings of anger

Preparing the participants for Feelings of Grief the Following Week
Many participants will have a week of grieving after the grief night. It is helpful to inform them of this and help them prepare for a week when many will feel down and somewhat depressed. The class exercise opens up their feelings of grief and it is helpful for them to continue the grieving process after the class.

Talking about this possibility during the huggle accomplishes two things. It makes them feel more normal and okay if they are having a "heavy" week. Secondly it will encourage them to do the actual grieving which they might tend to suppress if they aren't given permission to do it.

Life Stress and Physical Illness

Thomas H. Holmes and Richard H. Rahe conducted research that shows a connection between life stress and physical illness. The stress is either from internal sources or external sources; it is irrelevant where it originates. The stress comes from major changes in our lives and if the change is important enough, it may cause a crisis. If we do not adjust, there is an increased chance that a major physical illness will occur within two years after the crisis!

After researching about 5,000 people, they arrived at the following formula. The total life change units is calculated from the chart below, by adding up the number of change events that occur within a six-month period of a person's life.

Total Life Change Units	Percentage of Major Illness Within Two Years
150 LCU's	20% to 30%
300 LCU's	40% to 50%
450 LCU's	60%
600 LCU's	80%

Conclusion: Increasing your ability to cope with stress, will decrease your chances of having a major illness.

Social Readjustment Rating Scale

Rank	Life Event	Mean Value LCU's	Rank	Life Event	Mean Value LCU's
1	Death of Spouse	100	22	Change of Responsibilities at Work	29
2	Divorce	73	23	Son/Daughter Leaving Home	29
3	Marital Separation	65	24	Trouble with In-Laws	29
4	Jail Term	63	25	Outstanding Personal Achievement	28
5	Death of Close Friend or Family Member	63	26	Wife Begins or Stops School	26
6	Personal Injury or Illness	53	27	Begin or End School	26
7	Marriage	50	28	Change in Living Conditions	25
8	Fired from Job	47	29	Revision of Personal Habits	24
9	Marital Reconciliation	45	30	Trouble with Boss	23
10	Retirement	45	31	Change in Work Hours/Conditions	5
11	Change in Health of Family	44	32	Change in Residence	20
12	Pregnancy	40	33	Change in Schools	20
13	Sex Difficulties	39	34	Change in Recreation	19
14	Gain of New Family Member	39	35	Change in Church Activities	19
15	Business Readjustment	39	36	Change in Social Activities	18
16	Change in Financial State	38	37	Mortgage or Loan less than $10,000	17
17	Death of a Close Friend	37	38	Change in Sleeping Habits	16
18	Change to Different Line of Work	36	39	Change in Number of Family Get-Togethers	15
19	Change in Number of Arguments w/Spouse	35	40	Change in Eating Habits	15
20	Mortgage Over $10,000	31	41	Vacation	13
21	Foreclosure/Loan or Mortgage	30	42	Christmas	12
			43	Minor Violations of the Law	11

Reference:

Holmes, Thomas H. and Rahe, Richard H. "The Social Readjustment Rating Scale," *Journal of Psychosomatic Research*, Vol. II, No. 2, August, 1967, pp. 213-218

Use this page to take notes on during the presentation in Session Three on Grief

Letting Go

Letting go does not mean to stop caring,
it means I can't do it for someone else.

Letting go is not to cut myself off,
it's the realization I can't control another.

Letting go is not to enable,
but to allow learning from natural consequences.

Letting go is to admit powerlessness,
which means the outcome is not in my hands.

Letting go is not to try to change or blame another,
it's to make the most of myself.

Letting go is not to care for,
but to care about.

Letting go is not to fix,
but to be supportive.

It's not to judge,
but to allow another to be a human being.

Letting go is not to be in the middle arranging the outcome,
but to allow others to affect their own destinies.

Letting go is not to be protective,
it's to permit another to face reality.

Letting go is not to deny,
but to accept.

Letting go is not to nag, scold or argue,
but instead to search out my own shortcomings and correct them.

Letting go is not to adjust everything to my own desires,
but to take each day as it comes and cherish myself in it.

Letting go is not to criticize and regulate anybody,
but to try to become what I dream I can be.

Letting go is not to regret the past
but to grow and live for the future.

Letting go is to fear less and live more.

— Author Unknown

Then, Now, Tomorrow

Then *was the past.* Now *is the present.* Tomorrow *will be the future.*

Then *was memories, both good and bad It was friends of old.*
It was happiness and understanding. It was failures, success and compromise.

You cannot live in the Then. *You must hold onto the good and learn*
from the bad. You must remember the success and understand the failures.
You must use them to grow and become a more complete person.

Now *is painful. It is remembering the past, no matter how hard you try*
not to. Now *is looking at failures with a piercing mind. Success is hard to*
measure, or comprehend. Now *is recovery, thinking about life.*

You have to always live in the Now. *Everyday is* Now, *the present.*
Decisions made Now *will affect your tomorrow.* Now *is the present,*
Now *is the past,* Now *is the future. All these things are rolled into one,* NOW.

Tomorrow *is what will become. Happiness, sorrow, pain and LOVE.*
Will we be happy tomorrow? No one really knows that, but it can be determined.

Tomorrow *is dreams, hopes and prayers. It is change, for better or worse*
this change will come.

Tomorrow. *It must come or life becomes stagnate like a lifeless pond on*
the prairie of desolation.

Tomorrow *is what you make of it.*

—Author Unknown

Good-bye Letters

Dear Jane,

Even though it will probably only take you five minutes to read this, if you read it at all, it took me a long time to write it. It also took a lot of courage to speak my mind and my heart. I hope you don't see this as an attack on you, its not. Forgive me for my anger, its necessary. Anger is like a fire   I had to get it out and burn it up, so that I can be rid of it. I'm not trying to hurt you in any way. I know you've been hurt deeply already. I can't undo that, but I'm truly sorry. I've been hurt too, and I'm doing my best to forgive. I don't hold you responsible for my pain.

This is a letter to you, but not for you, it's for me. It's just a part of the work that I needed to do, so that I can get on with my life.   Good-bye.

Good-bye attorney's fees and custody battle

Good-bye frustration, wondering, waiting, never knowing

Good-bye foolish wishes and dreams

Good-bye to a marriage that was destined to fail, even before it began

Good-bye to the bitching when you couldn't get your way

Good-bye anger, at me, whether or not I had it coming

Good-bye sex, when you felt it

Good-bye trying to please you, which was practically impossible

Good-bye threats   who cares?!

Good luck kids, sorry you have to live with her for now

Good-bye insanity when my frustrations and anger overcame me

Good-bye your way, hello my way!

Good-bye being manipulated because I allowed myself to be

Good-bye feeling worthless, no matter what I did

Good-bye fear of what you'd do next

Good-bye looking for love elsewhere, and wishing I could come home to it

Good-bye   glimmer of hope   that someday it will work out

Good-bye pouring my heart out to you and feeling like you just didn't care

Good-bye craving to be loved by the woman I loved

Good-bye fear of failing, hello to being human

Good-bye abstinence

43

Good-bye resistance to every change I wanted

Good-bye to you planting a garden and me having to take care of it

Good-bye to being married once and having it work out

Good-bye to raising a family together

Good-bye to sticking together through thick and thin

Good-bye to no help from you, sometimes when I really needed it

Good-bye to your family, whom I grew to love

Good-bye to being an uncle to your sister's kid

Which reminds me, good-bye to your sister who will probably always take advantage of you

Good-bye to trying to understand your anger, maybe you were born with it

Good-bye to your hugs, which I'd die for when I could get them

Good-bye to growing old together

Good-bye to retiring to our mountain home together, my life long dream

Good-bye to my mother's friend, she really loved you, you know

Good-bye to our lake, and the happiest times of my life

Good-bye to catching fish with you there, 'til our arms hurt

Good-bye to hearing our kids saying "Mommy & Daddy" all in one sentence

Good-bye to being there as a team for them for the rest of our lives

Good-bye to being there, at home, for them whenever they need me

Hello to being a weekend father   great! Just what I've always dreamed of

Good-bye to the chance to put them to bed every night, reading books together, saying prayers and telling them I love them

Good-bye to showing them by example how two people can work it out, pray together and stay together and love their way through any problem no matter what

"Till death do us part"   the truth is, our marriage has died, and with it a part of me has died too. Now I'm alone, one of the "walking wounded"

Good-bye to loving you   damn, that's hard to say! But, there's no point in it now, what's the use?

Thank you Lord for the tears to wash away the pain, I've got to go on now. I can't believe how hard this is, but in a way it feels good to let go.

Someday, I've got to have faith that someday, I'll be healed. I wish you the best with all my heart.

Good-bye Letters

Dear Tony,

Good-bye to wonderful memories. Good-bye to a bitter ending.

Good-bye to our morning showers — together. What a wonderful way we started the day!

Good-bye to filling our photo album — family pictures — of yours and mine.

Good-bye to feeling secure in a blanket of love. Although our vows had not been "traditional," "our life" felt so very real.

Good-bye to the puppy's kisses, and our early-morning ritual of dog bones and tricks that we quietly shared, while my love lingered in dreams and the warmth of our bed.

Good-bye to my fish friends. I will miss your enthusiasm and joy when you hungrily saw me. Will you miss me?

Good-bye to a house that felt like mine — but wasn't — nor ever would be.

Good-bye to the adventurous couple — partners — the team.

Good-bye to hearing "How's My Babe?" You could make me feel so special with your smile!

Oh my love, I never got to say good-bye — with you — and be reaffirmed that our relationship had been meaningful. And it was, you know, so very meaningful to me.

Good-bye to my once best friend — and thoughts of "What did I do?" or "could have done."

Good-bye to the anger you have for me. Who are you really angry at?

> You know my only crime was loving you.

So Good-bye and Happy Holidays —

May your New Year be filled with love, happiness, tenderness, trust, courage, truth, and especially, peace of heart and peace of mind.

Good-bye to pain. I've learned — first hand — it doesn't have to last so long, but love can last forever — or for however long you believe you can love.

Our memories, our caring, and my hope for our future — I sealed them away in a tomb in my heart. Someday, when I am ready, I will remember how special it was, and you will be there for as long as I have that heart.

But now, most of all…

Good-bye to who I thought I was — your lover — your "other half" — your cook — your maid

> She doesn't exist anymore. A much stronger, wiser, independent, witty, beautiful,
>
> > and very stalwart, cautious woman took her place.

I like her — she's fun!

> And you know what? She doesn't need anyone to be that way,
>
> > but I don't think she ever really did — she just didn't know it.
>
> Good-bye to what once was — today is today — and welcome future, with love!

> Good-bye, my Babe. So long.

Affirmations

Writing and saying affirmations out loud can be a powerful experience. Here are some examples of affirmations. We invite you to write one or more affirmations that are important for you in your own personal growth and self-actualization. Post them in a prominent place and say them out loud at least once a day.

1. I am ready to acknowledge and grieve the losses I'm experiencing in my life.
2. I am committed to investing more in the relationship with myself so that I can become the person I am capable of becoming.
3. I am strong enough emotionally to allow myself to grieve appropriately.
4. I am open and ready to learn how to love myself more.
5. I am committed to reaching out to others and asking for what I need and want.
6. I am simply feeling my feelings and that's perfectly natural.

My first affirmation is:

My second affirmation is:

My third affirmation is:

My reactions to the reading assignment in *Rebuilding* are:

My reactions to the Grief session of the Rebuilding class are:

What were some of the important things I learned in Session Three?

What are some of the important changes I am making in my thinking and my actions?

Referral List of Therapists, Attorneys, and Clergy

We would like to compile a referral list of therapists, attorneys, and clergy to help people who are ending a love relationship. Would you list your recommendations in the spaces below?

I would recommend the following *therapist(s)* as being competent, helpful, and knowledgeable to help people who are ending a love relationship.

Name

Address

City   State, Zip   phone

e-mail address

Name

Address

City   State, Zip   phone

e-mail address

I would recommend the following *attorney(s)* as being fair, competent, and knowledgeable to help people who are ending a love relationship.

Name

Address

City   State, Zip   phone

e-mail address

Name

Address

City   State, Zip   phone

e-mail address

I would recommend the following *clergy person(s)*, and the church they are affiliated with, as being supportive, understanding, and caring to help people who are ending a love relationship.

Clergy Person

Name of Church

Clergy Person   Name of Church

Clergy Person   Name of Church

e-mail address

Session Four
Anger
"Damn the S.O.B.!"

You'll feel a powerful rage when your love relationship ends, whether you're the dumpee or the dumper. Those angry feelings are a natural, healthy part of being human. How you express them makes all the difference. Don't bottle your feelings up inside, but you needn't get aggressive either. You can learn to express both your divorce anger and your "everyday" anger constructively. And you can learn to reduce your anger altogether.

Lesson Plan for Session Four
Anger — Damn the S.O.B.!

Goals for Session Four:
1. To begin to view anger not as an enemy of love, but as an ally of love.
2. To learn that anger can help to cleanse relationships by helping to resolve issues.
3. To learn how to reduce inappropriate anger in your life.
4. To discover some new skills for coping with anger.
5. To discover positive, appropriate ways to express anger.
6. To identify some of the other feelings associated with your anger.
7. To learn and use affirmations that will help you become more comfortable with your anger.

Agenda for Session Four:

6:45 to 7:00 p.m. Arrive, greet new friends, get a hug, and a cup of tea or coffee.

7:00 to 7:10 p.m. Connecting and centering exercise.

7:10 to 7:55 p.m. Presentation: Anger.

7:55 to 8:30 p.m. Large group "Body Sculpture" exercise. Facilitator(s) demonstrate all body sculptures. Participants then break into dyads and try body sculptures. Discuss with dyad partner your experience while doing the body sculptures. Talk openly with your partner during this exercise — really play the part as much as possible. Act out any other creative body sculptures you can identify from your previous relationship. Which body sculptures describe the way(s) you related to your former love-partner?

8:30 to 8:45 p.m. Break.

8:45 to 9:00 p.m. Talk about homework assignments for next week.

9:00 to 9:55 p.m. Small group exercise: Be sure to allow each person a chance to share.
- How do I express my anger? (Explode, somatize, feel angry at myself, depression, sarcasm, passive aggressive, denial, own it and talk it out, misdirect it toward the wrong person, etc.)
- If I'm not happy about the way I'm expressing anger, what would work better for me?
- If I'm stuffing anger, what ways will I begin to let it go?
- What behaviors or situations "push my buttons"?
- How did people in my family deal with anger when I was a child?
- What have I done to nurture and take care of myself this week?
- What other feelings are related to my anger? (Fear, frustration, rejection, guilt, loneliness, low self-worth, etc.)
- What are my emotional blocks to expressing anger appropriately? (Nice guy, fear of rejection, anger is unhealthy, anger is destructive, etc.)
- What positive ways can I express and dissipate my anger that will not be harmful to me or to another?
- Share anger letters or other homework I've done that was important for me.

9:50 to 10:00 p.m. Big group time and closure. Time for "I feel _____" messages.

Homework For Next Week's Seminar: (*Indicates most important homework)
*1. Reading assignment: Chapter 11, "Self-Worth" in *Rebuilding*.
*2. Write a list of ten things you like about yourself.
 3. Call one or two people in the group and talk about adaptation, grief, and anger in your life.
 4. Continue to nurture yourself by doing things you like to do.
 5. Write "I am angry at you because _____!" as many times as you can. Do not share this writing with the person you are angry at. Instead, when you feel your anger is dissipated, go back over the letter and rewrite these anger statements into "I am angry at myself because _____!" Use anger as an avenue into understanding yourself better.
 6. Use some of the new skills you've learned for expressing and coping with anger.
 7. Read Chapter 10, "Letting Go" in the textbook.

Facilitating Session Four

Anger — Damn the S.O.B.!

Anger is a pervasive stumbling block. It pervades all of the other blocks. It affects our feelings of self-worth, our children, sexuality, denial, etc. Most people going through divorce at some time or another, if the situation is appropriate, are capable of committing a violent act. My research indicates the anger block takes the longest time to work through of any of the blocks. Strong feelings of anger can last for as long as three years after the separation. It is indeed an important stumbling block. Participants need all the help they can get to overcome this block.

Body Sculptures Exercise
Participants often need to perform an autopsy upon the past dead relationship. This body sculpture exercise is helpful in doing that. People are able to understand on a deeper feeling level the problems in their past relationship. This exercise also helps them to access feelings of anger so they can work through them.

Two people, usually the facilitator and a volunteer helper, demonstrate the different body sculptures. They illustrate how to hold their bodies but they also use appropriate words for each sculpture. The healthy one is hard to illustrate in the book because of the movement necessary. The healthy relationship sometimes has the couple embracing each other or walking together like when they are co-parenting, sometimes they are standing apart because each person is dedicated to maintaining their own identity while remaining in relationship with each other. An important aspect is choosing to share their lives together rather than resenting being in the relationship because of a feeling of obligation. The healthy relationship people are committed to personal growth, awareness and communication.

After the demonstration the participants break into dyads and experience the body sculptures themselves. It is important for them to experience both parts of the sculpture. For example, each one should take a turn at being on the pedestal and feeling how precarious and lonely it feels. The participants will readily discuss the experience with their dyad partner. Often they will be so involved discussing that the facilitator will have to end their discussion of the body sculptures in order to get on with other activities.

The Three Strikes of Anger Exercise
This is also a powerful exercise to help people understand the difficulties of expressing anger. I explain that we are going to be at bat as though we are playing ball. We will have three chances to hit the ball with each strike being a chance to find positive ways of dealing with anger.

1. First I ask them to share what they learned about dealing with anger from their family of origin. I put the list on a blackboard or flip chart. I usually get responses like:
a) anger was okay for adults but not for kids.
b) love was withdrawn when I was angry as a kid.
c) boys could be angry but all us girls could do was cry.

After the chart is full I point out that, "I asked what you learned about anger from your family of origin, not what *negative* things you learned. Do any of you have some positive ideas about ways to deal with anger?" Usually they can find a few. I suggest most of us missed the first chance to hit the ball and learn about anger.

2. I next ask them what they learned from society about dealing with anger. This would include schools, churches, movies, TV, etc. I get a similar list of negative ways of dealing with anger. Often I hear "anger and violence are connected." That anger "leads to power and control of others." It appears most of us have missed the ball on the second strike of learning how to deal with anger in a positive manner.

3) I next ask, "what does your inner critic voice say to you when you become angry?" The inner critic is the little voice inside your head that is usually critical of thoughts and behavior. I hear people report that their inner critic is saying things like: "You'd be out of control if you got angry." "Becoming angry is a sign of weakness." "People won't like you if you are angry."

I conclude by stating that it is no wonder so few people deal with anger in a positive manner. We have had three chances and most of us struck out. What do we do now?

Finding Positive Ways to Dissipate Anger

If we are going to overcome striking out we can start by sharing ways of dissipating anger energy. I then ask them to share ways they have found to dissipate anger that does not hurt them or another person. I often start the list.

- Exercise and physical activity. (I share the sticker on my refrigerator that states, "clean houses have angry housekeepers.")
- Finding an appropriate place to shout and scream.
- Making ten snowmen in your driveway, writing a person's name on them, and running over them with your car.
- Writing down angry feelings and then burning up the piece of paper in the fireplace.
- Putting on loud music and dancing.

Specific Ways of Changing to Minimize Feeling Angry Again

After the person has dissipated the anger energy how can they minimize the chances of becoming angry again? I ask for contributions from people again.

1) Learn to be more assertive so you don't have to pay the price of being nice.

2) Own the anger as yours. Stop blaming others for making you angry. They might be the trigger for you becoming angry, but they can't make you angry if you don't have those feelings inside of you.

3) Use anger as a mirror. Think of what pushes your buttons. Have you ever wondered why that specific behavior pushes your buttons? Learn more about yourself by looking at what makes you angry.

4) Realize that anger when dealt with properly can lead to intimacy. It can be the great cleanser that "tears down walls in your relationships with others so you can build bridges." Anger and love are allies, not enemies.

5) Anything you can talk out, you don't have to act out. Learning good communication skills using "I" messages will help you work through anger in a positive manner.

6) Improving your feelings of self-worth. People with low self-worth often feel they don't have the write to become angry.

Conclusion to the Three Strikes of Anger

This is a very powerful presentation on anger. It is tremendously helpful for people ending a relationship and experiencing what sometimes feels like overwhelming anger.

Micro Lab Small Group Activity

The purpose of this group activity is to build group trust and ability to share. Each group member can learn to invest of themselves into the group process. Questions are designed to start on a more superficial level and to delve deeper with each question. Expected time to complete will be five to ten minutes for each group member. A different person starts each time when answering the next question.

Questions

1. Share with the group your reactions to the body sculptures. Did any fit your love-relationship? Can you create another body sculpture for your relationship?
2. Share with the group how you usually express your feelings of anger.
3. Share with the group a specific situation in which you got angry.
4. Using this specific situation, tell how you:
   a. Recognized that you were angry.
   b. Identified the source of your anger.
   c. Understood why you were angry.
   d. Dealt with the situation.
   e. Could have dealt with the situation more realistically.
5. Generally, how can we deal with anger more constructively?

Looking Forward to Next Week.

Prepare participants by letting them know they may feel angry this next week. Remind them it is okay to feel anger but caution them about finding positive ways of expressing anger that will not hurt themselves or others.

Either before or during the huggle, talk about next week's topic of self-worth. Ask them to raise their hand if they would like to improve their feelings of self-worth. Usually 100% of the participants will raise their hand. Point out that the homework of writing twenty things they like about themselves is a powerful and effective way of improving their feelings of self-worth.

Healthy Ways to Work On Anger

(This list was compiled by junior high children in a summer activities program.)

1. Take a time-out to cool down, then talk out the problem.

2. Run as fast as you can.

3. Sing.

4. Bounce a ball as hard as you can.

5. Punch a pillow/mat/grass.

6. Cry.

7. Yell into a pillow (or away from others).

8. Scribble.

9. Draw what you are angry about.

10. Write in a "feelings journal."

11. Shred newspapers.

12. Count to ten (or 20 or 100 or ...).

13. Stomp and storm (alone).

14. Pretend you are a balloon and take in a deep, slow breath, hold it to the count of three, and let it out slowly.

15. Talk to a friend.

16. Squish marshmallows.

17. Do any kind of exercise.

18. Listen to music.

19. Make noise with a whistle, wooden spoon and a pot, etc.

20. Make faces about how you feel.

Using Anger to Become More Empowered

Many of you who are ending a love relationship are afraid of angry feelings in yourself and others. You believe anger is aggressive, destructive, and harmful to self and others. The extreme rage you might be feeling I have called "angerism."

I had to learn that it is okay to be angry toward someone I love or have an important relationship with. I had to learn that anger can be empowering instead of aggressive, productive instead of destructive, healthy instead of harmful. Many people in your position ask how you can use your anger to become empowered.

Imagine the woman who has no college education, put her partner through graduate school, and kept hearing how inadequate she was because she was not "educated." When she becomes divorced, she might discover she is feeling a great deal of anger about her lack of education. She may use these angry feelings to become empowered and give herself the determination to find the time and money to obtain her own college degree.

Imagine the man who was informed many times he had no feelings. When the divorce comes, he discovers large fires of anger burning inside of him. He takes the Rebuilding class determined to learn to access and share his feelings of anger. He finds it empowering to talk about feelings and is grateful for the opportunity to transform his anger into emotional strength.

How about it? Can you find ways to use your anger to become a more powerful and self-actualized person? It is worth looking into. You might discover how good it feels to be able to control your life instead of carrying around a burden of anger that keeps you emotionally tired and overwhelmed.

— Bruce

Use this page to take notes on during the presentation in Session Four on Anger

Illustrating Relationships With Body Sculpturing

A body sculpture is a way of experiencing different kinds of relationships by placing your body in a way that models or sculptures a particular kind of relationship. Doing this exercise may help you to discover aspects of your past and present relationships. This exercise—based largely on the work of famed family therapist Virginia Satir—is experiential and more meaningful when you actually model these relationships with another person. I recommend doing it on anger night because it often helps participants to discover angry feelings.

The A-Frame Dependency Relationship

This is the dependency relationship where two people lean on each other because they have not learned to be whole single people by themselves. The dependency upon the other person some-times feels good, but it is somewhat confining. When one person wants to change and grow, it upsets the other person. Try to put into words some of the feelings that you have while you are assuming this position.

The Smothering Relationship

The smothering relationship is quite frequently seen in high school and teenage relationships. The vocabulary for this relationship is, "I cannot live without you. I want to spend the rest of my life with you. I will devote myself completely to making you happy. It feels so good to be so close to you." Many love relationships start with this kind of a smothering relationship. They may grow and change into another body sculpture position because there is not enough space for the two people to grow in this position. The emotional closeness of the smothering relationship may feel good for a while, but eventually you feel smothered and trapped.

The Pedestal Relationship

The pedestal relationship is about worshipping the other person and saying "I love you not for what you are but for what I think you are. I have an idealized image of you. I would like to have you live up to that image." It is very precarious being up on the pedestal because there are so many expectations from the other person. As with all of these relationships there are problems of communication. Because you are in love with the person's idealized image, you are looking up to and trying to communicate with that image instead of with the real person. There can be a great deal of emotional distancing in this relationship.

The Master-Slave Relationship

"I am the head of this family. I am the boss. I will make the decisions around here." This relationship is not necessarily the male being the boss and head of the family. There are many females who are masters in the family and make all of the decisions. Many relationships have one of the partners with a stronger and more powerful personality than the other. This is okay until the relationship becomes rigid and has no flexibility. If one person makes all of the decisions, then emotional distancing and inequality will most likely result. The rigid relationship tends to take a great deal of emotional energy maintaining one person as master and the other as slave. There is often a power struggle going on that interferes with the communication and intimacy of the relationship.

The Boarding House Relationship

These two people are linked together by their elbows with a marriage contract or a relationship agreement. There is little communication in this relationship. Often the people watch TV while they are eating and spend time apart for the remainder of the evening. Communication is especially difficult in this relationship. It is a loveless relationship in the sense that there is no expression of love towards each other. Again, when you try this position, notice that when one person moves forward, changes or grows and matures, the other person is linked to that growth. This makes it a confining relationship.

The Martyr Relationship

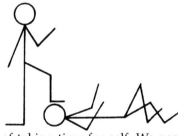

The martyr is the one on the hands and knees in the figure above and who completely sacrifices him or herself in trying to serve the other people in that family instead of taking time for self. We need to see and understand that the martyr position is a very controlling position. When the person on hands and knees moves, the other person who has a foot on the martyr is thrown off balance.

What emotion does the martyr use for gaining control? He/she controls through guilt. How can you be angry at the person who is doing everything for you, who is taking care of you completely? The martyr is very efficient at controlling people around him/her. It is very difficult to live with a martyr because you feel so guilty that you are unable to express your angry feelings and ask for what you want or need. Many of you have had a martyr parent.

Understanding the martyr relationship may help you learn to deal with your martyr parent.

The Healthy Love-Relationship

These are two people who are whole and complete and have found internal happiness within themselves. They are two upright people who are not leaning upon or tangled up with the other person. They have an abundance of life to share with the other person. These two people choose to *stay* together rather than having to *be* together. They can be emotionally close like the smothering position. They can walk hand in hand as they might do in co-parenting their children. They can move apart and have their own careers, lives and friends. They choose to stay together because of their love for each other rather than having or needing to stay together because of some unmet emotional needs. The healthy love-relationship is a relationship that gives both people the space to grow and become themselves.

Summary

Try these different positions with a friend and see how they feel. You may want to create another body sculpture to describe your relationship. Try to put into either spoken or written words, the feelings that you were experiencing while you were in each body position. Which of these positions describe your past or present love relationship? Did the healthy relationship feel uncomfortable? Many people state that their past love relationship went through almost all of the unhealthy body positions.

The reason for having you do this experiential exercise is to help you understand some of the difficulties that went on in your love relationship which may have been related to the angerism that you are presently feeling. Any of the above unhealthy body sculpture positions might result in feelings of anger.

So What Can I Do About My Anger?

(From Alberti and Emmons, Your Perfect Right. Reprinted with permission from the publisher.)

We'd like to offer you a simple, three-step method for dealing with anger in your life. We'd like to, but we can't. Anger is complex, and handling it is complex as well. Fortunately, however, there are some really helpful procedures which are of proven value. As it happens, they fall naturally within three general guidelines: (1) minimize anger in your life; (2) cope before you get angry; and (3) respond assertively when you get angry.

Minimize Anger in Your Life

Our first ten steps are borrowed from the Williams' recommendations in *Anger Kills*:

(1) Improve your relationships with others through community service, tolerance, forgiveness, even caring for a pet.

(2) Adopt positive attitudes toward life through humor, religion, acting as if today is your last day.

(3) Avoid overstimulation from chemicals, work stress, noise, traffic.

(4) Listen to others. Practice trusting others.

(5) Have a confidant. Make a friend, and talk regularly, even before you feel stress building.

(6) Laugh at yourself. You really are pretty funny, you know. (It goes with being human.)

(7) Meditate. Calm yourself. Get in touch with your inner being.

(8) Increase your empathy. Consider the possibility that the other person may be having a *really* bad day.

(9) Be tolerant. Can you accept the infinite variety of human beings?

(10) Forgive. Let go of your need to blame somebody for everything that goes wrong in life.

To the Williams' ten, we add two of our own to this "anger-in-your-life" section:

(11) Work toward resolution of problems with others in your life, not "victory."

(12) Keep your life clear! Deal with issues when they arise, when you feel the feelings — not after hours/days/weeks of "stewing" about it. When you can't deal with it immediately, arrange a specific time when you can and will!

Cope Before You Get Angry

Anger is a natural, healthy, non-evil human emotion and, despite our best efforts to minimize its influence in our lives, all of us will experience it from time to time, whether we express it or not. So, in addition to the steps above, you'll want to be prepared before anger comes:

(13) Remember that you are responsible for your own feelings. You can choose your emotional responses by the way you look at situations. As psychologists Gary McKay and Don Dinkmeyer put it, *How You Feel Is Up To You*.

(14) Remember that anger and aggression are not the same thing! Anger is a feeling. Aggression is a style of behavior. Anger can be expressed assertively — aggression is not the only alternative.

(15) Get to know yourself. Recognize the attitudes, environments, events, and behaviors which trigger your anger. As one wise person suggested, "Find your own buttons, so you'll know when they're pushed!"

(16) Take some time to examine the role anger is playing in your life. Make notes in your log about what sets you up to get angry, and what you'd like to do about it.

(17) Reason with yourself. (Another good idea from the "Williams collection.") Recognize that your response will not change the other person. You can only change yourself.

(18) Deflect your cynical thoughts. Williams suggests thought stopping, distraction, meditation.

(19) Don't "set yourself up" to get angry! If your temperature rises when you must wait in a slow line (at the bank, in traffic), find alternate ways to accomplish those tasks (bank by mail, find another route to work, use the time for problem solving).

(20) Learn to relax. Develop the skill of relaxing yourself, and learn to apply it when your anger is triggered. You may wish to take this a step further by "desensitizing" yourself to certain anger-invoking situations.

(21) Develop several coping strategies for handling your anger when it comes, including relaxation, physical exertion, "stress inoculation" statements, working out resolution within yourself, and other procedures,

such as those suggested by the Williams (items 1-10 above) and those we've noted in the box at the end of this chapter.

(22) Save your anger for when it's important. Focus instead on maintaining good relationships with others.

(23) Develop and practice assertive ways to express your anger, so these methods will be available to you when you need them. Be spontaneous when you can; don't allow resentment to build; state your anger directly; avoid sarcasm and innuendo; use honest, expressive language; let your posture, facial expression, gestures, voice tone convey your feelings; avoid name-calling, putdowns, physical attacks, one-upmanship, hostility; work toward resolution.

Now you've developed a healthy foundation for dealing with angry feelings. Go on to the following section and get ready to handle your anger when it comes.

Respond Assertively When You Get Angry

(24) Take a few moments to consider if this situation is really worth your time and energy, and the possible consequences of expressing yourself.

(25) Take a few more moments to decide if this situation is one you wish to work out with the other person, or one you will resolve within yourself.

(26) Apply the coping strategies you developed in step 21 above.

If you decide to take action:

(27) Make some verbal expression of concern (assertively).

(28) "Schedule" time for working things out. If you are able to do so spontaneously, fine; if not, arrange a time (with the other person or with yourself) to deal with the issue later.

(29) State your feelings directly. Use the assertive style you have learned in this book (see #23 above), with appropriate nonverbal cues (if you are genuinely angry, a smile is inappropriate!).

(30) Accept responsibility for your feelings. You got angry at what happened; the other person didn't "make" you angry.

(31) Stick to specifics and to the present situation. Avoid generalizing. Don't dig up the entire history of the relationship!

(32) Work toward resolution of the problem. Ultimately you'll only resolve your anger when you've done everything possible to resolve its cause.

Here are a few verbal expressions others have found useful for expressing anger:

"I'm very angry."
"I'm getting really mad."
"I strongly disagree with you."
"I get damn mad when you say that."
"I'm very disturbed by this whole thing."
"Stop bothering me."
"That's not fair."
"Don't do that."
"That really pisses me off."
"You have no right to do that."
"I really don't like that."
"I'm mad as hell, and I'm not going to take this anymore!"

Relationships Are My Teachers

It is easy to believe that others are responsible for your anger. "That person is a pain in the neck" is a common way of putting it. It is also easy to play the role of the victim and believe there is nothing you can do about the things that others are doing to you. This victim role often leads to stuffing anger and letting it smolder inside of you like the glowing embers of a campfire.

Instead of projecting the blame for your anger upon another, or believing there is nothing you can do about how they are making you angry, I suggest you think about each person being your relationship teacher. Each time you feel angry, think about the opportunity of using your anger to learn more about yourself. Take some responsibility for your anger. It's yours, not someone else's.

Where did you learn to be angry? What feelings are underneath your anger? What does it mean when another person pushes your buttons and you react emotionally to their behavior? Maybe the person that you feel angry around is actually helping you to access your feelings and learn about yourself. Maybe that person is your relationship teacher. Probably the relationship that is most stressful for you is your most important relationship teacher. Maybe one of your most important teachers is your ex!!

One of the great lessons you can learn when your relationship ends is learning about yourself through your feelings of anger. The person that you have been blaming because they are causing you so much anger, may be giving you a gift of pain. Can you embrace your anger and learn from it? Can that stressful relationship become your teacher helping you to become empowered? Can you change the "gift of pain" into a "gift?"

Have you thought about loneliness being one of your feelings underneath anger? Maybe feeling lonely is a passive and indirect way of feeling angry because it seems no one is there loving you, comforting you, and making you feel okay. I think I sometimes feel angry when I believe there is no one in the world who cares about me.

Maybe taking a journey back in time will be helpful to you in letting go of your anger. The reflection below, from an old friend of many years ago, is one of my favorite writings.

— Bruce

The Swing

Tonight I walked. It was warm, and something within me cried with tension and restlessness. So, I walked. My feet took me all around the town, past brightly lit houses with mothers doing dishes, and kids doing homework, and dads reading newspapers. And I walked. And I was alone, silent, unnoticed.

My feet took me to the old school playground — the one I hurry past every day on my way to classes. I chose my used-to-be favorite swing, and watched the last rose color left over at the earth's edge from the sunset.

*I was alone — yet close to something I cannot define. I began to swing. I pushed myself off the ground and pulled with my legs, going higher and higher. I leaned way back, and moved dizzily through the air. My soul felt free. **Free!** And for a moment I was a child again. Happy, alive, beautiful. I plotted to slowly die down to a certain level, then bail out. The best part is bailing out.*

Bailing out is when I'm able to fly — leaving my anger and loneliness behind. I wonder if my anger and loneliness are still swinging on that swing? I know when I bailed out, I felt more peaceful, happy, and contented.

— JoAnn

Affirmations

Writing and saying affirmations out loud can be a powerful experience. Here are some examples of affirmations. We invite you to write one or more affirmations that are important for you in your own personal growth and self-actualization. Post them in a prominent place and say them out loud at least once a day.

1. I can express my anger in healthy ways.
2. It's okay to be angry.
3. Anger can be empowering.
4. Anger comes from many different sources.

My first affirmation is:

My second affirmation is:

My third affirmation is:

My reactions to the reading assignment in *Rebuilding* are:

My reactions to the Anger session of the Rebuilding class are:

What were some of the important things I learned in Session Four?

What are some of the important changes I am making in my thinking and my actions?

Session Five
Self-Worth

"Maybe I'm Not So Bad After All!!"

It is okay to feel good about yourself. You can learn to feel better about yourself, and thus gain strength to help you adjust better to a crisis. As you successfully adjust to a crisis, you will feel even better about yourself!

Lesson Plan for Session Five

Self-Worth: Maybe I'm Not So Bad After All

Goals for Session Five:

1. To understand how important your self-worth is and how it's related to every part of your life.
2. To improve your feelings of self-worth.
3. To learn to accept "warm fuzzies" from yourself and others.
4. To learn to give yourself "warm fuzzies" in order to improve your feelings of self-worth.
5. To learn and use affirmations that will help you improve your feelings of self-worth.

Agenda for Session Five:

6:45 to 7:00 p.m. Arrive, greet new friends, get a hug, and a cup of tea or coffee.

7:00 to 7:10 p.m. Centering and Connecting Exercise.

7:10 to 7:50 p.m. Small group exercise:
- Share list of ten or more things you like about yourself.
- Share a recent experience of feeling angry. How did you handle it? (If you're not happy with the way you handled it, how would you like to have handled it?)
- How did the above experience influence how you felt about yourself?
- Share something you did to nurture yourself this week.
- Share what you plan to do next week to nurture yourself.
- Share my "I am angry at you (me) because ___" list (homework from last week)
- How was your week?

7:50 to 8:20 p.m. Presentation: Self-Worth.

8:20 to 8:35 p.m. Break.

8:35 to 8:50 p.m. Talk about homework assignments for next week. Discuss feelings about journaling.

8:50 to 9:50 p.m. Warm fuzzy exercise.

9:50 to 10:00 p.m. Big group time and closure. Time for "I feel ___" messages.

Homework For Next Week's Seminar: (* Indicates most important homework)

*1. Reading Assignment: Chapter 12 in *Rebuilding*, "Transition" (Read this one, there's a lot there!!)

*2. Read "Steps to Improving Your Feelings of Self-Worth" (page 42).

*3. Think of a behavior that you would like to change. Think of ways to change it by taking "baby steps" so that you make a specific change each day in your behavior. Keep it up for a week. Congratulate and reward yourself a lot. Share with a friend who'll encourage you. Next week think of another change you would like to make. Keep making positive changes for the rest of your life.
   It will help you to like yourself better and to improve your feelings of self-worth.

4. Write a list of ten or more things you like about another person, such as one of your relatives, son or daughter, or friend. Give the list to the person. (It could be a meaningful birthday or Christmas present.)

5. Practice the steps of improving your self-worth recommended in Chapter 11. Which of the steps are most important to you? Which one is the most difficult to do?

6. Read Chapter 15, "Trust" in *Rebuilding*.

Facilitating Session Five

Self-Worth:
Maybe I'm Not So Bad After All!

This is a very important night in the ten weeks. People have been in the divorce pits experiencing the difficult and often painful building blocks. Improving self-worth is a way to climb out of the divorce pits and resolve many of the other blocks. If a person scores high on the self-worth subtest in the FDAS they will often make an easier and more rapid adjustment to the ending of their love relationship.

Some facilitator's have rearranged the order of the ten week sessions and have self-worth later on in the ten weeks. One reason for this is that participants know each other better and are able to offer more meaningful warm fuzzies to each other. Another reason is that this night is such an emotional high it is a hard act to follow with the next week's session. However this night gives people so much emotional strength and ability to grow through the rest of the ten sessions that it is appropriate to have it as session five.

Small Group Sharing

The size of the large group will again determine whether to have small group sharing of the homework. Seminars of twelve or less will probably share in the large group.

It is one thing to write twenty things about themselves but it is another to share the list out loud with others. One of the volunteer helpers could share a list first. Ask them how they felt when they shared their list out loud as a participant and how it felt to share it this time. They will report how much easier it was to share the second time. This helps minimize the anxiety of participants sharing it the first time.

The other questions on the lesson plans are about the anger lesson. People will have had a week to process the anger work and may have important insights to share that they weren't aware of the week before.

Preparing Participants for the Warm Fuzzy Exercise

At the end of the presentation and before the break it is helpful to do a preview of coming attractions of what will take place after the break. It is somewhat traumatic for some to experience the warm fuzzy circle exercise. Some preparation is helpful.

Here are some sample comments. "After break we will be doing an exercise that can be of tremendous help in improving your self-worth. We want you to learn how to accept and internalize warm fuzzies better. Some participants have called it 'reprogramming my computer.' We usually remember more criticism from our childhood than we do compliments. The data we took in helped determine our feelings of self-worth. Now we need to put in more positive data so we can change the decision of how we feel about ourselves. The warm fuzzy circle will help us do that."

The Warm Fuzzy Exercise

Here are some ideas for doing the warm fuzzy exercise. "We are going to each take a turn at being on the hot seat by listening to people give us warm fuzzies. The lower our feelings of self-worth, the hotter the seat will be for us. We will go around the circle starting on my left, (again prepare the person on the left with a little warning). While that person is on the hot seat we will all verbally share a warm fuzzy with that person. Example: "I like your sense of humor." It is better to use "I" messages and speak directly to the person rather than third person comments talking about that person.

There are a couple of rules we will be following. The first is "You are not allowed to skip your turn in this exercise. Many times in the past four sessions if you didn't want to share it was okay. But we don't want you to miss this wonderful opportunity of improving your feelings of self-worth." (This prevents a possible problem. When it comes time for a person to be on the hot seat they may state they choose not to participate in this exercise. Telling them ahead of time they can't skip a turn prevents the potential problem.) Secondly, we want you to internalize and integrate the comments as deeply in your psyche as possible. You can say, "Thank you," "That feels good," "I didn't know that about myself," etc. These all indicate you were trying to take in the comments of others and believe them. But if you say, "That's not always true," "If you knew me better you wouldn't be saying that," "I like your sense of humor also," we all get to yell "foul." Either putting up defenses which are designed to not allow the warm fuzzies in, or grabbing the warm fuzzy and throwing it back at the other person are against the rules and the other participants get to yell "foul."

It is also powerful to have an "amen" corner. When one participant shares a warm fuzzy with the person on the hot seat and another participant really agrees or was going to say the same thing, the person or persons who agree can all say, "amen." This is reinforcing the comments and the person who is on the hot seat will internalize the warm fuzzies even better when more than one person is sharing them.

It is one thing to hear the comments but we need to send home valentines like we received when we were in grade school. Some people will have difficulty hearing the comments and will need to read them later on. Also in the future when a participant is having a bad day reading the warm fuzzies can make a big difference.

Pass out to each participant as many sheets of paper as there are participants in the warm fuzzy exercise. You may need to plan ahead in order to have enough sheets of paper. For example, if there are twenty-five in the class, you will need twenty-five times twenty-five or 625 sheets of paper. The five by eight inch pads of paper available in grocery stores work well for this exercise. You will need a pad of paper for each participant.

While each person is on the hot seat, the other participants can write comments while they are verbally sharing warm fuzzies. Each participant does not have to say and write the same warm fuzzy. Each person does not have to share a verbal warm fuzzy. In fact you may not have enough time for each to do so. Care should be taken to not interfere with the person hearing the warm fuzzies by passing the papers during the exercise. If you don't have a distribution system it may take a long time and a lot of confusion to distribute 625 sheets of paper. Here is a system that makes the process much easier.

Have each person write a warm fuzzy on a separate page of the pad of five by eight papers. When you have completed the warm fuzzy exercise, have the participants tear off the pages they have written on keeping them in order. Then have each one pass their completed pad of papers to the left or the same way you went around the circle when you were doing the verbal warm fuzzies. When the participant finds the sheet on top with their name on it, they simply take off their warm fuzzy sheet and pass it on to the next participant.

The above method allows the 625 sheets to be distributed with a minimum of confusion. Caution: There is usually one person in the group who doesn't follow directions and has to pass their sheets around individually. Has the warm fuzzy exercise helped them improve their self-worth? Being the odd one who didn't follow directions may make them feel lower feelings of self-worth. Make light of the situation with humorous comments.

If there is a blackboard or flip chart available, write an example of a warm fuzzy on it. Put the hot seat person's name at the top of the piece of paper. Write the warm fuzzy such as, "I like your sense of humor" next. At the bottom sign your name. A signed warm fuzzy is much more meaningful than one that isn't.

Time is important in this exercise. Allow about three minutes for each person to be on the hot seat. Plan ahead by allowing three minutes times the number of participants for the amount of time it will take to do this exercise. For example, twenty-five participants will take about seventy-five minutes to complete the exercise. Watching a clock or watch will help keep the process moving so that every person will have the same amount of time being on the hot seat.

It is difficult for the facilitator to keep the hot seat moving and still write warm fuzzies at the same time. If you can't write and facilitate at the same time there are a couple of things you might do. You may not want to take part in the exercise but encourage the participants to support each other. (Participants will be disappointed in most cases.) Or, you may want to write your comments ahead of time. Important: Be sure to ask about "I" feel messages in the huggle after this exercise. It is a powerful exercise and affects people in a profound manner.

Steps to Improving Your Feelings of Self-Worth

The Decision
"Whatever you think, so shall you be." The first step is deciding you really want to improve your feelings of self-worth. This is not a decision to be taken lightly because changing how you feel about yourself will change almost everything in your life.

Diminish Self-Judgments
I suggest you start your self-love process by making a list of all the negative messages you keep saying to yourself. Some examples might be "You are really stupid." "You are conceited." "You'll never amount to anything." (Note: self-judgments are usually "you" messages.) After you have made your list, try restating them into more positive messages. For example, you might change the one that says, "You're being selfish and self-centered" into "I'm learning do my self-care."

Make Your Relationships with Others More Loving
Most of us have relationships with others which may be destructive to feelings of self-worth. Sometimes these relationships are with spouses, family members, or close friends. You need to make these relationships more loving instead of letting them act in a negative way upon your self-concept. You need to do one of three things: (a) end these relationships — difficult to do sometimes; (b) improve these relationships so they help you feel better about yourself; and (c) get so strong inside that such relationships cannot be destructive to your self-worth.

Learn to Give Yourself Affirmations
Make a list of ten or more things you like about yourself. Secondly, ask a close friend, family member, or lover to make a list of ten or more things he or she likes about you. Put these lists in place where you will read them every day, such as on your bathroom mirror. Read them until you start to believe them!

Learn to Accept and Believe Compliments
Have you ever tried to compliment a person with a low self-concept? Compliments run off them like water off a duck's back. The next time you receive a compliment say, "thank you," "that feels good," or "I never knew that." Concentrate on letting the compliment penetrate you as deeply as you can so you feel different deep inside.

Nurture Yourself on a Daily Basis
Take time to enjoy the sunsets, to meditate, to have quiet time by yourself or with someone else, to read something stimulating, to enjoy the flowers. Do something so that when you go to bed you can say, "Today I did this for myself."

And so it is! You are a special human being. Unique and different from anyone else. It is okay to like and love yourself. You are a loving — and lovable — person.

**Grant Me The Serenity
To Accept the People I Cannot change
The Courage To Change the One I Can
And the Wisdom to Know**
It's Me!

Author Unknown

Rules for Being Human

You will receive a body.
You may like it or hate it,
but it will be yours for your entire lifetime.

You will learn lessons.
You are enrolled in a full-time informal school called life.
Each day in this school you will have the opportunity to learn lessons.
You may like the lessons or think them irrelevant and stupid.

There are no mistakes, only lessons.
Growth is a process of trial, error and experimentation.
The "failed" experiments are as much a part of the process
as the experiment that ultimately succeeds.

A lesson is repeated until learned.
A lesson will be presented to you in various forms until you have learned it.
When you have learned it,
you can go on to the next lesson.

Learning lessons does not end.
There is no part of life that does not contain lessons.
If you are alive, there are lessons to be learned.

"There" is no better than "here."
When your "there" has become a "here,"
you will simply obtain another "there"
that will, again, look better than "here."

Others are merely mirrors of you.
You cannot love or hate something about another person
unless it reflects to you something you love or hate about yourself.

What you make of life is up to you.
You have all the tools and resources you need.
What to do with them is up to you.
The choice is yours.

Your answers lie inside you.
The answers to life's questions lie inside you.
All you need to do is look, listen, and trust.

— Author Unknown

I'm Okay — You're Okay

You start out your life being smaller, younger, weaker, less intellectual, and more dependent than those people around you. It is easy to believe you are "not okay" or "less okay" than those around you. If you don't experience enough love, nurturing, trust, and attention, you tend to stay in the "not okay" belief.

As you begin to grow and develop, you begin to learn the other basic "okay" positions. These are: "I'm not okay and neither are you"; "I'm okay and you're not okay"; "I'm not okay and you're okay." It would be interesting to understand why some people stay stuck in one of these positions and are not able to attain the ideal of "I'm okay and you're okay."

Presently you are taking control of your life which includes determining which "okay" position you tend to believe about yourself, and working towards becoming more okay. Sometimes you will have to accept that you are a human being with some "not okay" parts to you. Sometimes you can find enough self-love to love those parts that you used to not like about yourself. Sometimes it is okay to be "not okay."

As you are ending a love relationship, it is normal to discover some "not okay" feelings you have about yourself. They may be old leftovers from the past that need to be accepted for what they are — beliefs that were learned at an earlier stage of your growth and development. You learned them once — now maybe you can relearn what you learned earlier.

Do you believe it is possible to have a "corrective emotional experience?" Can you accept the nurturing from others in this class that are able to accept parts of you better than you can accept yourself? Can you learn to give to yourself the things you believe you didn't receive earlier in you life? Can you learn to take compliments and warm fuzzies from others when you are not sure you believe them yourself? Can you talk about and become vulnerable about your "not okay" feelings?

One of the valuable lessons you are learning in this class is that you can feel "more okay" than you may have felt in the past. We call that "turning a crisis into a creative experience."

— Bruce

Hugging

Hugging is healthy: It helps your body's immune system, it keeps you healthier, it helps cure depression, it reduces stress, it induces sleep, it's invigorating, it's rejuvenating, it has no unpleasant side effects. Hugging is nothing less than a miracle drug.

Hugging is all natural: It is organic, naturally sweet, no pesticides, no preservatives, no artificial ingredients and 100% wholesome.

Hugging is practically perfect: There are no movable parts, no batteries to wear out, no periodic checkups, low energy consumption, high energy field, inflation-proof, non-fattening, no monthly payments, no insurance requirements, theft-proof, nontaxable, non-polluting, one-size-fits all and, of course, fully returnable.

Affirmations:

Writing and saying affirmations out loud can be a powerful experience. Here are some examples of affirmations. We invite you to write one or more affirmations that are important for you in your own personal growth and self-actualization. Post them in a prominent place and say them out loud at least once a day.

1. I am a special person.
2. I like the way I feel about myself.
3. I accept myself unconditionally.

My first affirmation is:

My second affirmation is:

My third affirmation is:

My reactions to the reading assignment in *Rebuilding* are:

My reactions to the Self-Worth session of the Rebuilding class are:

What were some of the important things I learned in Session Five?

What are some of the important changes I am making in my thinking and my actions?

Session Six
Transition

"I'm Waking Up and Putting Away My Leftovers"

Early experiences are extremely influential in our lives. The attitudes and feelings you developed in your childhood, and in relationships with family, friends, and lovers, are bound to carry over into new relationships. Some of these attitudes and feelings are helpful, others are not. If you are experiencing a personal identity-rebellion crisis, you may be seriously straining your love relationship. Recognize your valuable leftovers so you can keep and nourish them; work at changing those which get in the way.

Lesson Plan for Session Six
Transition: I'm Waking Up and Putting Away My Leftovers

<u>**Goals for Session Six:**</u>
1. To understand how "rebellion" may have affected your relationships.
2. To understand that *external rebellion* is an outward attempt to find one's identity, usually by acting out at someone who's perceived to be "parental."
3. To understand that *internal rebellion* is a process of working through inner-conflicts in order to create an identity separate from the expectations of others.
4. To help the partner of the person in rebellion to (a) grow and expand awareness instead of playing the victim role, and (b) to set appropriate boundaries with a rebellious person instead of acting "parental."
5. To give yourself permission to rebel when necessary in order to make positive changes.
6. To learn to use affirmations that will help you discover and maintain your own identity.
7. To explore how your childhood and family of origin influences may have contributed to the ending of your relationship.
8. To learn how "leftovers" and "power struggles" affect relationships.

<u>**Agenda for Session Six:**</u>
7:00 to 7:10 p.m. - Centering and Connecting Exercise.

7:10 to 7:45 p.m. - Small group sharing. What did you do this last week to improve your self-worth? What's a change in behavior that you could make this week that would really help you feel better about yourself? How are you doing at accepting compliments from others — not just being polite, but really taking them in? What changes in improving self-worth suggested in Chapter 11 did you make last week? What was your experience of writing "what I like about you" lists for friends or family members? Who else would you like to give this kind of list to?

7:45 to 8:30 p.m. - Presentation: Transition: four stages of rebellion, family of origin influences, childhood influences, leftovers and power struggles.

8:30 to 8:45 p.m. - Break.

8:45 to 9:00 p.m. - Discuss homework assignments for next week.

9:00 to 9:15 p.m. - Warm fuzzies for those who were missing last week.(Use whatever time necessary)

9:15 to 9:50 p.m. - Small Groups:
- What stage of Fisher's growth and development model are you in? (Page 70.)
- What stage is your former love-partner in?
- What is an example of a "should" and a "want" that you're struggling with right now?
- How has this inner-conflict been projected out onto your relationships?
- Are you clear about the difference between internal and external rebellion?
- How did your family of origin or childhood influences contribute to the ending of your love relationship?
- How have your relationships with family members been affected by the ending of your love relationship?
- What changes have taken place in you since the ending of your relationship?

9:50 to 10:00 p.m. - Big group time and closure. Time for "I feel ____" messages.

<u>**Homework For Next Week's Seminar:**</u> (* Indicates most important homework)
*1. Reading assignment: Chapter 13, "Openness" in *Rebuilding*.
*2. List some of the masks you've been wearing and begin to explore whether you need to continue wearing them.
 3. Find positive and constructive methods of rebellion that will improve your self-worth and help you establish your identity.
 4. Identify childhood and family of origin influences that are negatively affecting your relationships.
 5. Continue writing in your journal about these influences and how they are affecting your relationships.
 6. For more information on family of origin, childhood influences, power struggles, and finding identity through rebellion, we suggest you read *Loving Choices*, by Bruce Fisher and Nina Hart.

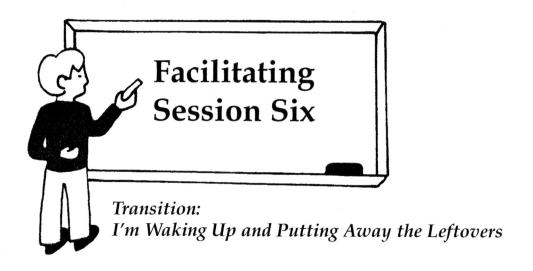

Facilitating Session Six

Transition:
I'm Waking Up and Putting Away the Leftovers

The Transition chapter is an expansion of the old Rebellion chapter. It is an attempt to help people continue to understand rebellion as an identity process helping us free ourselves from the shoulds.

It also helps in understanding some of the other influences that had a negative effect upon your past relationship that ended. All of the concepts introduced in this chapter are developed in greater length in my book, *Loving Choices.* I recommend that you the facilitator read this book in order to better understand the concepts in this chapter. I am attempting to introduce these concepts in the ten week divorce seminar and then further develop them in the succeeding ten week relationships class.

Participants are continuing to climb up the mountain. After using self-worth as a way of stepping out of the divorce pits we will see if improved self-worth will help them become strong enough to better understand how they contributed to the ending of the love relationship. The challenge for the facilitator in this chapter is to help participants understand the connection between family of origin, childhood, leftovers, and power struggles as obstacles in love relationships. Rebellion is a way to let go and transform beyond these obstacles so we can do a better job of taking control of our lives. I think this chapter in *Rebuilding* emphasized the immature aspects of rebellion but failed to explain the transformation possible in the rebellion process. Perhaps the presentation by facilitator's can help overcome this somewhat narrow viewpoint of rebellion. It is hard to appreciate the growth possible during the rebellion process until people have experienced this growth themselves.

Since the publication of *Rebuilding* in 1981, I have received many calls from readers of the book asking questions about the rebellion process. Most of the calls are from the partners of those in rebellion. It is not a coincidence the person in rebellion rebels against their partner — the partner is usually much like a parent personality. Facilitator's will need to help the partner of the person in rebellion see the need to invest in nurturing themselves instead of parenting others.

I found that often about half of the seminar participants were the partner of a person in rebellion. Seldom does the person in rebellion choose to take the class although this appears to be changing because more people in rebellion seem to be participating in the seminar. If the participant's partner has been doing external rebellion they will have difficulty appreciating the positive aspects of rebellion. They will be reluctant to rebel themselves because they think it might be as upsetting to others as it was to them. It is important to emphasize the difference between internal and external rebellion for these people. Calling internal rebellion "internal processing" might make the concept more palatable for those who were partners in rebellion. It is helpful for the partner to see the need to outgrow the adaptive behavior of being parental and over responsible that they were exhibiting in the past relationship.

I have found many participants unaware of how important family of origin and childhood influences have been in their past relationships. This chapter may help those going through a waking up process to become aware of their contribution to the relationship problems. It takes courage, good self-worth and commitment to look at ourselves. This session may be difficult for those who are intent upon proving the failures and weakness of their former love partner.

A sophisticated concept related to this chapter is that many couples tried to improve their love relationship and make it more healthy. When this process of change occurred there was an increase in emotional stress and pain and the relationship often ended just before the dawning of a new and healthier relationship. This chapter may lead to some couples understanding this concept and turning to the Healing Separation described in appendix B of *Rebuilding* as a way of finishing the stretch towards health and a new and revitalized relationship. Important: Continue to impress upon participants that healing separations only work when both partners are committed to individual growth and an improved relationship with themselves first.

There are many good books listed in the bibliography at the end of this chapter. I recommend that facilitator's read as many of them as possible. Some are starred and suitable for participants to read.

On the following page is the chart of the various stages of rebellion. It is important for participants to understand internal rebellion. It takes a long time to work through external rebellion but internal can perhaps be accomplished in months instead of years.

The connection between the adaptive-survivor parts in Session Two and rebellion is important. Many times a person has one of the adaptive parts controlling them and driving their personality car. An over responsible part might be an example. The person in rebellion is trying to become more balanced and to let other parts such as the little inner child have some power and control.

When you look at the charts of the adaptive parts in Session Two it is easy to see that the person in rebellion is often trying out the behavior on the opposite side of the part that has been controlling them in the past. One has to let the pendulum swing to the other side in order to find the happy medium or what Aristotle, the Greek Philosopher, called the "Golden Mean."

As I learn more about the person in rebellion I discover that they are truly seeking identity because they don't have a solid identity separate from the expectations of family of origin and society. The exercise on page 73 called "Affirmation of the Unlimited Person" is an important exercise for a person in rebellion. It is basically an "I am_____" exercise. It helps a person to define who they are and what their identity is. A good homework exercise for a person in rebellion is to write ten or twenty "I am _____" statements.

Of more interest in your seminar will probably be the partner of the person in rebellion. You will have few in rebellion but many partners of rebellion. The partner has an adaptive part of being parental, controlling, perfectionist, or some part that leads them to be rebelled against. They need to understand the connection between the partner rebelling and their own adaptive part.

In our next book on relationships it appears that the central unifying theme will be adaptive-survivor parts. It affects all of the other stumbling blocks in our divorce process. It also affects many of the problems in our relationships with others.

This chapter is the beginning for many participants to look at the influences from the past. Family of origin, childhood influences, rebellion, leftovers are all important stumbling blocks and will cause problems in future relationships if not attended to.

There is a lot to cover in this session. You the facilitator need to be well prepared in order to help the participants understand the many different concepts described in the textbook.

Safe and Sane
God.
Men webbed in that
Gray bunch of mediocrity,
Stuck together by a mass of
Rotting complexes.
There are the people —
Safe and Sane.

"You like me
And I'll like you."
Careful now — slowly,
One step at a time,
Adjust, conform.
This is our life —
Safe and Sane.

God!
I'll break though! !
Try honesty and truth
Even if it's *radical* —
And I swear, I'll *win!*
God, keep me from being
Safe and Sane.

—JoAnn

Fisher's Theory of Growth and Development

It appears in our society that people mature through four stages of growth and development while attempting to gain an individual identity separate from expectations of parents and society. Part of this process is to look at the adaptive/survivor behaviors you learned in your developmental years. Below is an outline of these four stages.

Stages	Shell	External Rebellion	Internal Rebellion	Love
Ages in each stage (Ages vary a great deal)	0-10 years	10-16 years	Anytime person finds courage and strength to do it.	16 years or more
Relationship with Parents	Stable. Child pleasing parent.	Unstable. Child rebelling.	More peaceful. Less projection.	Adult-to-adult. Compassionate.
Communication	Superficial. Few arguments.	Lousy. Many contradictions.	Child accessing adaptive voices from within.	Active listening. More self disclosure.
Attitude	Tries to please. What will people think?	Pushing for limits.	Ownership and responsibility.	Acceptance. I'm okay — You're okay.
Affect	Withdrawn. Identity hidden.	Gaining freedom and emotional strength.	Gaining identity and balance within.	Secure identity. Mature ability to love.

Psychologist Haim Ginot, in his book, *Between Parent and Child*, describes three stages of growth he calls organization, disorganization, and reorganization. Oscar Wilde mentions how children start out loving their parents, then reject them, and sometimes learn to accept them. Hegel, the 18th-19th century German philosopher, talked about the stages of thesis, anti-thesis, and syn-thesis. Plato in his *The Myth of the Cave*, talked about how people go through a process of leaving the shackles in the cave to search for the truth outside of the cave.

This model looks at rebellion as a search for mature identity and a much more positive emotion than commonly believed in our society. There are two malfunctions keeping people from growing through the stages. If children in rebellion fail to receive appropriate limits, they find difficulty gaining the emotional strength needed to grow out of the shell stage. Secondly, children find it difficult to grow beyond the stage that their parents are in.

The emotional and internal pressures that a person experiences, which motivate them to start seeking their identity, are often related to being out of balance. Usually one of the adaptive/survivor parts has been "driving their personality car." For example, the "shoulds" you have been feeling result in you being over-responsible and you experience the burdens of the whole world upon your shoulders. You are attempting to rebel in order to become responsible-for-self instead of being over-responsible.

People often do an external rebellion in which they project their lack of freedom upon others around them. They perceive others are keeping them from becoming mature and free. We recommend learning to do an internal rebellion where people learn to identify their adaptive/survivor behaviors which keep them from becoming free. Internal rebellion is where the search for mature identity happens.

External rebellion places great stress upon people's close relationships, and love-relationships become stressful and often end. Internal rebellion is possible to do within the confines of a marriage or important relationship, and allows people to find individual identity while in emotionally close relationships. If the partner of the person in rebellion will make the choice to look at their adaptive/survivor parts, which are usually parental, then they may make the crisis of their partner being in rebellion, a creative experience. Internal rebellion from one person, and ownership of parental behavior in partner, will allow love relationships to survive the crisis of rebellion.

72

Affirmations

Writing and saying affirmations out loud can be a powerful experience. Here are some examples of affirmations. We invite you to write one or more affirmations that are important for you in your own personal growth and self-actualization. Post them in a prominent place and say them out loud at least once a day.

1. The more I understand myself, the better I feel.
2. I appreciate my ability to apply the things I'm learning to my every day life.

My first affirmation is:

My second affirmation is:

My third affirmation is:

My reactions to the reading assignment in *Rebuilding* are:

My reactions to the Transition session of the Rebuilding class are:

What were some of the important things I learned in Session Six?

What are some of the important changes I am making in my thinking and my actions?

Session Seven
Openness

"I've Been Hiding Behind a Mask"

A mask is a false face — a feeling projected to others that's different from what you're really feeling. Some masks are appropriate; others are inappropriate. Masks may protect you from the emotional pain you feel or fear, but wearing masks takes a great deal of emotional energy. Masks distance you emotionally from others, keeping you from building intimate relationships. When you remove your masks appropriately, you find intimacy rather than emotional pain.

Lesson Plan for Session Seven
Openness - I've Been Hiding Behind A Mask

Goals for Session Seven:
1. To understand how you use masks to emotionally distance others.
2. To remove at least one of your masks by sharing it with others.
3. To learn how taking off a mask increases your emotional closeness and intimacy with others.
4. To learn to use affirmations that will help you become more authentic.

Agenda for Session Seven:

6:45 to 7:00 p.m. Arrive, greet new friends, get a hug, and a cup of tea or coffee.

7:00 to 7:10 p.m. Centering and Connecting Exercise. Discuss lesson plans.

7:10 to 7:50 p.m. Discussion of masks.

7:50 to 8:30 p.m. Small Groups:
What masks do you often wear? What's under each of the masks that you're afraid to expose? (Usually, some kind of fear or pain.) Which ones are really necessary (and why)? Which ones could you let go of? Who are the people you're in growing relationships with — those you'd find it easier to take your masks off with? Why? What would happen if you took off some of your unnecessary masks? How's your self-worth these days? What could you do to improve it?

8:30 to 8:45 p.m. Break.

8:45 to 9:00 p.m. Discuss homework assignments for next week.

9:00 to 9:55 p.m. Large group Unmasking Exercise:
Each participant:
1. Share a mask you have been wearing (take off the most difficult mask you are able to).
2. Share the feeling (usually fear or pain) underneath the mask which has kept you from taking it off before. It may feel scary to be this vulnerable! Remember that in reality, this is a powerful way of getting to know yourself better, as well as becoming intimate with others. Notice how many of us have been wearing similar masks and how good it feels to be yourself.

9:55 to 10:00 p.m. Closure and time for "I feel ____" messages.

Homework For Next Week's Seminar: (* Indicates most important homework)
*1. Read Chapter 14, "Love" in *Rebuilding*.
*2. Continue taking off some masks that you don't need to wear anymore.
*3. Write a definition of love as used in a love-relationship. Example, "Love is _____."
  4. What did you learn as a child, adolescent, and young adult about love?
  5. Fill out the Johari Window.

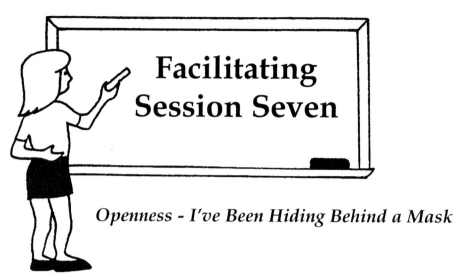

Facilitating Session Seven

Openness - I've Been Hiding Behind a Mask

The ten weeks class is shifting from divorce adjustment to transformation. This mask session helps participants have more open, honest, and healthy relationships in the future. This session helps promote group bonding and allows participants to discover taking off masks permits them to experience more intimacy with others.

The Johari Window

This is an interesting concept which many participants have not thought about before. The Johari window divides personality into four areas. We can change those areas by increasing how much we and others know about ourselves, and decreasing how much is hidden to ourselves and others. It is a concept relevant to the mask we wear. It is a good introduction to the mask topic and worth taking fifteen minutes of time to talk about.

Please Hear What I am Not Saying

If you are familiar with this anonymous writing, you may realize I have made some minor but important changes in the writing. The original writing placed a great deal of emphasis upon the other rescuing me. I made changes so the individual takes more responsiblity for asking for help and acceptance from other people. We are not victims but are able to ask for what we want and need as we struggle toward becoming more healthy.

I prefer reading this story out loud before sharing copies with participants. But after reading it most participants want a copy of the story so I make copies to hand out. Reading this is helpful and encourages participants to share their masks with others.

Small Group Discussion of Masks

This discussion is needed to help participants diffuse their fears and anxieties about sharing a mask. It provides an intellectual understanding of masks which will then make the emotional sharing easier. The questions on the lesson plans are suitable for small group discussion.

Large Group Sharing of Masks

This is a powerful exercise. It works well for either the facilitator or one of the volunteer helpers to share first. The example given is usually followed by the participants. It is important to not only ask the participant to share the mask, but it also important to ask what is the pain, feeling, hurt that is under the mask that the person is trying to protect.

For example, the mask might be "The joker. I continually make people laugh so they will like me. The pain underneath is a fear they will won't like me and will reject me." Be sure as a facilitator to keep asking what is the feeling or pain underneath that the person is hiding with a mask.

Be supportive to the people taking off a mask. It often leaves people feeling vulnerable and exposed. Point out when the exercise is over how close and intimate it feels to be in the group. We expect to feel rejected, not accepted, maybe abandoned when we share a mask. But when we take off a mask with appropriate people, we feel an increase in intimacy with others. It is an important lesson to learn on an emotional level.

Encourage the volunteer helpers to call participants this week because some may feel they shared too much of themselves and need reassurance for the sharing they did on mask night.

The Mirror Sees Through My Mask

Image, imprisoned in the glass,
Speak from your lofty realm of reality,
You, who see all and are seen by all,
Who are protected from all, but open to all,
Tell me what you see:

The mirror speaks:
Your smile only lifts one corner of my mouth,
Your single tear clings to my lashes,
You look at me with loathing, and I return your look,
For I am the prisoner of your hate,
And a slave to your whim.

But you are more an image than I,
Even though I am on the other side of the glass.
You see me through the mist of your own tears,
And the bitterness of the conjectures of your own mind,
Whereas I see you through the clearness of the glass.

Nancy

Building A Wall

I'm building a wall,
No one allowed.
You can't enter,
Unless of course,
I decide to open
the gate.
Try to understand, though,
The gate sometimes sticks,
And at times is very
Difficult to open.
Really should call
Somebody in
To oil the hinges.
But if no one comes in,
And I don't come out,
What's the use?

Help!
Somebody let me out!
Should have fixed it
A long time ago.
Now it's stuck,
And I want to get out,
I have to get out!
Help!
You pull from your side,
I push from mine,
But it's no use,
It won't open.
Guess I'll just go to sleep

Laura

Johari Window

from *Group Process: An Introduction to Group Dynamics,* Third Edition,
by Joseph Luft, Copyright © 1984, 1970, 1963 by Joseph Luft. Reprinted by
permission of Mayfield Publishing Company.

Known to self and others	Known to others Not known to self
Known to self Not known to others	Unknown to self and others

Before group experience

Known to self and others	Known to others Not known to self
	Unknown to self and others
Known to self Not known to others	

After group experience

The Different Areas of Your Personality

Area 1 (upper left):
The open area refers to the part of your personality that is known to yourselves and others.

Area 2 (upper right):
The blind area refers to the part of your personality that is known to others but not to yourself.

Area 3 (lower left):
The hidden area refers to the part of your personality that is known to yourself but not to others.

Area 4 (lower right):
The unknown area refers to the part of your personality that is unknown to you and to others. You know it is there because eventually many of these areas become known and you realize these unknown areas have been influencing your behavior more than you were aware.

Principles of Change

1. A change in any area will affect all other areas.
2. It takes emotional energy to keep feelings and motivations hidden or denied.
3. Threatening feelings and situations tend to decrease openness and awareness; trusting feelings and situations tend to increase openness and awareness.
4. Forcing openness, awareness, exposure is undesirable and usually ineffective.
5. Openness and free activity are helpful because more of one's resources and skills can be utilized.
6. Increasing the open area usually increases the ability to communicate meaningfully with another person.
7. There is a universal curiosity about the unknown area which often is referred to as the "dark" or "disowned" side. This curiosity is held in check by custom, social inhibitions, personal anxieties, etc.
8. We should remain sensitive to the hidden areas in ourselves and in others, and respect the desire of ourselves and others to keep the areas hidden until ready to be exposed.
9. The ten-week educational seminar helps to increase both individual and group awareness and to expand Area 1.
10. The size of the areas may change. For example, when you experience grief the open area may decrease in size until you have worked through the grief process.

Exercise

Draw a window for your present self. Draw what you would like your window to look like.

Please Hear What I Am Not Saying

Don't be fooled by me. Don't be fooled by the face I wear. I wear a mask, I wear a thousand masks. Masks that I am afraid to take off — and none of these masks are me. Pretending is an art that is second nature with me. Don't be fooled, for God's sake, don't be fooled. I give you the impression that I am secure, that all is sunny and unruffled within me as well as without, that confidence is my name and coolness is my game, that the water is calm and I am in command, and that I need no one. But please don't believe me. My surface may seem smooth, but my surface is my mask, my ever varying and ever concealing mask.

*Beneath lies no smugness, no complacence. Beneath dwells the real me in confusion, in fear, in aloneness. But I hide this. I don't want anybody to know it. I panic at the thought of my weakness and my fear of being exposed. That's why I frantically create a mask to hide behind, a nonchalant, sophisticated facade to help me pretend, to shield me from the glance that knows. But such a glance is what I need. And I know it. That is, if the glance is followed by acceptance and if it's followed by **love**.*

It can help me liberate me from myself, from my own self-built prison walls, from the barriers I so painstakingly erect. It will assure me of what I can't assure myself, that I am really something. But I don't tell you this, I don't dare. I'm afraid to. I'm afraid your glance will not be followed by acceptance and love. I'm afraid you'll think less of me, that you'll laugh, discover I'm just no good and reject me. So I play my game, my desperate, pretending game with a facade of assurance without, and with a trembling child within.

And so begins my parade of masks, the glittering, but empty parade of masks. My life becomes a front. I wildly chatter to you in the suave tones of surface talk. I tell you everything that is nothing and nothing that is everything, of what's crying inside me. So when I'm going through my routine, do not be fooled by what I'm saying. **Please listen carefully and try to hear what I am not saying. What I would like to be able to say. What for survival I need to say. But what I can't say.**

I dislike hiding. Honestly, I dislike the surface game I am playing, the superficial phony. I'd like to be really genuine and spontaneous even when that's the last thing I seem to want or need. You can help wipe away from my eyes the blank stare of the living dead. You can help call me into **aliveness.** *Each time you're kind and gentle and encouraging, each time you try to understand because you really care, my heart begins to grow wings, very small wings, very feeble wings, but wings. With your sensitivity and compassion and your power of understanding, you can breathe life into me. I want you to know that. I want you to know how important you are to me. How you help me find the real person that is inside of me if you choose to. Please choose.*

You can help me break down the wall behind which I tremble. You can help me remove the mask. You can help release me from my lonely prison. So do not pass me by. Please don't pass me by. It will not be easy for you. My long conviction of worthlessness builds strong walls. The nearer you approach me, the blinder I might strike back. It's irrational, but despite what books say about a person, I am irrational. **I fight against the very thing I cry out for.** *But I am told that love is stronger than strong walls, and in this lies my hope. My only hope. Please try to beat down my wall with firm hands, but gentle hands, for my inner child is very sensitive.*

Who am I you may wonder? I am someone you know very well. For I am **every man and woman you meet. I am the person right in front of you!**

— Author Unknown

I Am Me
My Declaration of Self-Esteem

In all the world, there is no one else exactly like me. Everything that comes out of me is authentically mine because I alone choose it. I own everything about me, my body, my mouth, my voice, my feelings, and my actions, whether they are expressed toward others or toward me. I own my fantasies, my dreams, my hopes, my fears. I own all my triumphs and successes, all my failures and mistakes. Because I own all of me, I can become intimately acquainted with myself. In doing so I can love myself and be friendly with myself and all of the parts of me. I know there are aspects about me that puzzle me and other aspects that I do not know. But as long as I am friendly and loving toward myself, I can courageously and hopefully look for solutions to my puzzles and ways to find out more about myself. However I look and sound, whatever I say and do, and whatever I think and feel at a given moment in time is authentically me. If I find some parts of how I look, sound, think and feel turn out to be unfitting, I can discard that which is unfitting, keep the rest, and invent something new for that which I discard. I can see, hear, feel, think, say and do. I have the tools to survive, to be close to others, to be productive, and to make sense and order out of the world of people and things outside of me. I own me, and therefore I can engineer me.

I am me, and I am okay.

— Author Unknown

"Micro-Lab" Small Group Activity

The purpose of this group activity is to build group trust and ability to share and for each group member to learn to invest themselves into the group process. Questions are designed to start on a more superficial level and to delve deeper with each question. Expected time to complete will be from one to one and one-half hours. A different person starts each time when answering the next question.

Questions

1. What are appropriate masks?

2. What are inappropriate masks?

3. When does the same mask change from one to the other?

4. Does your mask keep others from knowing you, or does it keep you from knowing yourself?

Affirmations

Writing and saying affirmations out loud can be a powerful experience. Here are some examples of affirmations. We invite you to write one or more affirmations that are important for you in your own personal growth and self-actualization. Post them in a prominent place and say them out loud at least once a day.

1. I can share with certain others what I am feeling and thinking without being afraid.
2. I'd rather be authentic than carry the weight of a mask.

My first affirmation is:

My second affirmation is:

My third affirmation is:

My reactions to the reading assignment in *Rebuilding* are:

My reactions to the Openness session of the Rebuilding class are:

What were some of the important things I learned in Session Seven?

What are some of the important changes I am making in my thinking and my actions?

Session Eight
Love

"Could Somebody Really Care for Me?"

Many people need to relearn how to love, in order to love more maturely. Your capacity to love others is closely related to your capacity to love yourself. And learning to love yourself is not selfish and conceited. In fact, it is the most mentally healthy thing you can do. There are a number of specific steps you can take to increase your self-love.

Lesson Plan for Session Eight

Love: Could Somebody Really Care for Me?

Goals for Session Eight:
1. To learn more about loving yourself.
2. To gain a better understanding of ways you can be more loving to others.
3. To learn that your capacity to love others (and to receive love from them) is closely related to your ability to love yourself.
4. To learn about some different styles of loving such as friendship, romantic, altruistic, game playing, possessive, practical.
5. To learn and use affirmations that will help you develop more love for yourself and others.
6. To touch on the need for boundaries in all your relationships, especially the closest ones.

Agenda for Session Eight:

6:45 to 7:00 p.m. Arrive, greet new friends, get a hug, and a cup of tea or coffee.

7:00 to 7:10 p.m. Centering and Connecting Exercise.

7:10 to 7:45 p.m. Share your definition of love with the group.

7:45 to 8:30 p.m. Large group discussion of Chapter 14, "Love."

8:30 to 8:45 p.m. Break.

8:45 to 9:00 p.m. Discuss the homework assignments for next week. Verify correct names, addresses and phone numbers for final class list.

9:00 to 9:55 p.m. Small group discussion:
- Describe your personal growth since the crisis that led you here began.
- What can you do that will help you to love and accept yourself more?
- How do you express your love? How would you like to be loved by others?
- How did your parents or primary caretakers express self-love?
- How did your parents/caretakers express love for each other?
- What is your primary style of loving? (See pages 182-185 in *Rebuilding*.)
- What was your primary style of loving in your last love relationship?
- How did it change over time during the relationship?
- What style(s) of loving would you like to be a part of your next love relationship?

9:55 to 10:00 p.m. Closure. Time for "I feel _____" messages.

Homework For Next Week's Seminar: (* Indicates most important homework)
*1. Read Chapter 16, "Relatedness" in *Rebuilding*.
*2. List the people you're in important growing relationships with and make some notes about the things you're learning from each of them.
3. Suggested topics to journal about or explore:
   Is there a balance between the love I'm giving and receiving?
   When I say, "I love you" to someone, what am I expecting to receive?
   How full is my cup? What do I need to do for myself to fill it up?
4. Read Chapter 15, "Trust" in *Rebuilding*.

Facilitating Session Eight

"Could Somebody Really Care for Me?"

This is an important night for participants. The question of "what is love?" is a difficult one for people who have ended a love relationship. The chapter in *Rebuilding* is a good one to stimulate people to think more about love.

I think it is one thing to write a definition of love but another to say it out loud. It is interesting for people to hear the definitions that others have come up with. It expands their concept of love to hear a wide variety of definitions. I suggest having a volunteer helper share their definition first because they have done it before as a participant. After having them share I ask how it was to share this time. They typically talk about how much easier it is to do the second time.

I like to collect each person's definition and compile a class list. It takes some time to do this but someone will usually volunteer to type all of the definitions on a computer and print out copies. It is meaningful for most people in the class to have the complete list.

A personal story. A female graduate of the seminar passed away about eight years after completion of the seminar. One of her class members had kept the copy of the definitions of love. Parts of this list were shared at her funeral. It was very poignant and touching to hear the deceased woman's definition of love.

I will always remember when I first started teaching the ten week seminars. There was no textbook. People did not know what I would be presenting until the night it was presented. I would always share my belief about the importance of self-love or loving yourself. I would say things like, "How can you expect another to love you if you don't love yourself?" "How can you truly love another if you don't love yourself?" "The capacity of loving another is directly connected to how much you love yourself. The more you love yourself, the more you can altruistically love another." It seemed to me to be obvious that it was okay to love yourself.

I learned after several seminars that many people would go home after class in a state of shock. It was uncomfortable for them to hear it was okay to love yourself. They had heard all of their lives that loving yourself was selfish and self-centered. I began to realize that a part of many people's unhappiness was their difficulty in accepting it was okay to love yourself. No wonder there are so many co-dependent relationships. If it is not okay to love yourself then you will have to find another to make you feel loved.

A major learning, or in many cases relearning, is important for this night. The shift in thinking can be enhanced by the class experience. When they read in the textbook about the values of loving oneself, when they write a definition of love which usually reflects their change in thinking about loving oneself, and when they hear in the group experience about the values of self-love, they often make a major shift towards giving themselves permission to love themselves. What could be any more important on this night of talking about love than having people give themselves permission to start loving themselves more than they ever have?

Do you remember session two when we talked about adaptive survivor parts? Many of our adaptive parts were an attempt to feel more loved. When we learn to love ourselves we diminish our need to continue to use our adaptive parts. Changing the way we feel about love and loving ourselves can be a very powerful transformational experience. Keep this in mind as you are facilitating session eight on love.

All About Love

There is a Law that man should love his neighbor as himself. In a few years it should be as natural to mankind as breathing or the upright gait; but if he does not learn it he must perish.

— Alfred Adler

To love is to place our happiness in the happiness of another.

— Gottfried Wilhelm von Leibnitz

We are shaped and fashioned by what we love.

— Johann Wolfgang von Goethe

There is a land of the living and a land of the dead and the bridge is love, the only survival, the only meaning.

— Thornton Wilder

Leave the hating for those not strong enough to love.

— Laura Plath

A coward is incapable of exhibiting love; it is the prerogative of the brave.

— Mahatma Gandhi

Love's like the measles, all the worse when it comes late.

— Douglas Jerrold

He that falls in love with himself will have no rivals.

— Benjamin Franklin

Love gives itself; it is not bought.

— Henry Wadsworth Longfellow

Love does not consist in gazing at each other but in looking outward together in the same direction.

— Antoine de Saint-Exupery

I hold it true, whate'er befall;
I feel it, when I sorrow most;
'Tis better to have loved and lost
Than never to have loved at all.

— Alfred, Lord Tennyson

Reply to a bored young man who asked a cynical question about love, because he never gave any!

It has everything to do with the price of beans,
And it cares after all about the mouse in the wall,
It has everything to do with a shell from the shore,
That doesn't sound like the sea anymore,
And everything to do with me and you.

— Nancy Thomas

Love is:
A warm comfortable feeling,
Being needed and feeling needed,
Giving completely
Without thought of getting.
Being able to ignite a sparkle
In another's eyes.
Knowing that no matter what you say or do,
Somebody, somewhere will
Understand,
Share,
Forgive,
Inspire,
Console,
And LOVE.

Not enough love is:
What will she think of this?
Did I say the right thing?
I'm not going to expose this weakness to her.
Will she be there when I return?
I wonder?
I doubt?
I must be close to her,
To make sure
She will understand,
She will forgive,
She will love.

Love, with a steadfast concern,
is the MOST.

— Bruce Fisher

What Do You Know About Love?

1. How do you know you are lovable?

2. What makes you afraid of being loved?

3. What makes you afraid of loving another?

4. What is love? How do you live it?

5. How do you express your love? How would you like to be loved?

6. How are you able to meet your own needs without feeling selfish?

7. What makes it possible for you to accept love from others?

8. How do others know you love them?

9. How do you love yourself?

10. Describe your personal growth since the crisis that led you here began.

11. How is your love becoming more mature? In what ways is your love immature?
    How is/was your love needy? How is/was your love overly dependent?

What we do not have, we cannot give. To love another, we must first love ourselves. Still, there persists the idea that to love oneself is an egocentric, infantile, destructive notion. Simple logic tells us that we can only give what we possess and that the more we possess, the greater our capacity to give. If you truly love someone, it follows that you want that person to have the best you have to offer, for the other's sake as well as yours. It is through an understanding and acceptance of yourself, your needs and what you require for happiness that you can comprehend and appreciate the needs of others. Love has acquired its tenuous reputation because for so long it has been left in the hands of amateurs who distrust it and themselves.

Love

Love, they said,
Is a passionate
Terrible thing.
A thing painfully exciting
And full of tortures.
This, they said,
Is love.

And so I thought…
Then, I loved… and was loved.
And then I knew.

Love, I say,
Is a gentle
Sacred thing.
A smile, caress, a look,
The holy touch of God.
This, I say,
Is love.

And so I know.

—JoAnn

You are your own best friend, and worst enemy.
As you think, so shall it be.
All the events in your life are there because you drew them there;
what you choose to do with them is up to you.
Argue for your limitations and sure enough − they're yours.
You are beautiful − inside and out!!
Give to yourself what you give to others.
When you stop needing to be loved so much,
And it dawns on you that you are the only person who can fill the void,
Perhaps true freedom will prevail.
It doesn't matter what other people think about you,
It only matters what you think about you,
And as you think, so it is!

—Bruce

Happiness — It's Only Natural

Once you see these factors as simply the unchangeable realities of your earlier life, rather than problems, you can put the responsibility for change where it belongs; on you today, and not on your background. How to go about it? Here are seven suggestions that should help.

1. Eliminate all *roles* that you've adopted in your life; behave as you want to rather than in terms of how you feel you're *supposed* to. If your behavior has been circumscribed by a role, then you as a person have been negated, and the role has taken over. There is no "right" way for people to behave. Be *you* each moment and rid yourself of roles.

2. Take constructive risks in your life. If you've always been shy and reserved, introduce yourself to a stranger. If you want to tell your mother how you feel about her behavior, do it. Most risks involve no personal danger, only anxiety. And you will find that the more you muster the courage to do the things you truly want for yourself, however risky, the more effective you will become at living happily.

3. Eliminate all blame sentences from your vocabulary. Stop saying, "*They're* to blame" for *your* unhappiness. Replace blame sentences, such as "she made me feel bad when I heard what she said."

4. Be assertive. You are an adult, responsible for your own life. You never need ask anyone how you ought to lead that life. While you may want to see how your behavior will affect people, that doesn't mean you must seek their permission.

5. Several times a day, stop thinking and analyzing, and let your brain slip into neutral. Take a minute to concentrate on a color, pushing out all other thoughts. Or take a walk, with your thoughts "free-wheeling." Just as the body needs rest and exercise periods, so does the mind.

6. Stop looking outside yourself for validation of your worth, beauty, intellect, and personality. When you fish for compliments, ask yourself if *you* are satisfied with your performance or looks. If so, ask yourself why you need anyone else to say so. You'll discover that the less approval you seek, the more you will receive.

7. Decide to appreciate life even when "nay-sayers" and grumps are determined to drag you down. Surround yourself with happy faces. Stop feeling it is *your* responsibility to change those who insist on being unhappy.

Your own expectations are the key to this whole business of mental health. If you expect to be happy, healthy and fulfilled in life, then most likely it will work out that way.

— Author Unknown

Affirmations

Writing and saying affirmations out loud can be a powerful experience. Following are some examples of affirmations. We invite you to write one or more affirmations of the affirmations that are important for you in your own personal growth and self-actualization. Post them in a prominent place and say them out loud at least once a day.

1. I am loving myself more and more each day.
2. I am giving myself the love I deserve to receive from myself and others.

My first affirmation is:

My second affirmation is:

My third affirmation is:

My reactions to the reading assignment in *Rebuilding* are:

My reactions to the Love session of the Rebuilding class are:

What were some of the important things I learned in Session Eight?

What are some of the important changes I am making in my thinking and my actions?

Session Nine
Relatedness

"Growing Relationships Help Me Rebuild"

It's okay to have an important relationship after your primary relationship has ended. We often need support, companionship, and feedback from others to help us rebuild. These relationships are often short-term, so we need to learn how to have "healthy termination." We need to take credit for creating these relationships as part of our growing process. And we need to become aware of how we can make these relationships as growing and healing as possible.

Lesson Plan for Session Nine

Relatedness: Growing Relationships Help Me Rebuild

Goals for Session Nine:

1. To understand how growing relationships can be a part of your personal growth process.
2. To understand the need for nurturing that can be a part of growing relationships.
3. To help you feel empowered to make necessary choices and to be yourself in your relationships.
4. To understand that growing relationships can happen with all kinds of people, such as other seminar members, friends, family, therapists, clergy, as well as love partners.
5. To understand ways of helping growing relationships to become long term relationships when appropriate, but they don't have to become long-term in order for you to grow and benefit from them.
6. To understand the difference between a *growing* relationship and a "running-from-knowing-myself/avoiding-loneliness" *rebound* relationship.
7. To give yourself permission to take some relationship risks and go out and "get your nose bloodied" (in other words, experiment with growing relationships).
8. To learn that some relationships just don't work for you or are toxic or destructive and need to end, and to learn about "healthy terminations."
9. To learn and use affirmations that will help you take more responsibility for your relationships.

Agenda for Session Nine:

6:45 to 7:00 p.m. Arrive, greet new friends, get a hug, and a cup of tea or coffee.

7:00 to 7:30 p.m. Complete and turn in the second *Fisher Divorce Adjustment Scale*.

7:30 to 8:30 p.m. Presentation and discussion of "Growing Relationships."

8:30 to 8:45 p.m. Break.

8:45 to 9:05 p.m. Large group sharing:
List the characteristics of an ideal love relationship. List hopes and fears about relationships.

9:05 to 9:50 p.m. Small or large group discussion:
- What kinds of improvements do you need to make in your relationship with yourself?
- What are the relationship skills you need to learn and/or practice?
  (Examples: communication, feeling expression, boundaries, ownership, trust, vulnerability, honesty, etc.)
- What kind of growing relationships would be helpful for you at this point in your process?
- If you can't imagine having another love-relationship in the future, what would you need to do before you would be ready to have one?
- What are your hopes and fears about dating?
- What can you do to reduce your fears? What can you do to make your hopes a reality?

9:50 to 10:00 p.m. Closure. Time for "I feel ____" messages.

Homework For Next Week's Seminar: (* Indicates most important homework)

*1. Reading Assignment: Chapter 17 "Sexuality" and Chapter 19, "Purpose."
*2. Make a list of sexuality questions. These will be asked anonymously of participants next week in a group discussion.
3. Extra-credit homework: Complete your lifeline. See example on page 246 of *Rebuilding*.
4. Practice using "I" messages as described on Page 211 of *Rebuilding*. This is the most important single behavior you can do to improve your communication skills!
5. If possible, read Chapter 18, "Singleness" in *Rebuilding*.
   Many facilitator's and seminar groups like to begin Session Ten with a potluck party. If this class plans to do so, we will start eating about 6:30 p.m. (Suggestion: Bring paper plates and silverware.)

Facilitating Session Nine

Relatedness:
Growing Relationships Help Me Rebuild

This chapter and chapter twelve on Transition are a preview of our book, *Loving Choices*. It would be helpful for you as a facilitator to read this book in order to help you facilitate this session better.

I have begun to realize the connection between growing relationships and the adaptive-survivor parts. Many times we felt stuck in our primary love relationship while acting out one of our adaptive parts. We had no awareness of what we were doing and our partners kept reinforcing our adaptive behavior with their adaptive behavior. Many times the reason the new growing relationship feels so good is that it is helping us gain freedom from our old adaptive parts. This theme is developed more completely in the *Loving Choices* book.

I had a tough decision to make when writing this chapter. The old yellow book, *When Your Relationship Ends* which many of you may not be aware of, had a chapter written for those recently separated when they were beginning to date and become social again. Because you may not have access to that original book I have reproduced those relationship blocks for people just starting to date on the next page.

Another concept that is helpful to introduce is boundaries. Many people have never thought about boundaries and it is a useful, pragmatic concept. The absence of boundaries increases people's emotional pain when they are ending a relationship.

Living in the present is mentioned in the rebuilding chapter. Do people know how to do that? Have they thought about whether they are living in the past or future? I learned in my Doctoral Dissertation when I used the Personality Orientation Inventory, that many recently separated people are other-directed instead of inner-directed — living in the past instead of living in the present. Think how much healthier participants could be if they could be more innerdirected and live in the present.

It is helpful to the participants to point out how they are living in the present much more than when they enrolled in the class. They are also much more inner-directed instead of looking for answers from others. Reinforce, affirm, and validate them for the growth they have achieved.

Notice that the lesson plans suggest that you have participants take the FDAS when they come to class. Mention to them not to try and answer the correct or more adjusted answer on the FDAS. They are somewhat test wise after getting the results back from the pre-test. Honest answers give more helpful feedback than correct answers.

You will discover that you need to have them take the FDAS in class. If you send it home with them, very few will bring it back. It is helpful to have as many take the post-test as possible. It is a warm fuzzy for them to see how much they have grown. It also gives the facilitator some feedback about the adjustment of the class as a whole. See the section in this manual on the FDAS in order to better understand the meaning of the post-test scores.

Notice lesson plans for session ten start at 6:30 with a potluck and don't end until 10:30 or later. There is a lot to do on the last night of class. Call attention to the participants that the last night will be longer than the other nine sessions.

I have found very few participants complete the sexuality questions before class. It is helpful to have it in the homework so they can be thinking about it. I suggest you point out chapter nineteen which explains the Lifeline. It is a powerful exercise and many facilitator's have figured out a way to include it in the ten sessions.

Relationship Blocks for Recently Separated People Starting to Date

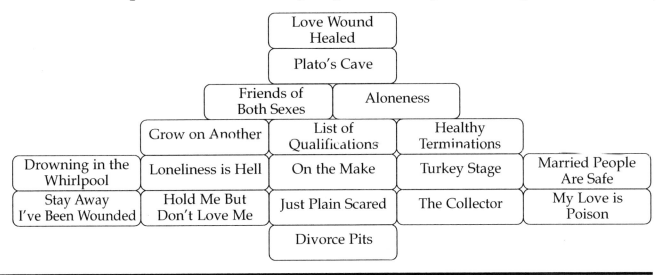

Divorce Pits
Ending a love relationship is often the "pits." Hopefully I have worked through this block by now.

Stay Away, I've Been Wounded
I feel so wounded. I am afraid to get close to anyone because it hurts so much.

Hold Me, But Don't Love Me
The scariest thing anyone can say to me is "I love you." But I do need to be held and comforted.

Just Plain Scared
I feel so full of fear that even going to the grocery store can be scary.

The Collector
I need to have a lot of relationships so I don't get too close to one person. I'm careful to not date the same person twice in a row.

My Love is Poison
I hurt the one I love. I don't want to hurt you.

Drowning in the Whirlpool
I got sucked into a whirlpool in my last relationship and lost my identity. I don't want to do that again.

Loneliness is Hell
It is terrible to be absolutely lonely all of the time. I'm too scared to do anything about it though.

On the Make
The only way I know to relate to the opposite sex is to have sex with them. It provides me with a physical release but I don't want anything intimate.

Turkey Stage
There ain't nothing out there to date but Turkeys. Not to be disagreeable but maybe it is because you are still a turkey yourself. An eagle doesn't want to associate with turkeys.

Married People are Safe
I don't want to be committed to anyone. I think I'll spend my time with those who are already committed so I don't have to worry about them wanting to commit to me.

Grow on Another
I'm just a wet little kitty who needs someone strong to take care of me. I think I will find that strong person and grow on them for a while.

Healthy Terminations
So many of my relationships have no future. I need to learn how to have healthy terminations to get those people out of my life.

List of Qualifications
I have made up this list of questions to ask the next person that I might have a relationship with. I want to know I can trust them to not hurt me.

Friends of Both Sexes
I have spent most of my life not having friends of the opposite sex because we might become romantically and sexually involved. I am learning that belief is not true.

Aloneness
I am finding it comfortable to be alone. In fact, I don't want a relationship that would interfere with my much needed aloneness.

Plato's Cave
I've been in a cave all of my life. I need a growing relationship that will allow me to come out of the cave into the warm sunshine of love.

Love Wound Healed
I am feeling healed and less afraid of intimacy. I guess my love wound is healing.

Today

Today was my day.
Once more God looked on me,
And blessed me,
And laughed with me.
Today.

Now I know the confidence
of strength,
I was afraid,
There is no fear.
I was hurt,
And the pain is gone.
Today.

Where are the trumpets?
Call them out!
Blow them loud . . .
For today was my day.

I cried,
And hurt,
And loved,
And lived.

Today
My cup runneth over.
What then of tomorrow?

—JoAnn

Growing Relationships

Just what is a "growing relationship" anyway? Here are some of the ingredients that I believe are important.

- It has good communication, using "I" messages rather than "you" messages.
- With obstacles and problems, you are committed to talking it out rather than acting it out.
- You take ownership for what you are creating in your life.
- There is a comfortable amount of being vulnerable — not too little, nor too much.
- There is dedication towards growing and learning about yourself.
- There is a commitment to embracing your pain and learning from it.
- There is a balance between giving and taking, between being responsible and having fun.
- There is a balance between following tradition and a willingness to try new things.
- There are flexible boundaries instead of walls.
- You are able to do self-care without feeling selfish.
- You are more inner-directed than other-directed.
- You live more in the present than the past or the future.
- You are committed to being you rather than looking for a committed relationship.
- You invest equally in your physical, emotional, social, and spiritual growth.
- You are dedicated to taming your adaptive/survivor parts instead letting them control your behavior.
- It can be with a therapist, friend, family member, relative, or a love relationship with the above traits.

Have you realized one of the most important things you have learned in the Rebuilding Seminar? You have been practicing and creating these growing relationships with the other class participants. Your challenge is easily defined. Keep on creating the same kind of growing and healthy relationships that you have experienced in the Rebuilding Seminar for the rest of your life. It may be one of the most valuable lessons you have learned in this class!

— Bruce

Listening is Loving

What is active listening?
> Listening actively rather than passively.
> Participatory: you give feedback and respond.
> Letting the other person know that you heard.

What does it do?
> Facilitates communication.
> Makes the other person feel important.
> Provides a place to air feelings and thoughts, non-threateningly.
> Allows and encourages expression of thoughts and feelings.
> Provides an atmosphere for each person to see what he or she has expressed more objectively.
> Affirms the value of the other person and his or her ideas, attitudes, feelings.
> Creates an equal relationship between two people, rather than, "I know more than you."

Effective Listening

(From Alberti and Emmons, *Your Perfect Right*, reprinted with permission of the publisher.)

Assertive listening involves an active commitment to the other person. It requires your full attention, and calls for no overt act on your part, although eye contact and certain gestures — such as nodding — are often appropriate. Listening demonstrates your respect for the other person. It requires that you avoid expressing *yourself* for a time, yet is not a nonassertive act.

Listening is not simply the physical response of hearing sounds — indeed, deaf persons may be excellent "listeners." Effective listening may involve giving feedback to the other person, so that it is clear that you understood what was said. Assertive listening requires at least these elements:

* *tuning in* to the other person, by stopping other activities, turning off the TV, ignoring other distractions, focusing your energy in his or her direction;
* *attending* to the message, by making eye contact if possible, nodding to show that you hear, perhaps touching her or him; and
* actively attempting to *understand* before responding, by thinking about the underlying message — the feelings behind the words — rather than trying to interpret, or to come up with an answer.

Attending Skills

(Adapted from Ivey, *The Skilled Helper*, reprinted with permission of the publisher.)

Ask open-ended questions.
Avoid yes-or-no questions.
Avoid "why" questions which block communication.
Use "what" and "how."
Use minimal encouragement:

* Nodding of head, eye contact
* "Uh-huh"
* "Yes"
* "Go on"
* "And"
* "Because"

Avoid rescuing.
Allow other person to have pain, confusion, sadness, and anger as part of their learning.
Nurture without bleeding with them; keep objective.
Believe that people can solve their problems if given a chance to talk in a non-threatening situation.

Questions for Discussion

1. What is required to trust members of the opposite sex?

2. How are men and women alike in their responses to feelings such as love, hate, intimacy and fear?

3. How are men and women different in their responses to feelings such as love, hate, intimacy and fear?

4. How do I know that I can trust myself and my feelings?

5. What feelings do I trust in myself and act upon?

6. What makes it possible to become emotionally close to a potential love-partner?

7. How do I distance myself from other people? How do I keep other people away?

8. What relationships am I building that help me heal my love wound? Why is this important?

9. What am I doing to build healing and trusting relationships with friends of both sexes?

10. What happens when I give mixed messages rather than communicate my real feelings?

11. How do I know when I can't trust another person?

12. How do I know when I can trust another person?

13. Why is it important to heal my love-wound? How will healing my love-wound help me experience intimacy?

14. What does it mean to live in the present in my relationships?

15. What is the primary difference between engaging in a short-term relationship versus a long-term relationship?

16. What kinds of risks am I taking in my relationship besides exposing my true feelings and thoughts?

17. How do I express true interest in my friends? How is that different from looking for another love relationship?

Affirmations

Writing and saying affirmations out loud can be a powerful experience. Here are some examples of affirmations. We invite you to write one or more affirmations that are important for you in your own personal growth and self-actualization. Post them in a prominent place and say them out loud at least once a day.

1. I can trust myself, and be myself in all my relationships.
2. I feel more internal peace when I connect with myself and others honestly and openly, with boundaries and with love.

My first affirmation is:

My second affirmation is:

My third affirmation is:

My reactions to the reading assignment in *Rebuilding* are:

My reactions to the Openness session of the Rebuilding class are:

What were some of the important things I learned in Session Nine?

What are some of the important changes I am making in my thinking and my actions?

Session Ten
Sexuality

"I'm Interested, But I'm Scared"

When you're first separated, it's normal to be extremely fearful of sex. During the adjustment process, you can learn to express your unique sexuality according to your own moral standards. The singles subculture emphasizes authenticity, responsibility, and individuality more than rules. You can discover what you believe rather than what is expected of you. The great difference in attitudes and values of male and female sexuality appears to be a myth. Your adjustment may be complicated by the major changes taking place in female and male sex roles. In any case, safe sex is the order of the day.

Lesson Plan for Session Ten

Sexuality: "I'm Interested But I'm Scared"

Goals for Session Ten:
1 To become comfortable with your own sexuality.
2. To feel more comfortable talking with others about sexuality.
3. To recognize that your questions and concerns about sex and sexuality are similar to those of the opposite sex.
4. To feel empowered to live your life to the fullest and to become the person you've always wanted to be.
5. To learn and use affirmations that will help you better appreciate the beauty of your sexuality.
6. To reflect on the things you've learned and the ways you've grown in the last ten weeks.

Agenda for Session Ten:
6:30 to 7:30 p.m. Arrive, greet new friends, get a hug. If a potluck has been planned, begin eating as soon as enough food has arrived. **Celebrate and enjoy!**

7:30 to 8:30 p.m. Large group:
Fill out seminar evaluations and recommend future volunteer helpers.
Complete sexuality questionnaire, and write out your favorite sexual fantasy.
Facilitator reads the sexuality questions. Those who choose to may read the answers they wrote.
Turn the seminar evaluations and sexuality questionnaires in to the facilitator.
Pass out "graduation diplomas" and *FDAS* post-test scores.

8:30 to 9:00 p.m. Break.

9:00 to 9:20 p.m. Small groups: (Men and women in separate groups)
(Choose one person in each group who writes quickly and legibly to list the questions, ideally someone with a strong voice who will be asking them in the following large group exercise.)
Suggestion: Get started writing questions right away!!
Write down as many questions as possible that you'd like to ask the opposite sex.
List pet peeves about behaviors of the opposite sex (allow at least five minutes at the end to do this).
Questions and pet peeves will be kept anonymous!

9:20 to 10:30 p.m. Large group: Alternating after each question, the men who choose to will answer the women's' questions and then the women who choose to will answer the men's' questions. Make every effort to offer answers one at a time so all can hear. We'd like to hear some answers from everyone, but no one will be made to talk if they don't choose to. (Writers: remember to list the pet peeves as well). From time to time the facilitator will read a sexual fantasy from the sexuality questionnaires.

10:30 p.m. Closure. Time for "I feel ____" messages.

10:30 to ? Continue large group with men and women answering questions, addressing pet peeves, from the lists drawn up by the opposite sex.

Homework for the Rest of Your Life:
Love yourself!
Be your own best friend!
Feel your feelings and listen to your heart!
Tell the truth as lovingly as possible and don't be attached to the outcome!
Build strong and healthy friendships where you can give and receive love and be comfortable being yourself!

Facilitating Session Ten

Sexuality: "I'm Interested but I'm Scared"

There is a great deal of difference from person to person, from class to class, and from one community to another, concerning the comfort level of participants on the topic of sexuality. Some classes are quite comfortable on this night, and others show their anxiety by making jokes and laughing a lot, changing the subject to something less threatening, or being very quiet.

I have suggested that the sexuality night could be a follow up class three months after the seminar is completed. It would allow people to adjust and be more comfortable with sexuality. It would be an exciting topic that many would come back for the extra night. It is an idea for you to consider but it takes time and effort to make it happen.

We suggest you make some comments to the participants at the beginning of this session. Talk to them about having fun tonight. Emphasize that it is okay for some people to not talk or share but just listen. It is a wonderful opportunity to discuss sex in a mixed group of men and women. How long has it been since you have done the same?

The *Rebuilding* book has a good section on safe sex. I suggest you point out that section to the participants to make sure they read it. We don't take time in class to expand upon what the book says.

Sex is different than sexuality. If your class, or you the facilitator, are uncomfortable talking about sex, you could emphasize sexuality. This would mean talking about such things as dating, changing male and female roles in our society, and sex education. Our society is polarized around abortion and homosexuality today, and these subjects would probably cause some heated discussion in most classes.

We designate a woman and a man to be spokespersons. After the male and female groups have written their questions, the spokesperson reads the questions to the class. Usually the questions are written to the opposite sex, but some

people will want to direct questions to the same sex. For example, we had a good discussion one night when one woman wanted to talk about how other woman handled the male being unable to have an erection.

Notice again the suggested times for this class. There is so much to do on the last night of class that we formally stop the class at 10:30. Often there will be people who want to keep talking for several more hours. The facilitator(s) has to make a decision as to whether you want to stay later on this night.

There are several questions which seem to arise in every class. Many want to know what it means to be a man, or to be a woman, in today's society. Usually someone wants to know if a woman expects to have a pass made, and if she thinks the male is a wimp if he doesn't. Often the question of when to start having sex is asked. Is it okay on the first date, the second, or just when is it okay? How you talk to your partner about safe sex is a good question. One woman said she had read everything she could about telling her partner she had Herpes. What the books didn't say was that males are impotent after you tell them that you have Herpes.

We suggest that participants learn to help each other in the area of sexuality. The frank, honest, and open talks taking place in tonight's session can continue on after the class is over. We have found that woman find it much easier to talk about sex than men. Why not help each other to be as comfortable as possible so that you can talk about sex with each other?

We suggest the facilitator keep the questions written by the participants. It is a wonderful piece of informal research into what people are wanting to know about sex today. It could be the basis for a future book on sexuality and divorce.

The first activity listed on the lesson plans is to complete the seminar evaluations. This could be done later in the class if you wanted to get reactions from them about the sexuality night. You might want to make a few comments about the voting on volunteer helpers. Emphasize the importance of selecting good people who will be helpful to future class participants but also be a good representative of the class.

The questionnaire on sexuality has merit. We ask them to write their favorite sexual fantasy on the back. These questionnaires are confidential but some people may not be comfortable sharing their sexual fantasies. We have found that sharing your fantasies with your love partner is an act of intimacy.

We have developed our own graduation diploma and a copy of it is on a page following. We purchase the printed paper that has it's own border which makes the diploma look like a certificate.

There is not much need to explain or interpret the FDAS post-test profiles because they are familiar with them from the pre-test results. It is helpful to have both pre- and post-test scores on the same sheet. (See the section in this manual concerning the FDAS.) It is also helpful and rewarding to share with them the class average profile sheets. They get excited observing the total class average gain scores.

Notice at the bottom of the lesson plans mention is made of the giant huggle picnic. This became an annual affair at the Learning Center. We did it the third Sunday in July. The largest huggle had around 350 former participants and their families.

We have huggle games. We ask them to form huggle groups of twelve people. An example of a game is to have each huggle group sit on the ground in a circle with their feet pointing out. Have the group lock arms and the first huggle group to stand up without breaking the locked arms wins that race. Be creative but be careful. We have had some people hurt doing huggle games.

Ask the people to plan a get together after the class is over. It is important that they have an ongoing social group where they can keep practicing the human behavior skills they learned during the Seminar. We suggest that you have the participants vote for a committee of three to be in charge of social activities. There is a place on the evaluation sheet at the bottom so they can vote for three to be on the social committee. When your next class graduates, vote again and add three more to your social committee. Set it up to have each person be on the committee for a year and then be replaced. Often there will be a person who becomes committee chairperson and may choose to stay on the committee instead of retiring.

We have devised a data base program on the computer to tabulate the evaluations. The form is enclosed which you can use to enter and calculate

by hand if doing a computer program is not possible. We have shared the evaluation results from one class. It would be more meaningful research to keep adding each new class to the results so you would have information from several classes instead of just one.

We suggest that single groups have a balance between growth and social. The seminar is a good growth experience, but people need to continue to having social contacts after the seminar is completed. We expect about two-thirds of the graduates to continue on and take the Reconnecting Class for singles. However that is another growth group and is not the same as having a singles support group that has an weekly meeting throughout the year.

A male participant made an interesting comment on the last night of class that I like to share with the group. He said, "This class is the springboard from which you jump into the river of life." Many people write poetry during the seminar and often some of the poems can be shared the last night of class.

I like to take a tool box full of tools and place it in the middle of the huggle at the end of the class. I say, "You now have a large inventory of relationship tools that you gained during this class. Are you going to keep using them? Keep them sharp? Or are you going to let them rust and become dull from a lack of use? It's up to you!"

Sexuality Questionnaire

Please complete the following questions about sex:

When I think about sex I _____

_____

When I was a child I thought sex was _____

_____

Now I believe sex is _____

_____

When it came to sex my father always said _____

_____

When it came to sex my mother always said _____

_____

I grew up thinking that sexual pleasure was _____

_____

When I first started my last love relationship I expected sex to be _____

_____

From my former love-partner I got the sexual message that _____

_____

My contribution to the sexual problems in my last love relationship was _____

_____

Since my last love relationship ended sex has _____

_____

In my next love relationship (as far as sex) I'll be sure to _____

_____

My favorite sexual fantasy is _____

_____

Affirmations

Writing and saying affirmations out loud can be a powerful experience. Here are some examples of affirmations. We invite you to write one or more affirmations that are important for you in your own personal growth and self-actualization. Post them in a prominent place and say them out loud at least once a day.

1. I am making loving choices in my life.
2. I am taking charge of the way I live my life.
3. I am able to build and create healthy relationships with friends of both sexes.
4. The more I get to know myself, the better I like myself.

My first affirmation is:

My second affirmation is:

My third affirmation is:

My reactions to the reading assignment in *Rebuilding* are:

My reactions to the Openness session of the Rebuilding Seminar are:

What were some of the important things I learned in Session Ten?

What are some of the important changes I am making in my thinking and my actions?

EXAMPLE OF FINAL CLASS EVALUATION
Averages From One Class Facilitated by Jere Bierhaus

Please rate the following areas of the Fisher Divorce and Personal Growth Seminar circling the appropriate number. The higher the number, the more valuable and worthwhile you found that activity to be. If you cannot evaluate a particular area, please circle "NA" for "Not able."

Class Sessions	Least to Most	Average
Session 1, Rebuilding Blocks of Divorce	1 2 3 4 5 NA	**3.4**
Session 2, Adaptive Behavior	1 2 3 4 5 NA	**4.2**
Session 3, Grief	1 2 3 4 5 NA	**4.6**
Session 4, Anger	1 2 3 4 5 NA	**4.7**
Session 5, Self-Concept	1 2 3 4 5 NA	**4.7**
Session 6, Transition	1 2 3 4 5 NA	**4.1**
Session 7, Masks	1 2 3 4 5 NA	**4.4**
Session 8, Love	1 2 3 4 5 NA	**4.4**
Session 9, Growing Relationships	1 2 3 4 5 NA	**4.3**
Session 10, Sexuality	1 2 3 4 5 NA	**3.9**
Taking the Fisher Divorce Adjustment Scale	1 2 3 4 5 NA	**4.1**
Textbook *Rebuilding: When Your Relationship Ends*	1 2 3 4 5 NA	**4.4**
Parties and activities outside of class	1 2 3 4 5 NA	**4.4**
Large Group Discussions	1 2 3 4 5 NA	**4.4**
Small Group Discussions	1 2 3 4 5 NA	**4.7**
Friendships you made during the class	1 2 3 4 5 NA	**4.9**
Huggles	1 2 3 4 5 NA	**4.7**
Volunteers	1 2 3 4 5 NA	**4.5**
Books and outside reading other than textbook	1 2 3 4 5 NA	**3.7**
Homework Assignments	1 2 3 4 5 NA	**3.8**
Total Class Experience	1 2 3 4 5 NA	**4.7**

This is an example of only one class. The feedback becomes more meaningful when you have results of the evaluations from several classes. You can compare various classes but you could also add the classes together in order to obtain average feedback from several classes. There can be important variations from class to class on the feedback sheets.

"REBUILDING" SEMINAR FINAL CLASS EVALUATION

Please rate the following areas of the Fisher Divorce and Personal Growth Seminar circling the appropriate number. The higher the number, the more valuable and worthwhile you found that activity to be. If you cannot evaluate a particular area, please circle "NA" for "Not able."

Class Sessions	Least to Most Worthwhile
Session 1, Rebuilding Blocks of Divorce	1 2 3 4 5 NA
Session 2, Adaptive Behavior	1 2 3 4 5 NA
Session 3, Grief	1 2 3 4 5 NA
Session 4, Anger	1 2 3 4 5 NA
Session 5, Self-Concept	1 2 3 4 5 NA
Session 6, Transition	1 2 3 4 5 NA
Session 7, Masks	1 2 3 4 5 NA
Session 8, Love	1 2 3 4 5 NA
Session 9, Growing Relationships	1 2 3 4 5 NA
Session 10, Sexuality	1 2 3 4 5 NA
Taking the Fisher Divorce Adjustment Scale	1 2 3 4 5 NA
Textbook *Rebuilding: When Your Relationship Ends*	1 2 3 4 5 NA
Parties and activities outside of class	1 2 3 4 5 NA
Large Group Discussions	1 2 3 4 5 NA
Small Group Discussions	1 2 3 4 5 NA
Friendships you made during the class	1 2 3 4 5 NA
Huggles	1 2 3 4 5 NA
Volunteers	1 2 3 4 5 NA
Books and outside reading other than textbook	1 2 3 4 5 NA
Homework Assignments	1 2 3 4 5 NA
Total Class Experience	1 2 3 4 5 NA

Write on back of this paper.
What did you like best about the class?

What did you like least about the class?

What would you like to see added in the future?

Selection of New Volunteers

The selection process for volunteers is: 1) voting by other class members, 2) feedback from the present volunteers, 3) decision by facilitator, 4) discussion between facilitator and prospective volunteer, and 5) attending the volunteer training workshop.
Please nominate people in the class who you think would be good volunteers in future classes.

Nominate three people you think would be good people to have on the social committee in charge of arranging an ongoing singles support group.

Class Evaluation Summary Sheet

Use this sheet to tabulate the class evaluaions. If possible, you can make a data base computer program to do the calculations on this sheet. Mark each participants rating in the vertical columns. Calculate totals and averages for each topic and for each participant. There are extra rows so you can add to the evaluations if you choose.

Participants Who Completed Evaulation Sheet

SESSIONS AND TOPICS	1	2	3	4	5	6	7	8	9	10	11	12	13	14	15	16	17	18	19	20	21	22	23	24	25	Total	Ave
Session 1 Reb Block																											
Session 2 Adaptive																											
Session 3 Grief																											
Session 4 Anger																											
Session 5 S. Conc.																											
Session 6 Transition																											
Session 7 Masks																											
Session 8 Love																											
Session 9 Grow Rel																											
Session 10 Sexuality																											
FDAS																											
Textbook																											
Parties																											
Large Group Discus																											
Small Group Disc																											
Friendships																											
Huggles																											
Volunteers																											
Other Books																											
Homework																											
Total Class Exp																											
Participant Total																											
Participant Average																											

Congratulations

For Completing the Fisher Rebuilding Siminar,

For Completing the Fisher Rebuilding Seminar,

For Making Your Crisis Into a Creative Experience,

For Surviving Instead of Drowning,

For Leaving the Chrysalis and Becoming a Butterfly,

For Taking Charge of Your Life!

FREEDOM

SINGLENESS · PURPOSE

SEXUALITY · LOVE · TRUST · RELATEDNESS

OPENNESS · ANGER · LETTING GO · SELF-WORTH · TRANSITION

GRIEF · FEAR · ADAPTATION · LONELINESS · FRIENDSHIP

DENIAL · GUILT REJECTION

_____
Facilitators

_____
Date

How to Facilitate the Rebuilding Seminar

This section of the Manual contains responses to the most frequently asked questions by people wanting to learn how to facilitate. I think that most of your questions on facilitating the Rebuilding Seminar will be answered.

Family Relations Learning Center

The main emphasis of the FRLC was to develop educational seminars designed to help people work through crises in their lives. Not only have these seminars proven to be practical and effective, but they also provide services at a reasonable cost to the participants. We perceive our work to be a socially concerned ministry caring about people in pain and people wanting to become more self-actualized in their relationships with others. The educational seminars are a way of carrying out this ministry.

Overview of Seminar

This model is designed to help people work through the process of adjusting to the ending of their love-relationship. It is designed specifically for people who are going through divorce; but it can be used to help people work through the ending of any relationship whether it be separation, divorce, death, a living-together arrangement, a homosexual relationship, or a friendship. In fact, the model has proven to be helpful to people working through any kind of crisis such as retirement, moving to a new community, terminal illness, or like my parents' adjustment process when they moved to town after living on the same farm for fifty-six years.

The seminar is an educational model rather than group therapy. It is educational with a textbook and reading assignments, specific homework assignments, a structured class format, and behavioral objectives. I believe it is more effective than group therapy, at least for the type of people who participate in this seminar and are dealing with crises.

The heart of the model is the nineteen rebuilding blocks listed in the textbook *Rebuilding: When Your Relationship Ends*. These rebuilding blocks provide a guide to the process and make the model

pragmatic in helping people to identify the specific steps they must take in adjusting to the crisis.

The *Fisher Divorce Adjustment Scale* is built upon the rebuilding blocks model and the subtests in the scale are six of the most important rebuilding blocks. The Scale is used as a pre-test, post-test instrument for the ten-week seminar.

The *Volunteer Support Program* is a vital aspect of this model. Volunteers are participants who go through a selection process at the end of the seminar and who then agree to volunteer their time and energy to other seminars. This support system is an important part of the model and is one reason for the tremendous growth that takes place in the people participating in this ten-week seminar.

The model was originally titled Fisher Divorce Seminar because it was believed at that time that divorce adjustment was the most important change that took place during the ten-week seminar. Gradually it became evident that divorce adjustment was a small part of their personal growth, and that the most important growth was using the crisis as motivation to take control of a person's life process rather than following the original life-script or learned pattern from childhood. Thus, the name was changed to Fisher Divorce and Personal Growth Seminar to reflect in the title the more important personal growth. Feedback from many participants indicates that the experience of participating in this class was one of the most important growing experiences of their lives.

History of the Seminar

The educational roots of this seminar become apparent when one learns that the Seminar was first offered at AIMS community college in Greeley, Colorado. It was offered as a pass-fail class and the ten weeks was the format used in the Community College.

The choice of the topics for each of the ten sessions (these later became the various chapters in the textbook) was pragmatic. The participants in the classes were given a questionnaire of sixteen possible discussion topics. It became apparent after a few classes which topics were more universal in nature. Every class picked relationships as the number one topic they were most interested in discussing. The males in the classes chose love as the second most interesting topic and sex as the third most interesting. Females in the classes chose sex as the second most interesting and love third.

No class chose children of divorce as a discussion topic. I asked them why they voted that way. They replied that they had so much to learn and work through emotionally themselves that they were unable to deal with helping their children. This led me to believe that the nicest thing one could do for your kids was to get your act together. If parents can learn to adjust, their children will also adjust in most cases. This doesn't mean we shouldn't be concerned for the large number of children whose parents do not adjust.

Originally there was no anger night and I had not listed that as one of the discussion topics to be voted upon. After completing my Dissertation and doing a statistical analysis of the Fisher Divorce Adjustment Scale, I learned there was an anger subtest in the scale that had not been identified. I re-scored the pre-test, post-test scores of former classes and discovered very little change during the ten weeks in the anger scores. Thus, the class was changed by adding an anger night and emphasizing ways of working through anger by the participants. Maybe computers and statistics can help us to become more human. It appears that I had not dealt with my own anger effectively at that point.

I started developing handout sheets for each of the ten sessions of the class and by 1978 there were approximately sixty pages of handouts. I had been telling people for about two years that I was going to write a book. Gradually people began to doubt my word. But in 1978 I put sixty pages of handouts into book form and printed my first book. The first 300 copies were copied on a copy machine and I bound them myself with spiral binders at the local voc-tech center. Even doing it myself the cost was about $5.00 per book and I realized that I would have to find a cheaper and quicker way. By March of 1979, I had been able to find a typesetter and printer for the book. I printed 3,000 copies which I thought might last me a lifetime, but to my surprise they were sold out a year later. By Christmas of 1979, I was able to purchase my dream home with the book sales making the mortgage payments.

Because of the success of the textbook, I decided to revise the book and find a publisher. Impact Publishers was interested and the book *Rebuilding* was published in 1981. *Rebuilding* has continued to sell very well with over 562,000 sold by the end of 1994. It has received good reviews and was excerpted twice in *New Woman* magazine. Several reviewers have stated that it is one of the best books on the divorce process. It has been published in eleven languages.

The model of the original fifteen rebuilding blocks came about in an interesting way. I was asked to make a presentation at the local NOW chapter on the divorce process. I took white sheets of paper and with a felt tip marker sat down at the kitchen table and devised the blocks. Have you ever created ideas and concepts that you were not totally aware of at the time? The rebuilding blocks have changed very little since that time but I didn't know all of the ideas and concepts that have later come to my awareness concerning the rebuilding blocks.

The Fisher Divorce Adjustment Scale was part of my Doctoral Dissertation completed in 1976, and is discussed in my Dissertation. The Scale is the biggest reason for the interest in my Dissertation, I have printed and sold about 1,000 copies of my Dissertation. (Imagine, a Dissertation becoming a best seller?) I wrote the original Scale after class one night with seventy items, then administered it to the classes and received feedback, revised it and administered it again to the classes, revised it again and began using it in research for the Dissertation. The statistics came back and there was an internal reliability of .915 for the Scale which is exceptionally good. I revised the Scale in 1978 and the internal reliability increased to .98. The Dissertation is titled "Identifying and Meeting the Needs of Formerly-Married People Through a Divorce Adjustment Seminar." I attempted to measure the adjustment of people taking the Seminar vs. those not taking the seminar and the research indicated statistically significant differences between the two groups. Participating in the seminar does help people in their divorce adjustment it appears.

The volunteer support system had its beginning in 1976 when a fireman took the class but was only able to attend every other week because of his work schedule. He asked to come back for the next class and make up the sessions he missed. I had been extensively involved in volunteer work as a juvenile Probation Officer and it suddenly dawned on me that this fireman could become a volunteer support person and continue to attend the classes. Gradually the support program grew until today it is a vital part of the model.

It gradually became apparent to me that marriages that ended in divorce were almost always a parent-child relationship with one party taking care of the other. These marriages are too rigid and the relationship is not able to adjust to changes or trauma. This concept was reinforced in the movie *Scenes from a Marriage* directed by Ingmar Bergman. I discussed this concept at great length in the chapter in the original textbook titled "T.A. for Lovers" and it appears that this is one of the major contributions to divorce adjustment theory to emerge from this book and model.

Another major contribution of this model to divorce adjustment theory has to do with the chapter in the textbook titled "Sometimes Grownups Rebel." Many people go through a transitional period trying to get free from the "shoulds" of the past and become free to be themselves. This transition period looks much like the rebel stage of a teenager in many ways, and it puts a tremendous strain upon love-relationships with many relationships ending. The Transition chapter outlines a practical and effective method of going through this transitional period, and helps people to understand what some have called a period of insanity.

I had at one time seriously considered entering seminary to become a minister. This has evolved until the present. I perceive I am carrying on a socially concerned ministry to people in emotional pain. The model has no direct connection to organized religion but is very spiritual in nature. Many churches are using the model with the Catholic Church using it the most. It is gratifying to have such a large congregation of class participants throughout United States and in many foreign countries.

Professional workshops to train professionals to facilitate the model were started in 1976. The model has caught on largely by word of mouth and in December of 1994, it is estimated there have been over 250,000 people who had participated in the model. It seems adaptable to many different types of facilitator's from churches, mental health agencies, private practitioners, and even to self-help groups discussing the textbook with no trained facilitator.

Philosophy of the Seminar

Because the Seminar is based upon the expressed needs and actual experiences, it is largely pragmatic in nature. Anything that worked and helped people adjust was incorporated into the model. The weekly homework assignments gradually evolved to meet a need for helping the participants change behavior and attitudes.

Systems theory has contributed much to this model. Divorce is looked upon as a process. The divorce didn't occur as a single and isolated event, but was a result of a breakdown in the system or pattern of interaction between the individuals and their environment. This book describes and explains some of the breakdowns or malfunctions of the system.

The model is cognitive with the belief that education can not only help us in dealing with our physical environment but can also help us deal with our emotional environment. Feedback from people frequently mentions having the book written in language that is easily understood helps them to gain information and understanding they were not able to learn from other sources. The belief that understanding intellectually leads to understanding emotionally is a belief in the value of cognitive thinking. The didactic aspects of this model make it cognitive in nature.

The seminar emphasizes the emotional, social, and psychological aspects of the divorce process. It is obvious that the legal and financial aspects of the divorce process are important, but we have found that solving the social and emotional issues makes the financial and legal issues easier to solve.

The model has incorporated changes in behavior which lead to changes in attitudes and a relief from emotional pain and this would be behaviorist in philosophy. Many times a change in behavior will bring about the quickest and most effective change in our lives. Thus, the model is eclectic in that it combines and incorporates many different philosophies.

The Educational Model

Here is what I have done to make the class an educational model:

1. My goal is to develop educational models that can be used in many different situations. I would estimate that less than 50% of the people teaching my Rebuilding classes are professional therapists. They are usually nonprofessional people teaching it in churches. My class is offered through Roman Catholic Churches more than any other group.

2. I have occasionally been able in the past to obtain college credit for the class through outreach programs. Several participants have obtained college credit on their own.

3. The class format is structured. It meets three hours a night, one night per week, for ten weeks. There are specific goals to be reached each night. There are lesson plans passed out for each of the ten sessions. The topics for each week are passed out opening night.

4. I do not accept any third party payments from insurance companies for the class. There is no diagnosing of the participants.

5. We do not expect people to self-disclose or share personal experiences. If they choose to do so during the small group discussion, we do not discourage them from sharing. Our goal is to learn skills and tools rather than commiserating. We state that with information, guidance, and emotional support people will be able to take charge of their lives.

6. We emphasize learning tools such as the communication exercises. About one-half of the class time is spent teaching the communication skills.

7. I wrote the textbooks for both of the classes. There are reading assignments for each of the ten sessions.

8. The most important learning takes place when the people do the homework outside of class. A typical homework exercise is for each person to make a list of what their ideal, dream relationship would be like so they can start creating a vision of what a healthy relationship would be like.

9. Participants are encouraged to keep a personal and private journal outside of class.

10. I have asked therapists and attorneys who have participated in the class to give statements that argue the class is educational and that the volunteer helpers do not perform therapy as part of the class experience.

11. The information sheet that is passed out to participants when they enroll in the class states the class is like a community college class. The sheet states most of the what I have listed above. Enclosed are copies of the sheets and lesson plans we pass out to participants in the classes.

Let's discuss the educational model further. Intellectual learning has to do with cognitive awareness. Much of what we learn in school or classrooms has to do with facts and the measurement of these facts by using a test. One of the reasons factual learning is so emphasized in formal school settings is because it is easier to test and measure, and because it is easier to agree on the facts. The more we get into human feelings, attitudes and beliefs, the less agreement there is as to the truth of these feelings and attitudes.

I once watched a college professor do an amazing demonstration with the faculty of a public school. He asked them what was the most important for children to learn, 1) facts about the world, 2) interactions among people, and 3) understanding of themselves. The teachers strongly voted in favor of understanding themselves as being the most important learning. He next asked them to vote which of these three topics they were spending the most time teaching their students. They strongly agreed they were spending more time teaching facts than the other two areas. To further illustrate this point, emotional learning would include learning how you feel about yourself, or in other words, your feelings of self-worth. How you feel about yourself probably affects more how you live your life than any other single factor. So emotional learning, which includes your feelings of self-worth and your understanding of yourself, has a profound effect upon your relationships with others.

I think this partially explains the dilemma facing public schools today. Many school administrators and teachers understand the importance of emotional learning. But in order to maintain accountability and to avoid criticism of the school program, more emphasis upon teaching facts is necessary.

The intellectual learning in this model is designed to lead the emotional learning, and to make the emotional learning more likely to happen. What does this mean as far as actual teaching methods used with this model?

In group therapy, the facilitator will go with the individual emotional sharing and direct the group energy to that person's sharing. In this educational model the facilitator will minimize the individual emotional sharing and emphasize instead covering the educational topic first. After the group has learned the intellectual concepts the participants are encouraged to do the emotional aspects of actually working through the problem.

Take the example of grieving. In group therapy the individuals might experience feelings of grief and the group energy is directed toward resolving those feelings. But in the educational model, the participants first learn intellectually about the grief process, learn what the grief symptoms are, learn the different losses we experience which cause us to grieve. This understanding gives participants permission to grieve because they have learned it is normal and healthy to grieve. It takes away the fears of being the only person in the world feeling these feelings. It breaks through the denial of these feelings which comes from not understanding the grief process.

Breaking through denial is a decided advantage of the educational model. A person who is denying feelings reads the textbook and learns intellectually the feelings and symptoms of grief. This not only eases their mind about being abnormal for feeling these feelings, but it also provides them an idea of what feelings to look for. It is common for participants in this seminar to enroll in the seminar with a great deal of denial of feelings, and to graduate from the seminar having broken through the denial. Overcoming denial is largely a process of learning to accept your feelings, and understanding them intellectually greatly increases the capacity to accept those same feelings.

There is an exception to the intellectual learning preceding the emotional learning. A participant may be experiencing emotional pain to the extent it keeps them from benefiting from the educational learning. This person may need to ventilate emotions to release the pressures and thus the emotional learning may precede the intellectual learning.

Basic Beliefs Affecting the Teaching of this Model

Part of the effectiveness of this model is certain beliefs underlying the philosophy and teaching of the model. These beliefs need to be clearly stated in order for the facilitator to do the most effective job of teaching. Let's discuss and examine some of these basic beliefs:

1) Motivation is always a determining factor in the effectiveness of learning. One of the reasons this model is so effective is the motivation coming from the pain associated with a crisis. Any crisis can be an opportunity or invitation for personal growth, and if the person does use the pain as motivation to grow, the crisis will likely become a creative experience.

2) One of the most important forms of personal growth resulting from participation in this seminar is the participant becoming free from their original life-script or pattern of interaction. The class helps people overcome their addictions and start making choices in their lives. This personal growth is probably closely connected to the increase in the improved quality of relationships participants experience after completing the seminar.

3) Many times during the seminar we suggest people work through the adjustment process before they become involved in another long-term, committed love-relationship. This is sometimes done in a subtle way and sometimes is done quite blatantly. Again, having a time period of singleness between relationships will tend to improve the quality of the relationships after the crisis.

4) Frequently we state in our material the belief that people, if given information, guidance, and support will be able to adjust to a crisis and make it into a creative experience. Underlying this statement is a belief in the abilities of people to solve their own problems rather than having some expert solve their problems or give them the answer to their problems. It is important that the facilitator agree with this belief in order to instill the belief in the participants they can solve their problems. A facilitator who talks about the "sickies" or "crazies" taking the class will probably not facilitate the class in the manner it was designed to be facilitated.

5) Similar to the previous idea is the belief that much of the important learning taking place in this seminar is the learning from the other participants. Each person sharing their own experience helps others to learn from them. The facilitator needs to encourage each person to share their own experience rather than preaching or telling others how to solve their problems. This sharing of themselves naturally includes the facilitator.

6) We believe the most important learning of any in this seminar is each participant learning to own their own feelings, attitudes, and beliefs. Owning rather than projecting or introjecting probably does more to improve relationships after completing the seminar than any other learning.

Time and Length of the Seminar

We have taught the seminar in various, time periods and believe the three-hour class periods once a week for ten weeks to be the most effective for several reasons. Participants need the thirty contact hours to be able to intellectually and emotionally learn enough to adequately, adjust to the crisis. Participants need the time outside of class to internalize the learning and to practice the homework assignments and the ten, weeks gives enough outside time. The three hours at each session gives enough time to accomplish the learning goals.

We have taught the seminar in six weeks rather than the ten weeks. Much of the important learning can be accomplished in the first six weeks of the seminar. We believe the last four weeks of the seminar help participants internalize the learning which minimizes the regression in adjustment taking place after the seminar is completed. All classes have an emotional high at the end of the ten weeks, but individuals have internalized enough to minimize the regression.

I did a follow-up of participants as part of my Doctoral Dissertation in 1976. I found that twenty-four of the twenty-eight who took the Divorce Adjustment Scale at the end of three months continued to improve their scores after completing the seminar. Four had a lower score indicating a regression in adjustment after the seminar. This is too small a sample to be statistically reliable but it indicates most participants continue to grow after the seminar but at a lower rate of growth.

I also have given the FDAS at two-week intervals to participants during the ten-week seminar. There was not an identifiable pattern of growth because some had tremendous growth early in the ten weeks, and others made their growth later in the ten weeks.

We have taught the seminar in various weekend schedules and with varying time frames. The all-day sessions are usually more intense and more like group therapy. We believe the regression after a weekend session is greater because of the lack of time to internalize the learning outside of class, but we have no research proving this.

It is not possible to get as many contact hours in a weekend unless you go to some sort of a marathon session meeting for twelve hours in a row. We don't recommend marathon sessions for an educational model because there is too much didactic material to cover and the participants feel overwhelmed. Usually the weekend session has seven hours a day which results in about fifteen hours a weekend or about half of the normal thirty contact hours. Thus a weekend session usually covers about the first half of the ten sessions.

We prefer the following schedule for a weekend class: Have the opening session with the presentation of the Rebuilding Blocks from chapter one in an evening meeting — maybe a Friday evening. Give the participants the textbook to read and wait one week until the following weekend, either Saturday or Sunday, and hold an all-day session. Then wait till the following weekend and hold another all-day session. This would result in about fifteen contact hours or about half of the regular thirty contact hours. If desired, you could continue the all-day sessions until the seminar was completed. By giving the participants time between all-day sessions, it gives them time to internalize the learning.

We do not have a favorite evening to hold the weekly three-hour meeting There may be conflicts on certain evenings such as some communities have an evening for church activities. Some communities have a large single's club and many participants in the seminar may want to attend the single's meetings. Some seminars held in churches meet on Sunday afternoons rather than evenings. We prefer meeting from 7:00 PM to 10:00 PM but some participants have difficulty meeting that early in the evening and prefer 7:30 or 8:00. We have always found it difficult to complete the session in three hours. The facilitator has to be very assertive and cut off discussion in order to complete the seminar in three hours. When they finally start talking about their adjustment process people want to continue to talk because it feels so good to talk.

The seminar has not been offered by many businesses as part of the employee benefits, but employers need to think about doing this. The loss of effectiveness by employees as they are going through the adjustment process is tremendous. For example, maybe an employee's salary is $40,000 per year. The year after separation from their marriage partner, they may be only operating at 50% effectiveness and this would be a loss of $20,000 per year for the employer. Participating in this seminar might decrease the down time, or the ineffective time, of the employee by half, resulting in a saving to the employer of $20,000. Whether these figures are researched or not, the saving for the employer would be great. Some businesses are offering the seminar and it can be offered during the noon hour or lunch break. This does not give enough contact hours to complete the seminar, but variations and compromises could be implemented. Possibly the employer could contribute an hour of the employee's time and in return the employee could contribute an hour or two of their time.

We have offered one-day sessions for participants with an emphasis upon the Rebuilding Blocks and the adjustment process, leaving it up to the participants to read the textbook and do their own homework rather than attending the ten sessions. This is not as effective but even reading the textbook without attending the seminar has been a growing experience for some.

There is enough material in the new edition of *Rebuilding* to have the class for more than ten weeks in order to cover the material. It often is difficult to find participants who will commit to more than ten weeks of class. Compromises might be needed. Perhaps ten weeks could be offered and then those who wanted to continue might be enrolled in a follow-up class.

In conclusion, I recommend the ten-week sessions as the most effective method of offering this seminar, but it can be offered in many different time slots.

Class Size
When I was first developing this model, I limited the class to fifteen participants. I gradually learned that larger classes could happen if more small group activities were implemented. We like a class size of from twelve to twenty-five members as being ideal. Less than twelve results in low energy. More than twenty-five in the class changes the interaction and the atmosphere of the class. It also makes it more difficult to meet in homes and increases the number of dropouts. People get lost in the crowd in a class with more than twenty-five members. On the other hand, single people are usually wanting to meet other singles, and the larger class size meets this need.

I suggest you start with smaller classes of twelve or less when you are learning to facilitate the class. Then as you get more experience, try larger classes and determine what size feels best for you. Obviously class size is often decided by your method of recruiting. Churches with a large membership can often attract large numbers for the class. Singles groups such as Beginning Experience often have large numbers for classes. A therapist with a small private practice may have to build a reputation with the class before recruiting large numbers of participants.

Dropouts and Absences

One of best testimonials to the value of this seminar is the minimal number of dropouts and absences. I used to hand score the FDAS answer sheets for classes all over the united States, and typically there would be the same number of participants at the end of the ten weeks as there was at the beginning. Participants have done things like talking their doctors into releasing them from the hospital in time so as not to miss a class. The participants find the class so valuable, they don't like to miss even a single session.

There are some patterns to the dropouts that do occur. Whenever a participant enters into a love-relationship, they tend to drop out. This relationship may be with their former love partner, or it may be a new relationship. We have tried diligently to welcome the new love partner into the class and let the two take the class together, but seldom has this happened. We have had the most success in preventing this type of dropout by discouraging the participants from entering into a love-relationship during the ten weeks.

A further word is necessary on the matter of going back to the former love partner. We believe the couple needs time apart after they have separated before going back together with each other. The old pattern of interaction is powerful and going back before the person has completed the ten weeks of the seminar is usually not productive. It gives too much power to the old pattern of behavior. We suggest participants wait until they complete the class before going back to the former spouse. This is especially true when it comes to living together. We suggest they do a courtship period before moving in together in order to encourage a new relationship developing rather than encouraging the old pattern of behavior. Going back to the former spouse too soon is usually going back for the wrong reasons such as a fear of becoming divorced, or a fear of not being able to make it by themselves. (For more information concerning this, see the "Healing Separation" in Appendix B of *Rebuilding*.)

We don't become too concerned about the person dropping out because they started a new relationship. We make them feel welcome to come back because we know the odds of that relationship lasting very long are not good, and we want them to feel welcome to come back when it ends.

There is an occasional dropout who is feeling overwhelmed. The class stimulates so much growth that some are not able to handle it, especially if they are experiencing outside stress such as court battles. This kind of dropout can be minimized by giving the person as much support from the volunteer helpers as possible But they just may not be ready to adjust and need more time before they are ready to adjust and grow.

There are some dropouts that come opening night and sign up for the class and don't come back. They may be caught up in the energy of opening night and sign up even though they aren't ready to grow. They may not want to deal with the buried feelings they have, such as unresolved grief. They may want to hang on to their pain a little longer before letting go. Some are in denial so bad that taking the class forces them to deal with their denial and the feelings of denial may win. This is especially true with dumpees who don't want the relationship to end.

As far as absences go, about the only thing that really needs to be said is to keep calling and checking with the participants who miss a class. Each class that you miss makes it that much harder to come back to class. It's not so hard to come back after one absence, but each additional absence makes it that much harder to come back.

I think a good teaching technique is to use the attendance sheet and let each person sign it to show they attended that night. This is sort of like taking attendance but leaves it up to them to be responsible rather than the teacher being the attendance taker. We also have offered a money-back guarantee for the class fee but they have to attend nine of the ten sessions in order to get their money back. Keeping attendance records helps to determine how many absences each person has during the ten weeks.

There is another aspect of absences. The person often will miss the night when we are talking about the feeling they are denying. One woman missed anger night when she took the class the first time. She volunteered in the next two seminars and again missed anger night both times. I don't think it was a coincidence she missed anger night three times in a row. We pointed out her behavior to her in the hopes she could learn from it.

Marital and Divorce Status

Usually a class has a large percentage of people recently separated — maybe half of the class are in this category. There is another large category of people who have obtained their final decree and are divorced. There are some who have never married but who are ending a love relationship, maybe a LTA (Living Together Arrangement). There are some who have not separated but are contemplating separation in the near future. Some of these go ahead and separate, but some take the class and find out how much work it is to divorce and they decide to work on their marriage some more. There are some widowed people taking the class and we will talk more about them in another paragraph.

We have not actively recruited people ending a homosexual relationship. The process of ending a homosexual relationship appears to be the same as for heterosexuals There may be some differences in finding a support group for homosexuals depending upon the community and the percentage of homosexuals in the community. We have had a few participants ending a homosexual relationship but they seldom share that information with the other class members.

We have had a larger number of people whose spouse came out of the closet and this was part of the reason for the divorce. These people have a special kind of process because usually they are not comfortable sharing the reasons for their divorce. It is one thing to be replaced by another person of your sex, but it is another to be replaced by a member of the opposite sex. Possibly it would be beneficial to have classes for these two groups of people so they would feel more comfortable sharing their situation.

Dumpers and Dumpees

How about dumpers and dumpees? Again, nationwide statistics for this seminar indicate about half of the class are dumpees, about one-third of the class are dumpers, and about one-sixth of the class are people who state it was a mutual decision. It is interesting to note dumpees usually take the class shortly after they separate, while dumpers usually take the class after they have been separated six months or more. There is dumper euphoria and the dumper usually has to be separated six months to a year before they overcome the euphoric feeling of being out of the relationship. I say that a dumper finally takes the class when they have been in the single's world long enough that their former love partner has begun to look desirable again. A possible conclusion might be: dumpees take the class to survive, while dumpers take the class for personal growth.

As for being a dumper or a dumpee, it is also interesting to note a comparison between how participants see themselves at the beginning of the class and how they see themselves at the end of the class. We found that 10% changed their dumper, dumpee, mutual status on the post-test FDAS compared to their pre-test FDAS answer sheet. We believe their post-test answer about whether they were dumpee or dumper to be the most correct.

Males and Females

As far as males and females are concerned, one-third of the class is male and two-thirds are female. This varies a great deal from class to class, as do all of the statistics. Some people ask why there are more females. Statistics indicate in the formerly-married subculture there is about the same ratio of two-thirds female and one-third male. If every divorce has one male and one female, how can this be? There may be many reasons for this but two important ones are: 1) Women live longer than men so each year of life the ratio becomes more predominately female, and 2) many formerly married men marry women much younger and many of these younger females have never been married before.

Some facilitator's state they have a preference for classes all of the same sex. They give two reasons for this preference. 1) The class members feel more comfortable being around members of the same sex rather than have some of the enemy in the class and are able to talk more freely, and 2) the class members do not become romantically and sexually involved with other class members.

We believe one of the most important aspects of the divorce process is working through the problems of interacting with the opposite sex. Divorce upsets male-female relationships and where is there a better place to work through this difficulty than in the safe atmosphere of an educational class? For this reason we strongly suggest you have a class which includes members of both sexes in order to facilitate maximum growth and adjustment.

Because the participants are often in an emotional space of being needy and vulnerable, we emphasize it is not a good time to become emotionally romantically and sexually involved with other class participants. We encourage them to make friends with both sexes but to invest in their own personal growth rather than in another relationship. Sharing these expectations with the class members usually results in a sigh of relief and a sort of safe feeling based upon the belief participants don't have to play the dating games while working through their adjustment process.

Some facilitator's state they are having nothing but females enroll in their classes, and how do we get classes with one-third males? We have volunteer helpers of both sexes and because these volunteers contact new class members, they may contact males. Having opening night in a more neutral setting such as community colleges and schools will bring more males than having opening night in a mental health center. Having both a male and female facilitator may help you to enroll more males. Males are more likely to be reluctant and having a volunteer or former class member bring them opening night often helps overcome the reluctance. Having a male volunteer displayed openly in the parking lot or at the door where the class is being held may help males to come into the class rather than driving around the block four times and then leaving. (Females have been known to do this also.)

We also have used this technique to enroll more males: We try to advance register as many as possible but limit the number of females enrolling in the class. Say you want fifteen to twenty people in the class. Advance register a limit of ten females and then aim to enroll as many males as possible. We have also found males are much more reluctant to advance register than females. They prefer to come opening night to check out the class before enrolling, and often don't bring a checkbook so can't pay the enrollment fee until the second night of class.

Widows and Divorced People

There is a problem of mixing widowed and divorced people in the same seminar This is too bad because the process of adjustment is very similar for both groups of people, and they could learn a great deal from each other. Widowed people feel the divorced person should not complain or be angry because they chose to end the relationship. Divorced people reply stating the widowed person has it easier because they don't have to talk to the S.O.B., and don't have to deal with visitation and legal problems. Also, money problems are usually easier for the widowed person. When a spouse dies, friends and neighbors bring food and visit the survivor. When a couple divorces, friends and neighbors usually avoid the divorcing person.

Widowed people find it easier to idolize the deceased spouse. It is easier to deny feelings, especially anger, when you don't interact with the deceased person There is no confronting the ex to bring this fantasy back to reality. We find it interesting how few widow support groups or educational classes such as this model there are even though there is as great a need among widows as there is for divorced people. We would like to see this model used for widows and believe it could be possible even though the word divorce is used throughout the textbook.

Another phenomenon occurs quite frequently and should be mentioned. Many widows report they wished they were divorced before the spouse died. They went through much of the divorce process and then had to go through the process of being widowed. These people are much more likely to benefit from participating in the class.

We also have had a large number of people who have been both widowed and divorced take the class. The question is often asked which is the more painful process. I have not kept a record of the responses but I usually ask them which was the more difficult. It appears to be about half and half and depends on the situation surrounding the death or divorce.

We have never refused to allow a widowed person to enroll in our classes, but there have been very few widows enroll. This is probably due to a selection process because the class is advertised as a divorce class. The occasional widow enrolled in this seminar has not been a problem. But there is always the potential for problems and if you enroll both groups, you need to be aware of the possible difficulties.

Meeting Place

The meeting place for the opening night is important. You will need to find the least threatening place because many of the participants will feel very anxious and uncomfortable on opening night. For many, it will be the first group and experience growth experience in their lives. We've already mentioned the problem is usually more difficult for males.

We recommend the most neutral place you can find. Churches are a good place to hold opening night and here at the Learning Center we frequently use them. We look for a church in the community that is a socially concerned church because holding the class there benefits us both. Many people going through divorce have left the church they were associated with and often we can encourage them to start attending a church that is concerned about meeting their needs. Many people are not only reworking their relationship with other people, but are also reworking their relationship with God and feel uncomfortable and guilty going to a church.

Community colleges usually are non-threatening and carry out the theme of the educational model. Mental Health Centers may lead some to think they are getting their "head shrunk" while taking the class and this conflicts with some of the philosophy of the class being a growth model. Private homes can be used but some people may not feel comfortable meeting in a home until they know the people. A public place like the meeting room in a motel is good and it is easier to find than many other locations.

We make opening night a free event and anyone is encouraged to attend. If they have not advance registered, they are free to do so after hearing the presentation. We like to have visitors because it meets our social worker needs to have them listen to the building block presentation. We know hearing the presentation will help them work through their process even though they aren't getting the full benefit of attending the ten week seminar.

After opening night we prefer meeting in the participants' homes. There are several reasons for this. It helps to get to know a person better by visiting their home. Many participants have had an empty, lonely home and having the class in the home helps fill it with warm vibrations. For many participants, it is the first time they have had guests in their home since the separation. And for many in a destructive marriage, it had been months before they separated since they had guests in their home. Meeting in the home provides an informal atmosphere that is conducive to learning because it feels safe and warm, rather than professional and cold.

There may be some problems meeting in homes. Class size of over twenty-five are difficult to handle in most homes although much larger classes can meet in much smaller homes than what you might think. It only causes the class to feel closer and cozier. Locating a different home each week can take time and cause classes to start late because many participants will have difficulty following directions and locating houses. Homemade and hand-drawn maps are helpful if passed out a week ahead of time. Children being put to bed and telephones ringing can cause disruptions to the class. I suggest the host disconnect the phone during class — after all, if they were meeting in another home they wouldn't be answering the phone. People really enjoy having the class in their homes and always are eager to volunteer their home. It is one of the positive experiences people remember about the class.

College Credit

When the seminar was being developed in the community college, pass-fail credit was available. This class is probably the most positive learning experience most people will experience and definitely deserves college credit. But we have had difficulty in arranging college credit. We have offered continuing education credit at various times, but it requires a great deal of time and effort to deal with the college and university bureaucracy and red tape unless you are on the teaching staff. Many community colleges are offering this seminar with the largest number being in Iowa. It is a perfect class for a community college to offer because it meets the needs of the community so well, and it gives the college such a good reputation in the community.

There are a few taking this class who desire college credit. Here in Colorado many teachers have taken the class to meet their requirements for continuing education credit. Many others, especially women, get college credit for this class as a start for their returning to college to obtain a degree. Seeing a person start back to college by using this class as a springboard is a good feeling. Many times a participant in this class who is a student in a college or university may find a professor who will allow them to take this seminar as an individual credit course. Bruce was able to use facilitating this class as an individual credit course as part of his Doctoral program.

Married Couples

We already mentioned the small group of people who are still married and living together taking the class. In addition there are some married couples who both desire to take the class. Should these couples take the class together? Usually, no, for the obvious reason they have too much anger towards each other and would not be able to benefit from the class as much as if they took it separately. They will need emotional space away from the other person and they will need to take the class separately. We have found a different way of enrolling both. One could take the class in this community and the other could take it in a neighboring community because at the Learning Center we had six or eight classes going simultaneously. If you don't have that option, you can have one take the class this time and the other take it next time it is offered.

We prefer having them take the class at the same time in different locations. Their timing has to be right in the sense each is ready to grow at the same time. Dumpers may be ready to grow before dumpees, but dumpees may be more motivated to attend the class. They experience the personal growth at the same time if they take the class at the same time. One taking the class before the other does can cause extra stress in the relationship tending to make it end rather than gaining time to facilitate carving out a new relationship.

In addition, we always suggest a couple which has separated not to move in together until they have begun to carve out the new relationship. Again, the old pattern is so strong and living together gives more power to the old relationship and encourages it to come back stronger and stronger.

We are finding many couples attempting to carve out a new relationship after both have taken the divorce seminar. It sounds like a contradiction but taking the divorce seminar often helps the marriage. Many don't have the skills needed to carve out a new relationship so we are encouraging them to enroll in the relationships class in order to increase their chances of creating a relationship which meets their needs.

We have asked ourselves what it is about the Divorce seminar that makes future relationships work better. We have decided the reason is people own their own feelings, attitudes, and behavior after taking the Rebuilding Seminar and this is one of the most important behaviors making relationships work.

Mediation

Many couples are finding mediation a way to overcome the destruction done to families by the court adversarial process. The couple meets with a mediation team, usually a therapist and lawyer, preferably of both sexes. Attempts are made to resolve the issues in order to avoid a lengthy and expensive court hearing. For the couples who are open to mediation, it provides a healthy and relatively inexpensive way of resolving the differences.

The mediation teams in our area have found participation in the Divorce seminar greatly increases the chances of mediation working. The teams often require couples to take the Rebuilding Seminar before they will agree to seeing the couple for mediation. There needs to be more communication between mediation teams and facilitator's of the Rebuilding Seminar because the two services compliment each other well.

Screening Applicants

It may be hard to believe but we have never done any screening of applicants. We seldom have emotionally disturbed people enroll in the seminar. How does this happen? We believe there is some sort of natural selection process happening. Those needing therapeutic, help don't look to an educational seminar for help.

We have had a few enroll in the class who are disturbed. Maybe five or six out of a total enrollment in our classes of 2,000. These few tend to take energy from the group, tend to keep the learning for the group from being as effective, and always report the class as being far more helpful than the hospitalization in a psychiatric ward or the years of therapy they had experienced in the past.

We have another theory to explain why disturbed people seldom take the class: Maybe they are looking for someone else to solve their problems and the theme of the class that you are able to solve your own problems causes them, internal conflict. Obviously the educational model has great value in teaching a disturbed person ways of coping and healing.

Individual Therapy During Seminar

We ask on the information sheet if the I person is in individual therapy. If they answer yes, we ask if they have consulted with their therapist about taking the class. We insist there be communication between the therapist and the participant before participation in the ten-week class. If the person does not feel comfortable talking to the therapist, (and we wonder why they don't) or if the therapist has questions concerning the seminar, we as facilitator's are glad to communicate directly with the therapist (given the client's consent). We see no conflict between the person being involved in individual therapy and participating in the class at the same time. In fact we see many advantages to this arrangement, and encourage it.

There may be some problems. Some therapists may become defensive when they see the class helping the client more than they were. Some therapists may realize the class decreases the adjustment time for a client and it may make the therapist glad or sad, depending on whether they are more interested in making money or more interested in the client's well-being. We are finding concerned therapists to be referring more clients to our class as they discover the value of the class.

Many people in the divorce pits may need individual sessions before they are ready to experience a group learning situation so the seminar becomes sort of a graduation from individual therapy. At one time I tabulated the number of participants in the seminar who were in individual therapy and it was running around 30%. If the person is not involved in individual therapy when they start the class, we suggest they wait to become involved in therapy until after the class is completed. We find the growing in the class to be as much as most people can handle, and another growth experience of individual therapy is overwhelming.

I will see a person while they are taking the class but only for single sessions. The value of these sessions is to help the person who is feeling overwhelmed to deal with the growth taking place within them. Normally the volunteer helpers fill this support role and the participants seldom come to me for therapy while taking the class.

We refer people to the class rather than seeing them individually if possible. It saves them time and money in most cases. We find maybe 10% of the participants ask to come for individual therapy upon completion of the class. We view this happening because the class helped them become strong enough to deal with the issues they needed to deal with. These therapy experiences after the class are usually short-term, and usually very positive.

Recruitment of Participants

We keep a record of how people find out about the class. About 95% have heard from a former participant and took the class because of that person's recommendation. This again speaks to the value of the class. But if you are just beginning to facilitate the seminar, you will have no former participants referring to your seminars. Here are some suggestions:

If you are associated with an umbrella agency such as a church, or a therapist with a mental health agency, your job of recruiting will be easier. Whatever your umbrella agency, it will provide with warm bodies ready for a tremendous growing experience.

There are many ways of making contacts. Usually ministers and lawyers have large numbers of people seeking help from them while they are going through the divorce process. When they learn the value of the class, they will be eager to refer. I would suggest you start with contacting these two groups of people in a professional manner such as sending them a letter with a brochure about the class, and then following the letter up with an individual conference.

We have a variation of this which is a positive way of making contact. After you start teaching the seminars, ask the participants to list lawyers, clergymen, and therapists whom they have found helpful to them. Make a list of the recommended ones. Not only will you have a list when a person asks you for an appropriate helping person, but you can write a letter to the professional person stating they have been recommended by participants and they are on your referral list. Ask them for referrals if they have clients who need a good personal growth and adjustment experience. It's a good way to gain positive professional contacts.

If you make your services known as a speaker, you may be asked to speak at several clubs and luncheons. They usually are looking for someone for their programs. I suggest the presentation title be "Rebuilding After a Crisis." Again, have brochures to pass out to the listeners and you may get several referrals.

We have found an ad in the personal column in the want ads section probably gets better results than paying for a large ad in newspapers. Sometimes a large ad will get good response, but people need to know more about the class and are reluctant to pay money until they know more about what is being offered. Having the opening night free and open to the public helps people come check out the program. Try putting a personal ad with one of the volunteer helper's phone number if you have a volunteer who would like to help people by answering the phone.

Brochures are an effective form of advertising. If you have been through our professional training workshop, feel free to mention in your brochure that you have been trained by us. Be sure you have a registration form

on your brochure to be filled out by people wanting to register. Do a good job of creating your registration form so it can be easily understood by everyone. It is amazing how you see it logical and easily understood, and how confused people can get filling it out.

If you are using either of Bruce's books in your classes, feel free to put an insert in the book with your name and phone number. Indicate you are teaching the Rebuilding Seminar locally. The books usually get passed around and you might be surprised how many contacts you get from these inserts.

Maybe you want make contacts with local bookstores to handle Bruce's books and make a deal with them to put inserts into the books. Bookstores will normally carry *Rebuilding*. We often get referrals from someone who has read the book. One fellow called from the bookstore. He reported he found the book, sat down immediately and started reading, and called me to see if he could enroll in the class when he realized how helpful and relevant the book was to him.

We always invite former class members to come again to opening night and bring a friend with them. Even though the person has completed the class, they may hear new things from each presentation of the rebuilding blocks. They enjoy seeing old friends and catching up on how each person is doing in their adjustment process. The guests they bring with them will often sign up for the class after hearing the presentation. It is not the primary goal of having volunteers to do recruiting, but they are good recruiters. Don't be afraid of asking them to contact others. You can still keep the program low key without it being high pressure sales job. The class is a fantastic experience and the volunteers can simply let people know this.

Be sure to invite professional people to come opening night as guests. They like to know what the class is all about. Hearing the opening presentation explains what the class is about as well as anything you can do. Ask your minister, your lawyer, or your accountant to come visit. It will be an interesting evening for them, and will make it easier for them to refer people in the future.

We have been training facilitator's to teach this seminar since 1976, and have learned that upon completion of the professional workshop there will be very few problems in teaching this seminar. (It almost teaches itself!) But the most difficult problem has been recruiting. So take some special time and effort and implement some of these recruiting ideas. If you do a good job of teaching and the people had a positive experience, your future recruiting will become easier and easier.

The marketplace does weed out some facilitator's because participants have not had a positive experience in the class. They won't refer others to take the class. Teaching the class privately is like building a private practice. It is slow at first, but the status and reputation of the class keeps building and pretty soon you may have more participants than you have time and space for.

Starting a Private Practice

The class is a perfect way to start your own business. Many have started moonlighting by teaching the class one night per week while they continue the regular job. Then as the class enrollment grows, they may go halftime in their job or take the big plunge and quit the 8 to 5 job in order to concentrate completely on teaching the seminars. Now that we have several different seminars you can teach, you will be able to teach the different seminars and reach a much larger audience.

If you already have a private practice but want to augment your income teaching the class, it will give you extra income. It may also increase your private clientele. If you are socially concerned about people as we are here at the Learning Center, you may find emotional job satisfaction from reaching so many people with such inexpensive services.

Have you done any figuring on potential income from teaching this class? If you have 20 in a class at $200 per participant, you will have $4,000 income every ten weeks. How many classes do you want to teach each week, or each year? Two classes per week would be eight classes per year which would be $32,000 gross income from only two nights a week of work.

Advance Registration

We strongly recommend having as many advance register as possible. The main reason for this is it speeds up the process of adjustment for the participants. As soon as the person registers with a $20 advance deposit, we send them a copy of the book and ask them to start reading. We also pass the names along to the volunteer helpers and ask them to start calling the person before opening night. This calling in advance makes a tremendous impression upon the person taking the class no matter where they are at in the divorce process. The result from reading the book and getting phone calls is that the person has already begun the adjustment process before opening night. You may encourage advance registration by making a cash discount for payment in advance. If the word gets out the class will be full by opening night, which often happens to us, it encourages advance registration because people learn they won't be able to enroll if they don't advance register.

It also helps you as a facilitator because you can have class lists printed by opening night. It is helpful to the participants to have everyone's name, address, and phone numbers on a class list. It helps to get better acquainted with each other opening night. Seeing your name on a class list is like finding your name in a phone book. It makes you feel accepted and okay.

Male and Female Facilitator's

Until I started using volunteer helpers, I always taught the class with a male and female co-facilitating. It seemed important to have input and viewpoints from both sexes. I still believe this to be important because some people will have difficulty with certain facilitator's. I once disclosed early in the class I was a dumper in my marriage, and one female dumpee never did forgive me and eventually dropped out of the class. Having facilitator's of both sexes will minimize this difficulty. If a person harbors anger toward facilitator's of the opposite sex, they might be able to relate to the facilitator of the same sex.

After I began to use volunteer helpers, I stopped having facilitator's of both sexes. It seemed the volunteer helpers were able to meet the needs of participants and there was no need to have facilitator's of both sexes. In fact, having several volunteers allowed participants to find a helping person no matter what their need was. For example, a female who is having difficulty because the ex has a girlfriend present when the children are visiting dad may find a volunteer helper who had experienced the same situation. The two people are able to relate in a meaningful manner.

As to the sex of the facilitator, many ask if participants relate to a male better than a female. There are some differences in how people relate. Having a class with a majority of females is common, and having a male facilitator makes the class more masculine in character. Many males relate to a male facilitator better. Many females need to learn to trust a male again and having a male facilitator is a good place to learn that trust.

As a single male, I found many females falling in love with me. I own some responsibility for that because when I was looking for available females, it was easy for females to pick up on those vibrations. My observation is many people need to have feelings of love as part of their process. It sort of makes them feel alive again, makes them feel they can love, and makes them feel like a man or woman instead of being neutered. If the facilitator can keep this adoration in perspective, it can be very helpful to those needing to know they can experience feelings of love.

Facilitator's dating and becoming involved with members of the class is to be avoided in all cases. Not only is it a violation of ethics and a way of using people while they are emotionally vulnerable, it is a lousy way to start a relationship. One big emphasis of this model is the of parent-child relationships. Starting a relationship with a class member is almost certain to be another parent-child relationship. The destruction is not only to the two people involved, but also to the total group process.

There is another pitfall to be avoided. If it is desirable to have a male and female facilitator, what is their relationship like? My suggestion is that it either be friends or a solid, committed love relationship. Being friends is ideal in many ways. When you are recently separated, the whole world appears to be coupled. If you come to a divorce class, and the facilitator's are coupled — it really reinforces that lonely feeling. Facilitator's who are friends provides a role model of a male and female friendship which is a good kind of role model to have for formerly married people attending this class. Facilitator's who are having some sort of relationship other than friendship can be difficult for the parties involved, but also can be stressful and painful for the participants. I once was teaching with a woman who fell in love with me and I had to distance and dump her while we were teaching the class. It was difficult for us and for the class members. I would avoid teaching the class with a person where the relationship was not clearly and solidly defined in order to prevent this from happening.

Qualifications of Facilitator's
This model appears to work well with a wide variety of facilitator training and experience. I advertise the model to be taught with a facilitator having a graduate college degree in a helping profession. In reality some of the most effective facilitator's I have known have not had college degrees, much less graduate degrees. It appears there are other factors related to effectiveness rather than education.

The effective facilitator usually has been through a divorce themselves but this is not a necessary qualification. They have to be sensitive to people and people's pain. They have to come across as caring and be able to relate to people in a manner that makes the people feel they care. It helps to be at a good place emotionally and not be working through their own adjustment process, although some have done a good job by being open and sharing with the class their own pain. The facilitator needs to believe in people's ability to solve their own problems, and to believe in people being able to grow and adjust without a

doctor or specialist doing it for them. Several times there has been a person who has been teaching the seminar, sometimes more than once, who has come to the professional training and found it to be a very positive experience.

Here at the Learning Center, we have had married people never divorced teach the class. Sometimes they have had a divorce within their marriage and were able to carve out a new relationship. It appears there are many ways to learn the adjustment process without the person having ended a marriage through divorce. I have found very little difference in the effectiveness of the facilitator whether they be clergy, nurses and doctors, mental health workers, teachers, or lay leaders. I strongly suggest anyone teaching the class without a graduate degree find a consultant person, preferably a trained counselor, who can be there if a problem should arise.

We have found some groups of people who get together without a facilitator. They use the book as a discussion guide, get together regularly on a weekly basis, do the assigned homework at the end of each chapter, and report they had a very positive experience.

There appears to be some value from having a trained person as facilitator. We did some research showing the gain scores on the pre-test, post-test FDAS scores for those facilitating the class after attending our professional workshop vs. those not attending our professional training. The numbers were small and maybe not statistically sound, but there was a marked difference in gain scores with those not trained showing much lower gain scores for the participants. I recommend you take the "Facilitator Training Workshop" in order to maximize the learning by the participants.

It would be easy to place too much emphasis upon the FDAS scores in evaluating the effectiveness of various facilitator's. Nationwide we have found the average pre-test, post-test gain score to be 66 points. The untrained facilitator's participants had a gain score of 43 points. The staff at the Learning Center expected to have an average gain score of 100 points. There are many variables in these gain scores with one of the largest variables being how low the person's score was at the beginning of the class. The lower the pre-test score, the larger the gain score as an average. I have learned to take statistics with a large amount of skepticism.

I spent a great deal of time trying to decide if I would sell textbooks and materials to those who had not been through our "Facilitator Training Workshop." Our decision to do so was largely based upon the belief many would be teaching the class without the training because of time and money. We believed they would teach the class more effectively if they had the textbook and teacher's guide. Presently there are far more facilitator's teaching the class without the training, than those with the training.

In summary, I believe this seminar will almost teach itself. But the better the training and experience of the facilitator, and especially the personal qualities and characteristics of the person, the more effective the class will be.

Fees for the Seminars

I do not make any recommendations as to the amount of fee you should charge for the seminar. I do believe participants should pay something because they will work harder, attend more classes, and respect the value of the class more if they pay even a small amount. Many churches offer this class for a small fee of $25.00, or just enough to cover the cost of the textbook and scoring of the FDAS. Their salaries are not paid from the class income. Others are working through an agency whereby the agency takes a cut off the top, and the person must charge $150 or more in order to make any money from teaching.

I already mentioned our basic philosophy of being able to offer a service which is effective but reasonable in cost. If we only looked at the value the participants received for the class, they would be paying a large fee. $200 is an average price for the ten-weeks seminar and this is only $6.60 per hour for the thirty contact hours. This is the best buy in town. Where else can you find this kind of positive experience for $6.60 per hour? Only in an agency like a church or mental health center where the salary of the facilitator is subsidized by other sources of income. As mentioned before, a large class of maybe 100 participants could be taught with a much smaller than average fee and still leave income for the participant if there were unpaid volunteers.

An Extra All-Day Session

For years I taught this seminar with an all-day session included, in addition to the ten sessions. The topic covered in the all-day session was the lifelines explained in chapter nineteen, This is a time-consuming topic and usually very heavy emotionally. It is appropriate for an all-day session, It is difficult to share everyone's lifeline in one evening, but it is possible to do.

Our format for that day was to start the day with solo time while each person completed their lifeline. I would normally share my lifeline as an explanation of how to do a lifeline because there was no textbook written at that time. Even now, with each person reading the chapter before coming to the all-day session, it would still be helpful to share a lifeline in order to help them

learn how to do one. I normally would do the all-day session toward the end of the ten weeks because, again, people needed to trust, just as they do with the mask night. It can be a tremendous exposure of themselves and often they would share events or trauma in their lives they had never shared before. One class of twelve had four women who had been sexually molested as a child and each of them shared that information for the first time as part of their lifeline. Having the all-day session near the beginning of the ten weeks would increase group trust and closeness and make the remaining weekly sessions more comfortable and trusting for participants. You may choose to do this, but I prefer waiting with the all-day session. The all-day session becomes more like group therapy with a lot of strong emotional sharing energy without a special topic to be covered or didactic concepts to be learned.

Journaling

Keeping a journal while participating in this seminar greatly enriches the experience. Writing helps a person to focus their confusing thought processes. It helps a person to identify feelings and thoughts they might otherwise not identify. It promotes going inside oneself rather than hiding behind helping others. It gives one perspective by going back and reading what one has written and then realizing the growth that has taken place. I would like to enclose the journals people have written into a book. It would be very interesting to read. Much of what I learned from people has been from reading their journals.

People will need encouragement in order to do the work of journaling. The best incentive is to have them hand them in and have someone read and make comments sharing reactions to their journal. Time is a factor because with a class of twenty writing journals it will take you hours per week to read.

You may try variations of reading the journals the first week or two until the people have gotten into the habit of writing, or reading every other week or every third week. My preference is to pass out notebooks the first night of class and have them write the first five weeks and then hand them in to be read. Any homework handed in needs to have a response from the facilitator.

You may need to give some instructions, such as start as many sentences with "I" or with "I feel" as possible. This is contrary to many writing styles but it tends to help people write feelings rather than intellectual comments about others. You might suggest they write each evening after class because many will have such an emotional high class night they will have difficulty sleeping.

Writing is a good way to wind down and prepare for sleep.

An alternative for some who have difficulty writing is to use a tape recorder. Most people are uncomfortable talking into a tape recorder but some find it easier to do. The end result appears to be the same whichever method is used.

Indications of the Value of the Seminar

There are many ways to evaluate the effectiveness of this Seminar. Here are some:

1) On the class evaluation sheet completed the last night of the class, the total class experience is usually 4.5 or more on a one to five basis.

2) The gain scores on the FDAS indicate positive adjustment during the class.

3) The seminar has spread world wide with basically no advertising.

4) I already mentioned there are seldom any absences or dropouts during the ten weeks.

5) The suicide rate for people ending a relationship is very high. I usually asked the participants how many had seriously thought about suicide while ending the relationship. Typically, 75% of the class would raise their hands. We had several thousand participants here at the Learning Center before we had a suicide of a class participant.

6) I followed up about seventy participants after the Seminar who had entered into a love relationship. Some of these went back to their former spouse. Over fifty of them had relationships that were working, which is about 80% success for these follow-up relationships. We joke and say on opening night the Seminar is better than a Caribbean Cruise in finding new love relationship — and is much cheaper.

7) Professionals are referring more and more people to our classes because they are seeing the difference the class has made with the people they are working with. The Fisher Seminars have a wonderful reputation all over the planet.

Welcome Volunteer Helpers

You are embarking on one of the most interesting and challenging experiences of your life. Welcome to the team! Your participation in the ten-week Rebuilding seminar has been an important experience, but now you will be involved in a different kind of growth experience. Observing the participants' growth from the perspective of a volunteer helper will be interesting and rewarding.

Hopefully you have learned from the ten-week seminar how to build authentic relationships instead of over/under responsible ones. Now you have a challenge and a test to see if you can be put into a potentially over-responsible position and still remain responsible to yourself. Will you be giving the hungry and hurting people a fish each week or will you be teaching them to fish?

Many of you are extremely motivated to help others as you have been helped but you may be feeling overwhelmed, fearful of hurting others or feeling inadequate as a volunteer. My suggestions are:

• Don't try to walk on water! Be real. Don't be afraid to show your pain. Give examples of how to deal with this pain rather than projecting an image of having worked through everything. The best set of volunteers I ever had in a class had five of the six volunteers ending another love relationship during the ten weeks. They were able to demonstrate to the participants how to make a crisis into a creative experience.

• Remember that active listening to participants is usually helpful and never harmful. On the other hand, preaching and advice-giving is usually detrimental. The old Indian proverb of trying to understand another by walking a mile in their moccasins before judging them is relevant here. Relax and practice your listening skills and know you can be helpful to others working through the process. After you have learned and practiced these listening skills, use them in all aspects of your life — with friends, children, loved ones, and fellow-workers.

The Rebuilding Seminar is being offered all over North America and in many foreign countries; we estimate nearly a million participants. One of the unique and important features of this model is the volunteer helper support system. Your volunteering makes this model effective in meeting the needs of participants. Thank you for agreeing to share yourself for the next ten weeks. You will be making a difference in this seminar, in your community, and in the world.

Lovingly,

Bruce and Jere

Volunteer Helper Agreement
Fisher Ten-Week Educational Seminars

My Duties and Roles as a Volunteer Helper

I understand the duties and role of a volunteer helper in this psycho-educational model are as follows:

1) To be supportive and be a good active listener to the seminar participants. I will *not* play the role of a therapist by offering advice, analyzing or diagnosing the participants' behavior, or attempting to change their behavior in certain prescribed ways.

2) To lead small group discussions with the participants during the weekly seminars.

3) To assist the facilitator by keeping attendance, helping with registration, seeing that absent seminar participants receive the handout sheets, organizing activities, and any other such duties as requested by the facilitator.

4) To attend at least nine of the ten sessions of the seminar. I will communicate with the facilitator before class time if I will be absent for that session.

5) To contribute to the large group discussion of the homework and topic for each session.

6) To contact the participants outside of the seminar in order to assist them in doing the homework and learning the material taught in the educational model.

Being a volunteer helper places me in a position of trust. When I am listening to the participant I may hear information of a confidential nature. People who are working through a period of adjustment to a crisis often feel vulnerable, may be looking for answers to relieve their emotional pain, may experience feelings of love for a friendly volunteer helper, and may become angry or emotionally upset at those attempting to help them.

7) I will not tell others about the personal information that is shared with me by the participants, other volunteer helpers, or facilitator's. I will ask permission from the participant to share important confidential information with the facilitator if I believe the facilitator needs to know. On the other hand, I understand that if a participant is feeling suicidal or threatening to do harm to another I am obligated to share this information with the facilitator or other appropriate helping person(s).

8) I agree to *not* become romantically or sexually involved with any participant during the ten-week class. I further agree to *not* become romantically or sexually involved after the completion of the class with any former participant who is not legally divorced.

9) I will conduct myself in an appropriate manner at all times when acting as a volunteer helper. I agree to *not* become involved in any illegal behavior with the seminar participants while I am a volunteer helper. I understand the facilitator is *not* responsible for any misconduct on my part while I am a volunteer helper.

Termination of My Role as a Volunteer Helper

I agree to terminate, or be terminated, as a volunteer helper under the following conditions:

1) I violate any of the above duties of a volunteer helper.

2) I experience emotional burnout resulting in my becoming insensitive to the needs of the participants and not interested in being supportive anymore.

3) I become engrossed with my own personal process such as feeling depressed, suicidal, homicidal, or overwhelmed emotionally in such a way that I am not able to be helpful to others.

I understand that I will not receive any financial remuneration for being a volunteer helper. I have read this agreement and understand it completely. I agree to comply with the terms of this agreement and be a volunteer helper during the ten-week seminar dates listed below.

_____   _____
Name of Seminar   Dates of Seminar

_____   _____
Volunteer Helper's Signature   Facilitator's Signature

Volunteer Helper Duties

Congratulations. You have been chosen to be a volunteer helper because you are a **special** person. I challenge you to make this a growing and healing experience for yourself and the participants you are helping. The following is a list of some of your duties:

Before Opening Night
- Convince your hurting friends who are having relationship difficulties to come hear the Building Block presentation on opening night. It will be helpful to them whether they participate in the class or not.
- Call as many participants that are advance registered for the class as you can. Ask your facilitator for names and phone numbers if you don't have them yet. Those participants receiving calls before opening night really appreciate it.
- Review the Volunteer Helpers Manual. Take the "Fisher Volunteer Assessment Scale" if you haven't already. Read the opening chapters in the textbook. Think about your experience as a participant in the class. How did participating in the class help you in your adjustment process?

Opening Night
This is the most important night for you as a volunteer helper. Do you remember how you felt opening night? Plan to arrive at least fifteen minutes early. Ask your facilitator what you can do to help. Be prepared to talk about one of the Rebuilding Blocks if your facilitator requests it. Here are some rules for opening night.
- Spend as much time as possible talking to people you don't know. Make them feel welcome. Be careful about hugging and spending too much time with your former classmates.
- Anytime during the ten classes, but especially on opening night, make sure if anyone walks out of class that at least one volunteer helper walks out with them. They may want to be alone, but be with them and actively listen to them if possible. Sometimes after talking they may feel strong enough to return to the class.
- Act like the winner that you are! Recently separated people believe that only losers end love relationships. You can help them realize that maybe they are a winner also.
- During break make yourself available to connect with the new participants. See if they have any questions or concerns. Encourage them to register for the class but make sure you give them emotional space to make the decision themselves. They will know when they are ready to participate and trying to pressure them to participate before they are ready will not be beneficial.
- Plan to be available to participants after class. A large percentage of participants will not have found a person they can talk to since the separation. Hearing the Rebuilding Blocks presentation may stimulate a multitude of feelings. I have known participants who talked for several hours after class.
- Determine which participants you are going to call. Work with your facilitator to make sure each participant gets at least two phone calls from volunteers the first week.
- Many times you can start your phone calls to participants immediately after opening night. Most of them will be processing the opening night and not go to sleep for hours after class is over.

Weekly Duties
- Call the facilitator if you are going to be late or absent from class.
- Read the assignments each week and do the homework. You might be surprised at how different the experience is as a volunteer from what it was during this class.
- Review your small group questions and be prepared to lead the small group discussion.
- Keep aware of the volunteer duties for yourself and others. Encourage the participants to avoid becoming involved romantically and sexually during the class.
- Keep the phone lines busy with your calls. Alert the facilitator if you are unable to make calls to the participants. Report important feedback that you receive from the participants to your facilitator.
- Keep nurturing yourself. Ask for help and support from other volunteers and the facilitator if you need it. Remember you may be going into a deeper layer in your process than you were able to do when you took the class. It's okay to still be in emotional pain sometimes.

Thank you for your efforts in becoming an effective volunteer helper.

Volunteer Special Assignment Sheet

Opening Night Date and Time _____

Name of Seminar _____

Opening Night and Second Night: (Please print your name next to the your assignment)

_____ Will bring refreshments to opening night.

_____ Make coffee — before and during the meeting. Clean up the coffee pot and refreshment area before we leave.

_____ Help set up chairs and couches before the meeting and put them back the way they were after the meeting.

_____ Put up signs leading from the front door to the room we're meeting in, and take them down afterwards. Also, use the sign-in sheet and transfer all the names and information on it to a current class list by highlighting correct information and adding new names to the class list. Give the class list to the facilitator at the beginning of the break for use during registration.

_____ Greet people at the front door of the building and direct them to the signs leading to the room we're meeting in.

_____ Greet people at the entrance to the room we're meeting in, have them put on name tags using a dark felt pen, and have them sign in on the "Sign-In Sheet." Be sure they have the "Rebuilding Blocks" handout sheet so they can make notes during the presentation.

_____ A male who, when asked to by the facilitator about the benefit you received from the seminar you attended, will share with large group during the presentation.

_____ A female who, when asked to by a facilitator about the benefit you received from the seminar you attended, will share with large group during the presentation.

_____ During registration be in charge of the Class Attendance sheet. Make sure each registered person signs their name and marks the week they would like to have the seminar in their home, and the week they would like to bring refreshments. Make sure someone signs up for week number two for both home and refreshments. Explain what we'll need: the largest room for the big group and as many smaller rooms as possible for small groups. Help arrange for additional chairs when needed. Try and obtain a map to the participant's home at least two weeks in advance so copies can be made and passed out a week ahead of time.

_____ An alternate volunteer who can help other volunteers with the assignments. You'll be the one they call if they are going to miss a class so you can carry out their assignment. Check with the facilitator(s) to see if there's anything special needed that night.

_____ Arrange get-togethers after class and between classes. Start having class parties after the 4th night of class. Be sure to ask only class members to the parties at first. You need to make it as safe as possible for participants.

_____ _All volunteer helpers_ _____ As soon as everything is cleaned up and ready to go after the first session, the volunteers will meet with the facilitator(s) to divide up the class list so that every participant gets a volunteer assigned to call them. This will happen at the meeting location if it can be done before 10:30 PM, otherwise we'll need to meet at a nearby location. See that everyone gets at least one call (two is better) each week for at least the first four weeks.

We are really counting on you to be responsible and carry out your assignments!!

Specific Suggestions for Volunteer Helpers

Be friendly, even if the person you talk to seems guarded or short with you. They're probably afraid or mistrusting — its not about you! Be positive and encouraging. Tell them a little about yourself, but be careful not to do all the talking (see self-disclosure section). If you're comfortable, they'll be more likely to be comfortable too. If you're nervous, they may become a little nervous also. If someone seems anxious, you might say, "Just tell me if you need to go, we can always talk again another time."

Get them talking by asking "open-ended questions," then all you'll need to do is be a good active-listener.

Open-ended Questions. (These are questions that can't be answered "yes" or "no")
How did you hear about the seminar? (If someone referred them, ask, "What did they say about it?")
What do you know about it?
I'd be happy to answer any questions you may have about the seminar.
What's your relationship situation?
What are you hoping to get out of this seminar?
What have you been doing to take care of yourself during this time?

Don't Give Advice!!!
If you need to, you can say: "This is what I (or someone I know) did, and this is how it turned out." Instead of telling them what to do, you can say, "I have felt pretty confused sometimes too, but the answers seem to come to me the more I learn and trust myself to make good decisions." Encourage them to make their own decisions, that will ultimately empower them the most! If you're not sure how to answer a question, say "I don't know, maybe you could ask the facilitator about that." Let them know it's okay if feelings come up for them while they're on the phone, or at any time. Let them feel you don't need to fix it by trying to feel for them, or to diminish their feelings and pain.

Be sure to repeat your name, give them your telephone number, and the best time to reach you at the end of the conversation. Let them know its okay to call you if they have questions or feel like talking. We recommend you call them before opening night. You might say, "Of course I'll be there opening night. I'll be wearing a name tag, so please be sure to come up and say 'hi' to me. Will I see you there?"

Telephone Calls
If you're not in a centered place, don't take or make calls. Take care of yourself. If you get someone very talkative and you need to go, just say, "I've really enjoyed talking with you. I've got some things I need to take care of; hopefully we can connect again soon."

Hello, This is _____ with the Fisher Rebuilding Seminars. The facilitator asked me to give you a call about the upcoming Rebuilding Seminar. Is this a good time to talk?" If yes, "Great!" (If no, "When would be a good time for you?")

"Did you receive the letter we sent you, with directions to the first night? Do you think you'll be able to make it?" (If no, see the "Resistance" section.)

"Were the directions clear about how to get there? I'd like to verify the spelling of your name, your address, and telephone numbers for our class list, would that be all right? This is the information I have (read slowly). Is this all correct? Would you like me to change or add anything?"

Small Groups

- Sit next to the most talkative person.
- Try not to interrupt or cut people off — however sometimes you may need to. Say something like, "I really appreciate your openness, maybe we could talk some more about that at break or during the week. I need to give everyone a chance to share. Who'd like to be next?" (or pick someone). Be sure to follow up one to one!

Come-ons

If someone approaches you to be more than a supportive friend, even if it's asking you to go out after the seminar is over, say something like, "I am really flattered that you like me. I have agreed not to get romantically involved with any of the participants during the 10 weeks. It's nice that you're feeling comfortable enough with me to ask. I want you to stay focused on yourself as much as possible during this time, that's what seems to help people the most. Romantic relationships sometimes have a way of getting in the way of that. You start thinking about the other person all the time instead of working on yourself. Working on yourself is what this seminar is all about."

Resistance Because of Time

"It seemed like a lot of time to me at the beginning, too, but I found that the nights actually went by really fast. I think it was some of the best time I ever spent on myself. I learned a lot and it helped me work through some pretty difficult feelings (or changes). Why don't you just come to the opening night presentation and check it out? It's free and open to the public!"

Resistance Because of Money

"Don't worry about the money. The facilitator's know people are often going through money problems at a time like this. He or she will let you work out a payment plan or special arrangements if you need to. Be sure to come opening night, which is free and open to the public. You can talk with the facilitator about your financial concerns at that time."

Fear of Groups and Confidentiality (though they might not bring it up)

"You know everything that's said in these groups is totally confidential, and that includes our telephone conversation, too."

After you have handled basic resistance and they still don't want to come, ask if they'd like to be contacted about future seminars. If they're not interested, be cordial and support them to come sometime in the future. Let the facilitator know they are not interested in coming to the Seminar at this time.

Self-disclosure

"My relationship(or marriage) ended about _____ months/years ago. It was pretty tough, it still hurts sometimes, but things are getting better. Its really working out for the best. I don't mean to say it's been easy, but the group has helped a lot.
"The Rebuilding seminar really helped me:

- I learned a lot about the kinds of things that almost everyone goes through when an important relationship is in trouble or ends.
- I learned a lot about myself too.
- I understand more about my part in the problems in my relationship.
- I found a lot of understanding for the feelings I was having.
- Many people in the seminar were going through the same kinds of things as me.
- I made some good friends I could really talk to, about anything, without worrying about what they'd think of me."

General Guidelines About Volunteering

Make the calls assigned to you. It's easier to make them soon after the meeting night. Make a note on your class list of the people who are in your small group so if they are assigned to you to call, you will remember them. After the third night of class, call the people who were in your small groups, so keep track of participants in your small group on that night. No other calls will be assigned. Encourage participants to call each other. It will help them tremendously, and it will make your life easier too. Carry out your special assignments responsibly. If you are going to miss a class or commitment, contact the "alternate" or another volunteer to handle your responsibility. Be on time if at all possible, especially early on in the seminar, in order to set a good example. Help the facilitator(s) get people back from break as fast as possible when "big group time" is called. Set up carpools with people in your area. Start on opening night when we come back from break by saying, "Everyone from _____ who'd like to carpool, let's meet over there right after class." Have a place in mind to meet, (like a park-n-ride), and be familiar with the directions to get there.

If a participant is really having a hard time, or you are having a problem dealing with them, talk to a facilitator about it right away. Be sensitive to the participants and to each other. If someone is feeling a lot of feelings and needs some extra nurturing, give it to them! If someone doesn't wish to talk in a small group, at break or over the phone, let them gracefully "pass." Be supportive of each other! Talk to another volunteer if you need some support. The more you feel supported, the more you'll be able to support others. Please don't tell participants your problems to the point where they start feeling the urge to take care of you. They need to be focusing on themselves. Sometimes volunteers arrange their schedules so they can get together before or after group to talk about how they're doing, who needs extra support, or check out ideas for outside group gettogethers. It can be very helpful; we strongly recommend it if at all possible.

Make the most of this volunteer opportunity. Just be yourself, because you're the best! That's why you were chosen.

Thank you very much for your help!!

Fisher Seminars Volunteer Assessment Scale

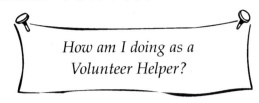

How am I doing as a
Volunteer Helper?

This is a self-assessment instrument designed to help evaluate your own readiness to be a volunteer helper. The assessment is divided into various sections to identify the various helping skills better. Please be honest and objective in order to learn as much about yourself as possible. We do not expect you to be perfect. Use your responses as a guideline in your continuing growth process.

Active Listening   Almost Never to Almost Always

 1. I am a good listener.   1 2 3 4 5
 2. I concentrate well when I am listening.   1 2 3 4 5
 3. I can easily paraphrase in my own words what I heard the helpee say.   1 2 3 4 5
 4. I normally maintain eye contact when listening.   1 2 3 4 5
 5. My body language indicates to the helpee that I am listening.   1 2 3 4 5
 6. My responses indicate that I have been listening.   1 2 3 4 5
 7. My responses might be called assertive rather than passive or aggressive.   1 2 3 4 5
 8. I respond with "I" messages rather than "you" messages.   1 2 3 4 5
 9. I listen rather than give advice.   1 2 3 4 5
10. I believe helpees are capable of solving their problems by talking them out.   1 2 3 4 5
11. I interrupt the helpee only when it is appropriate.   1 2 3 4 5
12. I respond with open-ended questions.   1 2 3 4 5
13. I use helpful active-listening responses.   1 2 3 4 5
14. I do not detract from the helpee's concerns and feelings.   1 2 3 4 5
15. I help the person focus on the main problem and feelings.   1 2 3 4 5
16. I help the person find choices and alternatives without telling them what to do. 1 2 3 4 5
17. I help the person become aware of their own feelings.   1 2 3 4 5
18. I am aware of my judgmental attitudes as they relate to the helpee concerns.   1 2 3 4 5
19. My feedback is descriptive rather than evaluative.   1 2 3 4 5
20. My feedback is specific rather than generalizing.   1 2 3 4 5
21. My feedback meets both my needs and the helpee's needs.   1 2 3 4 5
22. My feedback is directed toward behavior the helpee can change.   1 2 3 4 5
23. My feedback is requested rather than imposed.   1 2 3 4 5
24. My feedback is given as soon as possible after the helpee comments.   1 2 3 4 5
25. I check out my interpretations with the helpee to make sure I am not assuming. 1 2 3 4 5
26. I am comfortable with appropriate silences.   1 2 3 4 5
27. I use physical touching and hugs in an appropriate and helpful manner.   1 2 3 4 5

Barriers to Communication   Almost Never to Almost Always

28. I avoid using generalizing terms like "always" and "never."   1 2 3 4 5
29. I communicate by using first person pronouns.   1 2 3 4 5
30. I avoid leading questions in order to get the answer I want the helpee to say.   1 2 3 4 5
31. I avoid intellectualizing, non-feeling responses.   1 2 3 4 5
32. The helpee talks more than I do.   1 2 3 4 5

Authentic Rather than Adaptive/Survivor Active-Listening

33. I build authentic relationships with helpees.   1 2 3 4 5
34. I can choose to use an adaptive part if it is helpful to the helpee.   1 2 3 4 5
35. I avoid over-responsible adaptive rescuing of the helpee.   1 2 3 4 5
36. I understand adaptive behavior can appear to be authentic when it's not.   1 2 3 4 5
37. I am aware which adaptive/survivor part I normally operate from.   1 2 3 4 5
38. I practice self-monitoring of my adaptive/survivor parts when active listening.   1 2 3 4 5
39. I can stay in control of my outer critic when active listening.   1 2 3 4 5
40. I am generally aware which adaptive/survivor part the helpee is using.   1 2 3 4 5
41. I am dedicated to continue nurturing myself when working as a volunteer.   1 2 3 4 5

Appropriate Self-Disclosure

42. I can openly share my feelings and experiences with the helpee.   1 2 3 4 5
43. I share my own feelings and experiences in a helpful manner.   1 2 3 4 5
44. I self-disclose only when it is helpful to the helpee.   1 2 3 4 5
45. My self-disclosure aids the helpee in sharing personal feelings and experiences   1 2 3 4 5

Sensitivity

46. I genuinely care for the helpee.   1 2 3 4 5
47. I can identify and understand the problems and concerns of the helpee.   1 2 3 4 5
48. I can nurture and listen objectively.   1 2 3 4 5
49. My voice tone and language are copsistent with those of the helpee.   1 2 3 4 5
50. I am sensitive to what the helpee is "not saying.'   1 2 3 4 5

Creativity

51. I am creative in responding to the helpee.   1 2 3 4 5
52. I am creative in finding new ways to active listen that are helpful to the helpee.   1 2 3 4 5
53. I am creative in offering new ideas and attitudes to the helpee.   1 2 3 4 5
54. I am creative in finding new ways of being helpful.   1 2 3 4 5

Emotional Burnout   **Almost Never to Almost Always**

55. I have trouble concentrating when I am listening to the helpee.   1 2 3 4 5

56. I would rather be doing something other than listening.   1 2 3 4 5

57. I am tired of being around hurting people.   1 2 3 4 5

58. I want to do things for me instead of always helping others.   1 2 3 4 5

59. Helping others is hard work and not enjoyable.   1 2 3 4 5

60. I am listening to avoid feeling rejected or guilty.   1 2 3 4 5

Mechanics

61. I usually arrive at class a few minutes early.   1 2 3 4 5

62. I remain aware of the time when I lead small groups so I can return on time. 1 2 3 4 5

63. I contact my facilitator if I am unable to complete my assigned phone calls. 1 2 3 4 5

64. I am usually available when participants wish to contact me.   1 2 3 4 5

65. I only make commitments when I know I can follow through with them.   1 2 3 4 5

66. I contact my facilitator any time I have doubts or concerns.   1 2 3 4 5

67. I give my facilitator feedback on how I am feeling about my role as volunteer. 1 2 3 4 5

General Rating

68. If I were a helpee, I would want to talk to someone like me.   1 2 3 4 5

69. The participants in my class would rate me as a warm and caring volunteer. 1 2 3 4 5

70. I would rate myself as an effective volunteer helper.   1 2 3 4 5

I'm doing great!!

How To Set-Up and Implement a Volunteer Helper Program

An important aspect of this educational model is the Volunteer Helper Program. Volunteers are former class participants who agree to return and become part of the group process. They attend the weekly sessions as participants and as small group leaders. One of the main roles of the volunteers is to help the participants complete the homework. They spend time outside of class making phone calls and being an active listener to the participants. We have found one volunteer for each five class participants is a good ratio.

Realistically speaking, many volunteer programs are not successful. There are many ingredients that go into making the program successful. We have attempted to identify those ingredients and share them with you. Following is a list of important criteria needed to make the volunteer program successful:

Goals and Objectives
The primary goal of the Volunteer Helper Support System is to assist people who are working through the process of ending a love-relationship. Not only will the volunteers help intensify the growth experience of the participants in the divorce adjustment seminars, but the volunteers will also become a network of "people helping people" in the community. Because doing the homework is an important part of the educational model, one of the volunteer duties is to help the participants complete the homework.

Selection Process
The volunteers actually become representatives of the Seminars to the outside world. It is important that you select people who will be a good representative of your seminars. The volunteers are role-models for the class. It makes a tremendous impression upon a prospective class member to see a group of "winners" who are going through the divorce process, because many felt that only "losers" became divorced. We need to have good quality people acting as volunteers if we are to have a successful seminar. We have devised a very effective selection process to choose volunteers. The five steps are listed below.

1) The participants vote during the last meeting of the ten-week session on which present class members would make good volunteers for future classes. They can vote for as many as they choose ranging from none to the whole class. We have had classes where there was not a single person qualified to be a volunteer, and we have had classes where a majority would be good volunteers. We don't tell the class members that we will be voting the last night in order to minimize campaigning by class members. The voting is done as part of the class evaluation and is anonymous, written, and secret. Because the class members have watched the volunteers in action, they have a good idea of what volunteers are supposed to do. This helps them do a better job of voting. Very seldom has the voting been just a popularity contest. I have grown to respect participants' votes a great deal.

2) The present volunteers also fill out the evaluations and vote for future volunteers. Usually there is agreement between the voting of the class members and the volunteers, but sometimes there is not. For example, one class had a quiet member who seldom asked for help from the volunteers but who was good at reaching out to help others. The class voted her to be a volunteer but the volunteers didn't.

This voting procedure has lots of advantages but one advantage is the way it spreads the responsibility for choosing volunteers. Frequently a class member will talk to the facilitator about the fifth week of class and ask to be a volunteer. Often the person eager to be a volunteer is not the person you want. So when a person asks to be a volunteer, I can thank them for their interest and let them know there is a selection process. It provides an easy way to say no without making the person feel rejected.

3) The voting is tabulated and I discuss individually with one or more of the current volunteers, or with the co-facilitator, the results of the voting. It provides a chance to consider different qualifications of the prospective volunteers. This is a confidential talk because we do not disclose the results of the voting to class members.

4) After the facilitator has talked with one or more volunteers, or with the co-facilitator, a decision is made by the facilitator to ask certain class members to be volunteers. The law of supply and demand is in operation here because you usually choose as many volunteers as you need. Frequently there can be a standby list with people you might be able to use in the future. Normally we have plenty of female volunteers but are sometimes short of good male volunteers. Often we try and have extra male volunteers so the class ratio of males and females will be more even. (Nationwide class average for participants is 1/3 males and 2/3 females.)

5) The facilitator asks the class member if they would like to become a volunteer helper. This is one of the most pleasant jobs a facilitator has because it is a real compliment to be asked to be a volunteer. The typical reaction is one of self-doubt — "I don't know if I could be a good volunteer or not." This is a good time to mention the volunteer training workshop which is an all-day session to train class members to be better volunteer helpers. We will discuss the training workshop later.

Sometimes the timing is not right for a person to be a volunteer helper immediately after the seminar. They may have done so much growing they will need some time to assimilate and internalize what they have learned. They may still need more time to recover from being in the divorce pits. They may choose to spend time with their children now that they have grown by taking the seminar to a place they can be better parents. They may have other time commitments keeping them from volunteering. It is important to not miss any of the ten sessions as a volunteer.

Normally , the energy of the person is high and they want and choose to volunteer immediately after completing the ten-week seminar. When asked why they choose to spend so much time and energy helping others, they will usually state two reasons. 1) "I benefited so much from the class and I want to pass that help on to another," or 2) "I learned so much but I still need more growth, and being a volunteer is like taking the class again for free."

If you read the textbook for the seminar, or have taught the divorce class before, you know a big part of the class is helping people to be responsible to self rather than being over-responsible. Just when they are learning to do that, we ask them to be in an over-responsible role again. What a wonderful opportunity to practice self-care while helping others!

Selecting Volunteers the First Time You Teach the Seminar
New facilitator's always ask the obvious question, "How do you select volunteer helpers when you have not taught the class before and there are no graduates to select?" It is a good question and here are some possible answers. 1) Do you have a college or university nearby? There often are students in the helping professions looking for experience in the field who would be willing to volunteer their time for the experience. 2) If the facilitator is a therapist there may be clients or former clients who have been through the divorce process and are at a place emotionally where they could be volunteer helpers. 3) Do you have friends who have worked through the divorce process and would be able to be volunteer helpers? 4) Do you have other colleagues in the helping professions who would like to understand the divorce process better and would be willing to be a volunteer helper? Be sure and think of professionals of all kinds such as ministers, doctors, nurses, social workers, lawyers, and not just therapists. 5) Do you have another person of the opposite sex who could be a co-facilitator with you? Having a co-facilitator diminishes the need for volunteer helpers.

Roles and Functions of the Volunteers
Volunteer helpers will serve three main functions during seminars: 1) Be a member of the group process attending the weekly seminars, and 2) Be a small group leader during the weekly meetings of seminars, and 3) Be a one-to-one listening person outside of the regular class meetings.

The most important part of being a volunteer takes place the first night of class. We ask volunteers to be there early and make sure each new prospective member feels welcome. It is against the rules to talk to old friends. The volunteer needs to spend as much time as possible getting to know the new class members.

We ask a volunteer to share with the group how they felt the first night of class. It comforts new participants to learn that others are feeling anxious. It is important when a volunteer states how ten weeks ago they were in the pits, and now the class has helped them get in control of their life again. Think what a powerful testimony that is for the new class member in the divorce pits. We may also ask the volunteer to share their experience with a particular building block during the Building Block Presentation.

Before opening night volunteers perform two functions. They are contact people who let their friends and acquaintances know about the class, and they call new class members who have advance registered to get acquainted before opening night. They may make sure the new class member has a ride to class, or may need to be picked up because of fear about attending opening night. Hopefully the class members will learn to build their own support system and by the time the ten weeks are over, participants will not need either the volunteers or facilitator's.

Supervision and Support of Volunteers

When I used to supervise volunteers who worked with me as a Juvenile Probation Officer, they needed a lot of support to keep from burning out. There was a lot more energy invested in the teenagers, and less energy being returned. With the divorce class, there is so much energy from each class meeting, and it is rewarding to watch how rapidly people adjust. There is less of a need for support for the divorce class volunteers. As a facilitator, you will always need to be there for support when needed. We train the volunteers to reach out for support and place the responsibility on them to see they get the support they need. We encourage them to reach out to each other, especially new volunteers reach out to the older ones for support. It is helpful to have a weekly meeting of volunteers outside of class, especially during the first three or four weeks of class. It is a time to talk over with the volunteers what is happening in the class and with the individual class members.

It is helpful to the facilitator to learn where each class member is before the actual class meeting. For example, one volunteer alerted me that a quiet class member had made a decision to talk and share in the class that evening This helped me to look for that person's hand and be sure they had the opportunity to carry out their commitment to talk.

I have always had an open door policy with volunteers whereby they could come for a free counseling session in return for volunteering. Many times a volunteer will dig up old garbage and need to work through an issue, and it is really a by-product of being a helping person. I have had a policy of not allowing a volunteer to be a regular client because of the conflict in roles. I once had a volunteer who had begun to think about suicide a great deal, and felt she was not helpful to the class members. If she had been a client, it would have been difficult asking one of my clients to stop volunteering because of their emotional condition.

Does a Volunteer Helper Program Save Time and Energy for the Facilitator?

If you are thinking of implementing a volunteer program in order to save time and energy, then forget it. Having a volunteer for the participant to call does minimize the phone calls you receive from class members. The time and energy you put into selecting, training supervising, terminating volunteers is far greater, than any saving in time you might experience.

The advantage is when you put one hour of time into the volunteer program, they may put ten to twenty times that much time into the class members. It is like an investment of time and energy. We ask for and expect five to ten hours per week outside of class from each volunteer.

Volunteers can do certain helping things while you as the facilitator can do certain other helping things. Together it is synergistic in that your total output is more than the individual time added together. Many professionals find themselves threatened when they find out how effective volunteer helpers can be. Volunteers can be role models for learning to be a single person. They can share their own personal growth in surviving the breakup of their relationship. As one class member stated when she looked at the facilitator, "You look like you have climbed to the top of the mountain and I will never be able to climb that high. But the volunteer in class is only a little way ahead of me on the mountain and I know I can climb that far."

Before I used volunteers in the seminars people would want to have more than ten sessions. They would not feel finished at the end of the ten weeks. After I started using volunteers, people felt finished and did not ask for extra sessions. I believe the class experience is so enriched by having volunteers present that people experience more growth than is possible by not having volunteers. The benefit from having volunteers is not to save you time as a facilitator, but to have a more in-depth experience for the participants.

Ethics for Volunteers

Because the volunteers are lay people and not professionals, a different set of ethics is in order. Instead of the confidential protection with professionals, we ask the volunteer to not tell or share anything confidential that they see or hear. We suggest they get permission from the participant if they want to share confidential things with the facilitator. On the other hand, we emphasize that if the participant is in personal danger from violence or suicidal feelings, the volunteer is obligated to share that information with the facilitator or with an appropriate person such as a crisis line.

We ask the volunteers to learn about burnout and not over-extend themselves. We ask them to learn to deal with dependency and manipulation from participants. We ask them to learn to deal with the vulnerability of participants in the area of dating, romance, sexual involvement by refraining from becoming emotionally involved with participants. In the volunteer all-day training workshop, we talk about and discuss the possibility of participants hitting on them, or wanting to become personally involved with them. It complicates the helping process to have the participant fall in love with the volunteer. It is not a compliment or an ego boost to have a participant want a personal relationship with the volunteer. It is an example of their neediness and desire to want to be with another who is warm, who listens, and who isn't like their ex.

Litigation

Volunteers are an extension of you the facilitator. Even though they are not professional and are not paid, they still have a certain amount of power in their volunteer role. They can cause damage by becoming personally involved with a participant. They can gossip or share things they shouldn't share. They can become overwhelmed emotionally with their own process, and can also suffer emotional burnout. They can become involved with their own divorce in the court system and lose their effectiveness as a volunteer.

Some insurance companies will charge extra liability premiums for insurance if you are using volunteers. You can possibly be liable for some of their behavior. I strongly encourage you to use the Volunteer Helper Agreement Form. Having them sign the form may give you some legal protection if they should violate the Agreement. The form has a positive value in that it clearly states what the role of the volunteer helper is so not only volunteers but participants who are using the *Rebuilding Workbook* can also become aware of the volunteer roles and expectations. The Agreement Form specifies the reasons for termination which makes terminating the volunteer helper easier if s/he does violate the Agreement.

Termination of Volunteers

Volunteer programs consistently have a high turnover of personnel. We normally have had volunteers help with up to five seminars, but we have had one volunteer help for sixteen class seminars. Many will volunteer for only one or two sessions. When you think of the time and energy and possibly money for baby-sitting, gas for cars, it makes you really appreciate having people willing to volunteer. But we need to be clear about termination. Normally it is an easy decision

because termination naturally occurs when the ten-week class ends. Volunteers don't expect to continue to volunteer unless asked for the next class. Sometimes a situation arises such as already mentioned whereby a volunteer either breaks the ethics, or gets into a needy position where they will need to be terminated even though the class is not ended. If it is made clear as part of the training that a volunteer can be fired just as an employee can be, then the termination can be easier. Hopefully the professional and volunteer can communicate with each other when the need to terminate happens.

Training of Volunteer Helpers

We carried out our training program by having a all-day Volunteer Training Workshop from 9:00 AM to 4:00 PM. Our policy is to the volunteer helper to attend the training workshop before volunteering. We do the training after they complete the ten-week seminar, and before the next seminar begins. It is helpful to build up a large number of volunteers who have been trained so when the next seminar starts, you can find enough volunteers for the seminar.

The goal of the workshop is to train people to become better active listeners. We point out active listening has great potential to help people and the possibility of doing harm is almost nonexistent. This is in contrast to giving advice or preaching with the potential of great harm. Helping volunteers understand this concept is a great relief to them because they almost always have a concern about their ability to be a helper. They believe they must learn to walk on water so part of the training is to help them understand being human and being real is more important than being completely adjusted.

We do some training in suicide prevention as part of the all-day workshop. I asked many of my classes to raise their hand if they had seriously thought about suicide since they have been separated. About three fourths of the class would typically raise their hands. One of the successes of the Fisher Seminars has been that suicide has been almost nonexistent among the participants. The volunteer helpers have had a very positive impact and minimized the suicide thinking among the participants.

Volunteer Training Workshop Agenda

We have conducted an all-day workshop from 9:00 AM to 4:00 AM. The facilitator(s) of the Seminar do the training. It is a very powerful day because volunteer helpers are a great group of high energy people.

8:30-9:00 AM

Registration and get acquainted time. We like to use name tags. We make sure each volunteer has a copy of the *Rebuilding Workbook*. We have usually made the volunteer training free, but sometimes charge a small fee to cover expenses. Ask each person to complete the sign-in sheet from **Session 1. 9:00-9:30 AM**

Words of welcome to the volunteers from the facilitator's. A relaxation and centering breathing exercise. An outline of the day's activities.

9:30-10:30 AM

An introductory exercise using active listening skills. Choose someone as a partner that you don't know. Converse with each other for about 5 minutes sharing with the other person information about yourself. Form a large group again and take turns introducing the person you just met to the group.

10:30-10:50 AM Break With Refreshments

10:50-12:00 AM
- Relax and be yourself. No one has all the answers!
- Telephone calls. Call people before opening night if possible. Get names of those registered for the seminar, or those who expressed interest in registering but have some reservations.
- Telephone calls outside of class are important. See making calls suggestions in *Rebuilding Workbook*.
  - Show up early for classes if at all possible, especially on opening night. Call the facilitator if you are going to be absent so a substitute volunteer can be called.
- Explain Volunteer Agreement and Special Assignment Sheet. Make sure both are filled in by the volunteer helper. Explain the need for the Volunteer Agreement Form. The Seminars cannot continue if volunteer helpers don't follow the expectations explained in the Agreement Form.
- Opening night responsibilities. See list in *Rebuilding Workbook*.
- Encourage the volunteers to again read the assignments and do the homework. Be prepared to lead small group discussions on reading assignments and homework.
- Talk about after class and between class activities. It is helpful to meet after the class for coffee and connecting. It may be helpful after the first few weeks to have parties and activities outside of class.

12:00-1:00 PM Potluck Lunch. Homework during and after lunch is to let your "inner-child" out and do something fun!

1:00-2:00 PM
- Difficult situations and what to do. Suicide prevention. Make copies of the suicide pages found below. Dealing with participants wanting a personal relationship. Learning to use boundaries and limits. Don't allow yourself to become burned out and to give more than you have time and energy to do. A good question is to share what behavior did a volunteer helper do in your class that was especially meaningful and helpful to you.
- How to facilitate small groups. Give each person an opportunity to talk. Limit those who monopolize the small group. Set time limits at the beginning of the small group — "We have thirty minutes which means each of you will have about five minutes to share." Ask people to talk about themselves instead of talking about the ex. Finish each of your sharing times with the phrase, "But I'm working on it."

2:00-2:15 PM Break With Refreshments

2:15-3:30 PM
- Divide into groups with others you'll be volunteering with. Fill out Volunteer Agreement, Special Assignment Sheet, and Class List of those advance registered. Decide who will call participants.
- Simulated small group facilitation. For five minutes one person be small group leader with two people being over talkative, and two being very quiet. Take turns so each person has a chance to practice being small group leader. Each group share your experience in large group.

3:30-4:00 PM
- Turn in Volunteer Agreements, Special Assignment Sheet, Referral List of Therapists — Attorneys — and Clergy. Closing Statements by Facilitator's. Huggle-time. Make sure you have copies of the Volunteer Agreement Form, Special Assignment Sheet, the sign-up sheet with all the names, addresses, and phone numbers of the volunteers who attended the training workshop.

Helpful Information for Volunteer Helpers

The following pages are helpful information for volunteer helpers. We suggest you make copies of this information and have them available for the volunteer helpers as part of the Training Workshop.

What is Active Listening?
It is listening actively rather than passively. Active is participatory, meaning you give feedback and appropriate responses. Listening means you let them know you heard what they said. It may include paraphrasing what you heard them say, and repeating it back to them.

What does it do?
It demonstrates good communication skills. It provides a place for the person to express feelings and thoughts in a non-threatening situation. It validates the person's self-worth, and makes them feel important.

Theoretical and Philosophical Basis
The central tenet is a belief in the person being able to solve their own problems without an expert coming to "fix it" for them. It is based upon equality between people rather than on one person being the expert and authority. It establishes an "I-thou" relationship between the helper and helpee based upon interdependence. It emphasizes the value of talking out problems and decisions with another, and using the other person as a mirror to more clearly see oneself.

Ingredients of Active Listening
Empathic Understanding. Learn what is going on with them, what it is like for them.

Unconditional positive regard. Respect each as an important human being.

Genuineness or congruence on your part. Be real, be yourself, be honest and tactful. If you don't know, say so.

Specificity. Say what you mean with straight messages. Don't pussyfoot around.

Be non-judgmental. Let them explore their own feelings. Share your own feelings and experiences to help shed light on their situation.

Stay in their space. Concentrate on what they are saying, thinking, feeling.

Avoid Rescuing. Allow the other person to have pain, confusion, sadness, and anger as part of their learning. Trying to take their pain away is a mean and harmful act of rescuing.

Nurture and support the other person without bleeding with them.

Stay objective. Believe and learn that people can solve their problems if given a chance to talk in a non-threatening situation.

Ask open-ended questions. Avoid questions that can be answered with a yes or no. Avoid "why" questions. They put the person into intellectual answers rather than feeling answers. They also make the person feel defensive.

Use Minimal Encouragement Responses (You will be amazed at the effectiveness of these next five responses)
• Nodding of your head with eye contact.
• Uh,huh. . .
• Yes. . .
• Go on . . .
• And. . .

Criteria for being a good listener:
• To be able to actively listen to a person in a way that does not detract from the person's concerns and feelings.
• To be able to focus with the person on the main problem or concern.
• To be able to help the person generate and select alternatives in a way that keeps responsibility for decision-making with the person.
• To be aware of your own feelings, and be able to share them or set them aside appropriately.
• To be aware of your own judgmental feelings and attitudes. To be able to share them or set them aside while you are a listener.

Barriers to Good Communication
Barriers to communication are those habits of speech and ways of communicating which frequently appear in our everyday conversations. They are more common than we like to admit. Becoming aware of and eliminating such barriers improves our communication kills.

Generalizing. Taking one or two incidents and applying them to all situations. It is worse when the generalization is evaluative or judgmental. Examples: "You always say things like that. Everybody here is tired. You never listen to me when I'm talking."

Using second and third person pronouns results in either over-responsible speaking for others, or under-responsible speaking for no one. Examples of over-responsible speaking for others: "We are tired." "Everyone had a good time."

Examples of under-responsible speaking for no one: "When you get up in the morning, it's really hard to get moving." "It makes one feel good to exercise."

Examples of responsible speaking: "I am tired." "I feel good when I exercise."

Leading questions or statements disguised as questions. These are questions used to get the answer you wish. They make the respondent feel set up and trapped. Examples: "Don't you agree that my ex was unfair?" "Don't you think we should end our marriage?"

Intellectualizing. Using intellectual and rational approaches to avoid feelings. Example:

"I think you act just like your mother when you are angry."

Advice giving or preaching. People who give advice are often doing it to avoid dealing with their own pain or feelings. The critical personality is especially good at giving advice. Examples: "Just stop wallowing in pity and feeling sorry for yourself and you will be okay."

Interrupting a person leaves them feeling diminished, discounted, and not listened to.

Excessive speech. The person who talks excessively and never listens usually has underlying feelings of insecurity and anxiety. They are trying to cover up these feelings by talking. As a volunteer you may need to learn gentle and loving ways of confronting these people to prevent them from monopolizing small group discussions.

Assessment of Suicide Potential

An uncommon, but important, part of facilitating and/or volunteering is dealing with participants who are feeling suicidal. Several attempts at suicide have been prevented by volunteers. Probably the most helpful thing you can do is to actively listen to people who are having suicidal thoughts. That may be enough to prevent them from acting out their feelings. You may be feeling anxious reading and talking about the possibility that you may have to face this situation. Please share your fears with other volunteers or your facilitator. It is unlikely that you will encounter this problem, but we want you to feel prepared. *If you have not been able to get the person to talk out their suicide feelings, and if you believe the potential for suicide is real — or if the person has already made an attempt, call another volunteer, your facilitator, crisis line, or law enforcement person immediately.* We have an ethical responsibility to do everything in our power to prevent someone from taking their life.

Here is some information and possible questions to help you determine the suicide potential of the person you are helping.

Age. The highest risk age groups are between fifteen and thirty years, and over fifty.

Gender. Men are at greater risk. More women attempt suicide, but men choose more lethal methods and are more likely to succeed.

Method. The more dangerous the method, the more likely it is to succeed. Drugs are less likely to succeed than jumping out of the top floor of a building.

Suicide Plan. The risk increases in proportion to the organizational clarity and detail of the plan.

Important Losses. Suicide potential increases when the person has experienced real or imagined losses such as job, status, prestige, and loved ones.

Support Group. The better the support group, the less potential there is for suicide. The support of the class greatly diminishes suicide risk.

Resources. A greater risk exists for those experiencing financial or employment problems.

Medical Status. There is a greater risk for those with chronic, debilitating illness, or for those who have had unsuccessful experiences with the medical profession.

Prior Suicide Attempts. Those who have made attempts in the past, or those who have had close friends or loved ones attempt suicide, are more likely to attempt suicide.

Symptoms. Watch out for sleep disturbances, depression, feelings of hopelessness, change in eating habits, evidence or complaint of stress, alcoholism, or homosexuality. Watch especially for a sudden improvement in attitudes or moods. This can mean that the person has made a decision to commit suicide and is feeling a sense of relief.

Questions to Ask the Person. If you get an answer to these questions indicating thoughts of suicide, go on to the next question. Stop when you get a response indicating a strong reason to continue living.

• Have you ever thought of suicide? (This question will usually get a positive response.)
• Do you have a plan?
• Do you have the means to carry out your plan?
• Have you ever attempted suicide?
• Has anyone close to you attempted or succeeded at suicide?
• What are the odds you will?
• How do you see yourself in the future (tomorrow, one week, etc.)?

The most important thing is to find out what keeps them living. Ask questions like, "What keeps you from committing suicide?" Hopefully, they will give answers like "I'm too chicken." "I don't want to hurt my loved ones." "What would happen to my kids?" "Morally and spiritually I believe it would be a sin."

Dealing with Violence

Many class participants are experiencing intense anger. You may hear threats of violence from some of them to property or to people. Again try and help the person talk out these feelings of anger, and actively listen to their feelings. If you believe the person is likely to act out these feelings of anger and is likely to commit an act of physical violence, you have a legal obligation to inform your facilitator or law enforcement personal of the potential act of violence immediately.

Participants of this Rebuilding Seminar will most likely have found ways of dissipating their anger. Their former partner may be more inclined to be violent. Help the participants to protect themselves and to use common sense in order to prevent a situation where violence might occur. The chances are very small you will have to deal with physical violence as part of being a volunteer-helper, but we want you to feel prepared if the situation should arise.

Social and Emotional Needs of Volunteers

In order to grow as a person as well as be an effective volunteer, you must learn to continue to meet your individual needs. Class meetings will tend to help you meet these needs by:
• Continuing the emotional high from participation.
• Making new friends in the present class.
• Gaining a better understanding of the group process.
• Developing better small group and leadership skills.
• Improving your effectiveness as a helping person.
• Gaining a better understanding of the divorce process, which will help you continue your own adjustment process. (Facilitator's learn more about themselves each time they teach the class.)

You may also need to meet your needs by activities outside of the class. Volunteers need to have contact with people not hurting, or people not adjusting to a loss. You may need relaxation or exercise to break the pattern of being in a helping situation. Please be sure and continue to meet your social and emotional needs while acting in the role of a volunteer.

Fisher Divorce Adjustment Scale

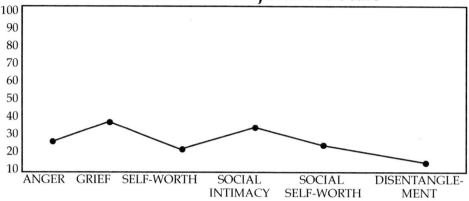

Description of the FDAS

The FDAS was designed as a pre-test, post-test instrument to be used with the Divorce Seminar. It was developed as part of Bruce's Doctoral dissertation in 1976 and was revised in 1978. It attempts to measure a person's adjustment to the ending of a love relationship. It is not designed to measure a person's mental illness. The Alpha Internal Reliability of the FDAS is .98 for the total score and a range from .87 to .93 for the various subtests. High test retest reliability statistics like this mean that if a person were to retake the FDAS their scores would be similar to the first time they took the test, assuming the test taker had not changed between taking tests.

Validity has to do with whether the test measures what it states it is measuring — in this case does it measure divorce adjustment? *There are no numerical statistics for the validity of the FDAS.* However, there are three indications of validity for this instrument.

Face Validity

When people take the FDAS they frequently state, "These test questions are right on. This is exactly what I have been feeling." Often they feel good after taking the test because they feel understood and accepted and not so different from everyone else. Thus it appears the face validity is good for the FDAS.

Time Validity

It appears divorce adjustment is time related. The longer you are divorced, the more you have adjusted to the divorce. The mean scores for length of separation with the FDAS indicate scores increase the longer the time interval since separation. Or stated another way, there is a high correlation between length of time since separation and scores on the FDAS. This would indicate the FDAS has time validity.

Seminar Members Evaluations

I usually ask at the end of the ten-week seminar to have seminar members vote for the three participants who have experienced the most improvement in divorce adjustment while taking the seminar. There is a correlation between their votes and the participants having the highest gain scores between the pre-test and post-test on the FDAS. Thus, it appears the FDAS is measuring the same thing participants in the seminar define as divorce adjustment.

In spite of the good statistics for the FDAS, keep a healthy skepticism toward it and any other personality test results. There are so many variations and errors in testing and statistics. Many people will take a test and believe the results are the gospel truth when in reality the scores are only indications concerning the person's personality.

My suggestion to people when they receive the scoring results is to think of them as feedback similar to feedback they may receive from a friend who knows them well. The feedback may agree with the person's perceptions of themselves and may be meaningful and relevant. But if the feedback from the scores disagrees with the person's perception of themselves, then either the person needs to think about the feedback because it may teach them something about themselves, or else the feedback from the test may be incorrect or inaccurate.

As mentioned before, there is a total adjustment score for the FDAS plus the six subtest scores of self-worth, disentanglement, anger, grief, social intimacy or trust, and social self-worth. As with any personality test, the total score is much more important statistically. When giving feedback to participants or when doing any sort of evaluation using the FDAS, be sure to place the most emphasis upon the total score.

People enjoy taking the FDAS. They find it a healing experience. They often state, "I thought I was the only person in the world who was feeling what I have been feeling. When I took the test and found that many others were also experiencing the same feelings I felt much more normal and not different from everyone else." Many also state, "I would have answered those questions differently a few weeks or a few months ago. I guess I have grown and adjusted more than I thought." Taking the test validates people and helps them realize their emotional growth and adjustment even before they receive any scoring results.

The FDAS is designed for people ending a love-relationship and not for a person who is widowed. I devised the Adjustment Scale for widowed so they could also take the Scale. The grief subtest works very well for widowed people and can be used by itself even though the total test was not completed. The Widowed Adjustment Scale has not been normed and standardized for widowed people, so be cautious about interpretations of their profiles.

Some therapists have used the FDAS with clients in individual therapy. It works well for this purpose. It is helpful for clients to take the test, helpful to have scoring results, and also helpful to use the FDAS as a checklist for possible areas and concerns to discuss in individual therapy. It could be used as a pre- and post-test to evaluate a person's therapy progress.

Administering the FDAS

The question arises as to when it is best to administer the pre-test and post-test FDAS during the ten-week seminar. The best time to give the pre-test is to have people advance register for the seminar and take the FDAS before opening night. Listening to the Building Blocks Presentation or reading the textbook will affect their scoring results. In many cases it is not easy to advance register, therefore, my second recommendation is to give them the FDAS when they register for the seminar opening night. Have them take it home to complete. Have them mail back the completed answer sheets immediately so you can score them and share the results the second night of the seminar. Realistically it is difficult to get everybody's answer sheet back and scored that quickly. Many times it will be the third meeting of the seminar before you can share the scoring results with them. Because that is often the reality you may want to have them bring back the completed answer sheets to the second meeting of the seminar and then score them and share the results the third meeting. I would keep aiming for the quickest possible way to get scoring results back. I would attempt to have them mail them back with the hope of sharing scoring the second meeting of the seminar.

The test has 100 items and takes approximately thirty minutes to complete. Directions for completing the FDAS suggest marking the first answer that comes to mind. Usually this will be the most accurate response. In its present form the FDAS has some questions which might be identified as double negatives. These questions are difficult for some people to answer. They only think of the frequency they think or feel the concept asked about in the test item and mark that response on the answer sheet.

My preference for administering the post test FDAS is to take time during the ninth meeting of the seminar and have them complete it during seminar time. Participants are not as uptight as they were opening night and can easily take it during seminar. Spending this time during the ninth night does not interfere like it would the first night. Aim to have 100% of the seminar participants take the FDAS both pre- and post-test in order to be able to make seminar averages as meaningful as possible. In order to get 100% to take the post-test, you will probably have to give it during seminar time.

I have given up trying to have someone take it after the tenth night of the seminar and return the completed answer sheets. Their commitment ends when the tenth session is completed and to get them to complete the test and return it does not work.

FDAS Scoring Results

The individual answer sheets are scored using the scoring masks, or keying the answers into the computer scoring program. (It is possible to take the test on the Computer with the FDAS Scoring Program. This allows the scoring to be done automatically without having to type in the answers.) Individual scores are transferred to the FDAS profile sheet and the summary sheet along with the basic information of sex, age, length of separation, and dumper-dumpee-mutual status.

The summary sheet has room for both pre-test and post-test scores so seminar averages can be easily computed. The average can be entered on a seminar average profile sheet. It is helpful in gaining an overview of the seminar in order to total the number of males and females, number of dumper - dumpee - mutual, various lengths of separation times, and age of participants.

You may not be aware of some of the differences in your seminars until you complete these items. For example, the typical seminar has 1/2 dumpees, 1/3 dumpers and 1/6 mutuals. I had one seminar with 11 male dumpees and one female dumper. Seminars with a majority of dumpers are different than seminars with all dumpees. Seminars of mostly recently separated are different than seminars with many people separated for a longer period of time.

It is helpful for the seminar participants to see both the seminar average and their individual score on the same profile sheet. Usually there are participants who have very low profiles on the pre-test. Seeing the seminar average which isn't usually much different from theirs, is very comforting. A helpful hint: One way to put seminar average profiles on the individual sheets easily is to trace the seminar average on a plain piece of white paper. Use this as a master and run the individual profile sheets through the copy machine. This will put the seminar average on each individual profile sheet.

Next, make a copy of each individual profile sheet before you hand it back. When you are ready to plot the post-test profile you already have a copy of the profile sheet with the pre-test score on it. Plot the post-test score and the person can easily see the difference between the pre-test and post-test scores.

Rather than an individual explanation, a group explanation of the scoring results can be used. A profile sheet with the seminar average can be used as a demonstration model to show the six subtests and the total score. Emphasize the importance of the total score rather than the various subtest scores. Show how the higher the profile is, the more it indicates divorce adjustment in all areas, especially in the anger subtest which is confusing to many people. They think a high score means more anger when it means less.

Explain that the raw score is a total of the marks from each item in that subtest. Thirty of the hundred items are reversed scoring which keeps people on their toes when completing the answer sheet. This means the points on the answer sheet range from 5 to 1 rather than from 1 to 5. Without some items having reversed scoring people may determine which is the most desirable way to mark the answer sheet.

Percentile is probably the easiest comparison score to use. A percentile score of 75 means of every 100 people who take the test, 75 will score lower and 25 will score higher than the 75 score. Emphasize that it is not a percentage score with 75% of the answers scored correctly. There are no correct or incorrect answers on this Scale.

The first four subtests of self-worth, disentanglement, anger, and grief are similar to the building blocks with the same title. The social intimacy subtest is a combination of the rebuilding friendships, trust and sexuality blocks. The good social self-worth block has been referred to as the miscellaneous block because the items in that subtest cover a variety of subjects. Suggest that people read the helpful hints for interpreting the scores on the back of the answer sheet. Those hints will answer most of the questions people have about the scoring results.

After sharing the group interpretation of profiles, pass out individual profiles and check with each person to make sure they understand the profile and how to interpret it. It is advisable to pass out the profiles before the break in order for people to have time to process results and decide if they have questions or are feeling uptight and anxious about scoring results. Check again at the end of the seminar meeting to make certain everyone is feeling okay about scoring results.

It is helpful for the facilitator to see each participant's individual profile in order to better understand their needs. Look for low spots and high spots in the profiles to see which subtests the participant needs to work through. Look for scores under 300 total raw points and be especially aware of how much emotional pain they are feeling. Check to see if they are thinking about suicide. 300 points is not a critical cut-off point but the lower the score the more likely the person will be needing extra help and support.

Not only is it helpful to see the individual profiles but the seminar profile is also very helpful. Normally, the seminar profile will be quite flat with very little variation between the different subtests. However, some seminars will have peaks and valleys in the profiles. A seminar that is much lower in grief, for example, may need more time spent on the grief chapter.

There may be a lot of variation from seminar to seminar. Some seminars have low profiles and others have very high profiles. We have had one seminar where the seminar average was below the 16 percentile line. With this seminar we talked about suicide feelings and asked more volunteer helpers to be present with the seminar members. Other seminars may have had a growth experience before starting the seminar. They may have a seminar average profile over the 50 percentile mark. A high scoring seminar like this is most likely growing rather than surviving like the hurting seminar. The growing seminar is usually more fun to teach than the hurting one.

Post-test scores are not as important to participants as pre-test scores. However they do enjoy seeing an indication of their growth on a piece of paper. Participants grow so much during the ten-week seminar and giving them back post test scores is a great big warm-fuzzy. Seeing their growth on a profile sheet really reinforces and affirms their growth.

It is useful to examine the pre-test and post-test seminar averages for objective feedback about the effectiveness of the seminar experience. Always be careful in using test scores to evaluate teaching techniques because it is easy to teach toward having good gain scores instead of caring about the participants' individual pain. I have often learned a great deal about improving the seminar experience by looking at the seminar gain scores.

In the FDAS Research Data there are seminar average gain scores showing that the average person gains about 66 total score points while taking the seminar. Our experienced facilitator's here at the Learning Center often have seminar average gain scores of over 100 points. Some facilitator's who have not been through the Professional Workshop training have seminar average gain scores much less than the average 66 points. It appears that taking the Training Workshop makes better facilitator's. As a general rule, the more experience you have teaching the model, the higher the gain scores in your seminars.

Some facilitator's need to have objectivity in helping them teach more effectively. For example, one facilitator was very intent on helping people work through addiction (disentanglement). There was a big gain score in the disentanglement subtest in his seminars. However, the test scores showed there was no difference in the anger subtest scores from pretest to post-test. He used the test results to improve his big picture of divorce adjustment and was able to change his seminar procedures and help participants work through anger more effectively.

I would encourage everyone teaching the Rebuilding Seminar to use the FDAS as a pretest, post-test tool. It adds greatly to the effectiveness of the model.

Note to the Facilitator

Published "psychological tests" are expected to meet certain criteria of standardization, including statistical verification of reliability and validity, standard procedures for administration and scoring, and norms (published reports of data on tested groups). Moreover, it is expected that such assessment instruments will be administered, scored, and interpreted by qualified professionals with training and experience in psychometrics. Standards for such qualification are established by the American Psychological Association, as summarized in the following statement:

> *"The test user's key function is to make valid interpretations of test scores and data, often collected from multiple sources, using proper test selection, administration, and scoring procedures. For test users to provide valid interpretation, it is important that they be able to integrate knowledge of applicable psychometric and methodological principles, the theory behind the measured construct and related empirical literature, the characteristics of the particular tests used, and the relationship between the selected test and the particular testing purpose, the testing process, and, in some contexts, the individual test taker."[1]*

The *Fisher Divorce Adjustment Scale*, while it has been the subject of a number of studies of statistical reliability and validity, does not meet the qualifications of a standardized psychological test. The *FDAS* was developed as a tool to measure progress in divorce recovery, and is used primarily as *an aid to self-assessment* for individuals who are participating in the Fisher Rebuilding Divorce Seminars. No inferences should be drawn regarding personality characteristics of individuals who take the *FDAS*, nor should clinical decisions be based on *FDAS* scores without appropriate supporting evidence.

The statistical data and profiles provided in the following pages are for the information and guidance of facilitators who use the *FDAS* in conjunction with the Fisher Seminar. It is hoped that readers will better understand the *Scale*, its potential usefulness, and the effort Dr. Fisher undertook to create a meaningful benchmark for seminar participants.

— Robert E. Alberti, Ph.D.
Impact Publishers, Inc.

1. Turner, S.M., DeMers, S.T., and Fox, H.R. (2001). APA's Guidelines for Test User Qualifications: An Executive Summary. *American Psychologist*, December 2001, p. 1104.

Fisher Divorce Adjustment Scale

The following statements are feelings and attitudes that people frequently experience while they are ending a love relationship. Keeping in mind one specific relationship you have ended or are ending, read each statement and decide how frequently the statement applies to your present feelings and attitudes. Mark your response on your answer sheet. Do not leave any statements blank on the answer sheet. If the statement is not appropriate for you in your present situation, answer the way you feel you might if that statement were appropriate.

The five responses to choose from on the answer sheet are:

(1) almost always **(2)** usually **(3)** sometimes **(4)** seldom **(5)** almost never

1. I am comfortable telling people I am separated from my love partner.
2. I am physically and emotionally exhausted from morning until night.
3. I am constantly thinking of my former love partner.
4. I feel rejected by many of the friends I had when I was in the love relationship.
5. I become upset when I think about my former love partner.
6. I like being the person I am.
7. I feel like crying because I feel so sad.
8. I can communicate with my former love partner in a calm and rational manner.
9. There are many things about my personality I would like to change.
10. It is easy for me to accept my becoming a single person.
11. I feel depressed.
12. I feel emotionally separated from my former love partner.
13. People would not like me if they got to know me.
14. I feel comfortable seeing and talking to my former love partner.
15. I feel like I am an attractive person.
16. I feel as though I am in a daze and the world doesn't seem real.
17. I find myself doing things just to please my former love partner.
18. I feel lonely.
19. There are many things about my body I would like to change.
20. I have many plans and goals for the future.
21. I feel I don't have much sex appeal.
22. I am relating and interacting in many new ways with people since my separation.
23. Joining a singles' group would make me feel I was a loser like them.
24. It is easy for me to organize my daily routine of living.
25. I find myself making excuses to see and talk to my former love partner.
26. Because my love relationship failed, I must be a failure.
27. I feel like unloading my feelings of anger and hurt upon my former love partner.
28. I feel comfortable being with people.
29. I have trouble concentrating.
30. I think of my former love partner as related to me rather than as a separate person.

31. I feel like an okay person.

32. I hope my former love partner is feeling as much or more emotional pain than I am.

33. I have close friends who know and understand me.

34. I am unable to control my emotions.

35. I feel capable of building a deep and meaningful love relationship.

36. I have trouble sleeping.

37. I easily become angry at my former love partner.

38. I am afraid to trust people who might become love partners.

39. Because my love relationship ended, I feel there must be something wrong with me.

40. I either have no appetite or eat continuously which is unusual for me.

41. I don't want to accept the fact that our love relationship is ending.

42. I force myself to eat even though I'm not hungry.

43. I have given up on my former love partner and I getting back together.

44. I feel very frightened inside.

45. It is important that my family, friends, and associates be on my side rather than on my former love partner's side.

46. I feel uncomfortable even thinking about dating.

47. I feel capable of living the kind of life I would like to live.

48. I have noticed my body weight is changing a great deal.

49. I believe if we try, my love partner and I can save our love relationship.

50. My abdomen feels empty and hollow.

51. I have feelings of romantic love for my former love partner.

52. I can make the decisions I need to because I know and trust my feelings.

53. I would like to get even with my former love partner for hurting me.

54. I avoid people even though I want and need friends.

55. I have really made a mess of my life.

56. I sigh a lot.

57. I believe it is best for all concerned to have our love relationship end.

58. I perform my daily activities in a mechanical and unfeeling manner.

59. I become upset when I think about my love partner having a love relationship with someone else.

60. I feel capable of facing and dealing with my problems.

61. I blame my former love partner for the failure of our love relationship.

62. I am afraid of becoming sexually involved with another person.

63. I feel adequate as a fe/male love partner.

64. It will only be a matter of time until my love partner and I get back together.

65. I feel detached and removed from activities around me as though I were watching them on a movie screen.

66. I would like to continue having a sexual relationship with my former love partner.

67. Life is somehow passing me by.

68. I feel comfortable going by myself to a public place such as a movie.

69. It is good to feel alive again after having felt numb and emotionally dead.

70. I feel I know and understand myself.

71. I feel emotionally committed to my former love partner.

72. I want to be with people but I feel emotionally distant from them.

73. I am the type of person I would like to have for a friend.

74. I am afraid of becoming emotionally close to another love partner.

75. Even on the days when I am feeling good, I may suddenly become sad and start crying.

76. I can't believe our love relationship is ending.

77. I become upset when I think about my love partner dating someone else.

78. I have a normal amount of self-confidence.

79. People seem to enjoy being with me.

80. Morally and spiritually, I believe it is wrong for our love relationship to end.

81. I wake up in the morning feeling there is no good reason to get out of bed.

82. I find myself daydreaming about all the good times I had with my love partner.

83. People want to have a love realtionship with me because I feel like a lovable person.

84. I want to hurt my former love partner by letting him/her know how much I hurt emotionally.

85. I feel comfortable going to social events even though I am single.

86. I feel guilty about my love relationship ending.

87. I feel emotionally insecure.

88. I feel uncomfortable even thinking about having a sexual relationship.

89. I feel emotionally weak and helpless.

90. I think about ending my life with suicide.

91. I understand the reasons why our love relationship did not work out.

92. I feel comfortable having my friends know our love relationship is ending.

93. I am angry about the things my former love partner has been doing.

94. I feel like I am going crazy.

95. I am unable to perform sexually.

96. I feel as though I am the only single person in a couples-only society.

97. I feel like a single person rather than a married person.

98. I feel my friends look at me as unstable now that I'm separated.

99. I daydream about being with and talking to my former love partner.

100. I need to improve my feelings of self-worth about being a wo/man.

Fisher Divorce Adjustment Scale **Answer Sheet**

First name _____ Last name _____

Address _____ City _____ State _____ Zip _____

Home phone _____ Work phone _____ Date _____

I am ___ male ___ female.   I am _____ years old   I have been separated _____ months

Who decided to end my relationship? ___ I did ___ my spouse did ___ both of us did ___ widowed

Please fill in the following circles to answer the questions on the *Fisher Divorce Adjustment Scale.*
The five responses to choose from are:

1) almost always	2) usually	3) sometimes	4) seldom	5) almost never
1 2 3 4 5	1 2 3 4 5	1 2 3 4 5	1 2 3 4 5

	1 2 3 4 5		1 2 3 4 5		1 2 3 4 5		1 2 3 4 5
1.	0 0 0 0 0	26.	0 0 0 0 0	51.	0 0 0 0 0	76.	0 0 0 0 0
2.	0 0 0 0 0	27.	0 0 0 0 0	52.	0 0 0 0 0	77.	0 0 0 0 0
3.	0 0 0 0 0	28.	0 0 0 0 0	53.	0 0 0 0 0	78.	0 0 0 0 0
4.	0 0 0 0 0	29.	0 0 0 0 0	54.	0 0 0 0 0	79.	0 0 0 0 0
5	0 0 0 0 0	30.	0 0 0 0 0	55.	0 0 0 0 0	80.	0 0 0 0 0
6.	0 0 0 0 0	31.	0 0 0 0 0	56.	0 0 0 0 0	81.	0 0 0 0 0
7.	0 0 0 0 0	32.	0 0 0 0 0	57.	0 0 0 0 0	82.	0 0 0 0 0
8.	0 0 0 0 0	33.	0 0 0 0 0	58.	0 0 0 0 0	83.	0 0 0 0 0
9.	0 0 0 0 0	34.	0 0 0 0 0	59.	0 0 0 0 0	84.	0 0 0 0 0
10.	0 0 0 0 0	35.	0 0 0 0 0	60.	0 0 0 0 0	85.	0 0 0 0 0
11.	0 0 0 0 0	36.	0 0 0 0 0	61.	0 0 0 0 0	86.	0 0 0 0 0
12.	0 0 0 0 0	37.	0 0 0 0 0	62.	0 0 0 0 0	87.	0 0 0 0 0
13.	0 0 0 0 0	38.	0 0 0 0 0	63.	0 0 0 0 0	88.	0 0 0 0 0
14.	0 0 0 0 0	39.	0 0 0 0 0	64.	0 0 0 0 0	89.	0 0 0 0 0
15.	0 0 0 0 0	40.	0 0 0 0 0	65.	0 0 0 0 0	90.	0 0 0 0 0
16.	0 0 0 0 0	41.	0 0 0 0 0	66.	0 0 0 0 0	91.	0 0 0 0 0
17.	0 0 0 0 0	42.	0 0 0 0 0	67.	0 0 0 0 0	92.	0 0 0 0 0
18.	0 0 0 0 0	43.	0 0 0 0 0	68.	0 0 0 0 0	93.	0 0 0 0 0
19.	0 0 0 0 0	44.	0 0 0 0 0	69.	0 0 0 0 0	94.	0 0 0 0 0
20.	0 0 0 0 0	45.	0 0 0 0 0	70	0 0 0 0 0	95.	0 0 0 0 0
21.	0 0 0 0 0	46.	0 0 0 0 0	71.	0 0 0 0 0	96.	0 0 0 0 0
22.	0 0 0 0 0	47.	0 0 0 0 0	72.	0 0 0 0 0	97.	0 0 0 0 0
23.	0 0 0 0 0	48.	0 0 0 0 0	73.	0 0 0 0 0	98.	0 0 0 0 0
24.	0 0 0 0 0	49.	0 0 0 0 0	74.	0 0 0 0 0	99.	0 0 0 0 0
25.	0 0 0 0 0	50.	0 0 0 0 0	75.	0 0 0 0 0	100.	0 0 0 0 0

Note: If you copy this answer sheet on a copy machine, make sure the copy is exactly the same
spacing as the original if you want to hand score the answers using the transparencies.

Fisher Divorce Adjustment Scale Profile

Name: _____ Identification Number: _____ Sex: _____

Age: _____ Months Separated: _____ Dumper, Dumpee, Mutual (Circle one)

> The higher your score, the more you approach the values at the top of the profile graph.
> The lower your score, the more you approach the values at the bottom of the profile graph.
> Further explanations of your scoring results are given on the reverse side of this page.

— Sub-Test Scores — Total Score

percentile scores	Good feelings of self-worth	Disentangled from former love partner	Anger at former love partner dissipated	Grief work completed	Open to social intimacy	Good social self-worth	Adjusted to ending of love relationship	percentile scores
95	125	110	60	120	40	45	500	95
90	117	106	58	114	38	40	458	90
85								85
80	112	103	53	110	35	37	440	80
75								75
70	106	100	50	105	33	36	420	70
65								65
60	101	96	47	101	31	34	401	60
55					29	33		55
50	97	92	43	95			377	50
45								45
40	91	85	39	88	26	31	361	40
35								35
30	85	77	35	81	24	29	340	30
25								25
20	79	66	31	76	21	28	310	20
15								15
10	70	56	26	64	17	25	280	10
5								5

	Low feelings of self-worth	Emotionally investing in past love relationship	Angry at former love partner	Grieving loss of relationship	Fearful of social intimacy	Low social self-worth	Not adjusted to ending of love relationship
Post-Test points							
Pre-Test points							
Pre to post gain							

The pre- and post-test point scores are obtained by counting the one through five marks on your FDAS answer sheet. These point scores are compared to a sample population group giving a percentile comparison score. The percentile scores listed on the sides of the above graph are rank order scores. If you scored 280 points on the total score, your percentile score would be 10. This means that out of every hundred people who took the FDAS, 10 would score lower than you, and 80 would score higher than you. The total score is the most important score. The sub-test scores are interesting but not as significant statistically. For those interested in statistics, the line at the 84th percentile is one Standard Deviation above the mean. The line at the 16th percentile is one Standard Deviation below the mean.

Reprinted with permission from *Facilitator's Manual for Rebuilding When Your Relationship Ends*, © 2004 by Bruce Fisher and Jere Beirhaus.

Dates of Seminar:

FDAS Scoring Class Summary Sheet
Location:
Facilitator:

Personal Information					Pre-Test Scores								Post-Test Scores								
Name	Age	Sep	Sex	Dr/de	FSW	DLR	FOA	SOG	RST	SSW	Total	FSW	DLR	FOA	SOG	RST	SSW	Total	Gain
1.																			
2.																			
3.																			
4.																			
5.																			
6.																			
7.																			
8.																			
9.																			
10.																			
11.																			
12.																			
13.																			
14.																			
15.																			
16.																			
17.																			
18.																			
19.																			
20.																			
21.																			
22.																			
23.																			
24.																			
25.																			
26.																			
27.																			
28.																			
29.																			
30.																			
Total																			
Average																			

It is helpful to know how many dumpers, dumpees, and mutuals there are in the class. Add up each and enter in total square in personal information column.

Abbreviations: Feelings Self-Worth, Disentanglement Love Relationship, Feelings of Anger, Symptoms of Grief, Rebuilding Social Trust, Social Self-Worth

Helpful Hints for Interpreting the Fisher Divorce Adjustment Scale Profiles

Did it feel good to take the FDAS and find out you are not the only person experiencing those feelings? Maybe you are more normal then you thought your were? Did you realize your score would have been different if you had taken the Scale last week or last month? The FDAS questions are designed to be marked differently as you work through the adjustment process. If you marked different answers than you would have in the past, this indicates you are adjusting to your loss. Normally your score will be lowest at the time of your physical separation.

The FDAS is designed to measure your adjustment to the ending of your love-relationship. It is NOT designed to measure your mental or emotional health. The feedback you receive from this scoring profile should help you identify your strong and weak areas in the process of adjusting to your loss. Your scores will be affected by the way you felt the day you took the test. Take this into account when you look at your scoring results.

The numbers listed at the bottom of the profile sheet are your raw scores. The six subtest raw scores are computed by giving points to the marks on your answer sheet. These are then totaled to give you total raw scores. Raw scores have no meaning until they are compared to others taking the test. Using a comparison group of 492 people, I computed percentile scores from the raw scores. These are the vertical rows of numbers five through ninety-five at each side of profile.

Percentile scores are a rank order method of comparison. A score of 75 means that out of every 100 people taking the FDAS, 75 scored lower than you and 25 scored higher. A percentile score of 75 does NOT mean you marked 75% of the answers correctly, because there are no right or wrong answers to this test. Your profile line is drawn to show how your scores compared to the comparison group of 492 people.

The most important score is the total score located on the vertical line on the right-hand side of the graph. The four subtests starting on the left are self-worth, disentanglement, anger, and grief. These are similar to the building blocks with the same title. The social intimacy subtest is a combination of the friendships, trust, and sexuality blocks. The social self-worth subtest is not a homogeneous group of questions and it is hard to define what it is measuring.

Have you taken both pre- and post-tests? If so, the gain score is shown in the lower row on the profile sheet. The nationwide average gain score pre-test to post-test for the total score is 66 raw score points. Did you gain more or less than the average?

Hopefully, you were able to be completely honest when you took the test so your test results will be meaningful. Some of you may still be in some denial, especially in the anger subtest, which will affect your scores. Some of you may have a lower post-test score than the pre-test. Usually this means you were denying feelings when taking the pre-test. The post-test score, after participating in the ten-week seminar, usually is more meaningful because you may have overcome any denial you had when taking the pre-test.

This FDAS is a research instrument and scoring results may change as more research data is gathered.

Good luck on working through the ending of your love relationship! – Bruce

Facilitators:
Please copy this sheet on the back of every profile sheet you return to the person taking the FDAS.

Fisher Divorce Adjustment Scale
Scoring Transparency

Scoring Transparency #1 is Feelings of Self-Worth

Make a transparency of this sheet making sure it is exactly the same size between numbers as this sheet. Place the transparency over the completed answer sheet. Give each mark on the answer sheet the number value just to the right of the mark. Add the total value of the marks on this sheet, and write the total points on the profile and summary sheets in either the pre- or post-test squares.

The maximum score is 125, and the minimum score is 25 for this self-worth subtest.

1) almost always	2) usually	3) sometimes	4) seldom	5) almost never
1 2 3 4 5	1 2 3 4 5	1 2 3 4 5	1 2 3 4 5	
1.	26. 1 2 3 4 5	51.	76.	
2.	27.	52. 5 4 3 2 1	77.	
3.	28. 5 4 3 2 1	53.	78. 5 4 3 2 1	
4.	29.	54.	79. 5 4 3 2 1	
5	30.	55. 1 2 3 4 5	80.	
6. 5 4 3 2 1	31. 5 4 3 2 1	56.	81.	
7.	32.	57.	82.	
8.	33. 5 4 3 2 1	58.	83.	
9. 1 2 3 4 5	34.	59.	84.	
10.	35. 5 4 3 2 1	60. 5 4 3 2 1	85.	
11.	36.	61.	86.	
12.	37.	62.	87.	
13. 1 2 3 4 5	38.	63.	88.	
14.	39. 1 2 3 4 5	64.	89.	
15. 5 4 3 2 1	40.	65.	90.	
16.	41.	66.	91.	
17.	42.	67. 1 2 3 4 5	92.	
18.	43.	68. 5 4 3 2 1	93.	
19.	44.	69. 5 4 3 2 1	94.	
20. 5 4 3 2 1	45.	70 5 4 3 2 1	95.	
21. 1 2 3 4 5	46.	71.	96.	
22.	47. 5 4 3 2 1	72. 1 2 3 4 5	97.	
23.	48.	73. 5 4 3 2 1	98.	
24.	49.	74.	99.	
25.	50.	75.	100. 1 2 3 4 5	

153

Fisher Divorce Adjustment Scale
Scoring Transparency

Scoring Transparency #2 is Disentanglement from Love Relationship

Make a transparency of this sheet making sure it is exactly the same size between numbers as this sheet. Place the transparency over the completed answer sheet. Give each mark on the answer sheet the number value just to the right of the mark. Add the total value of the marks on this sheet, and write the total points on the profile and summary sheets in either the pre or post-test squares.

The maximum score is 110, and the minimum score is 22 for this disentanglement subtest.

1) almost always	2) usually	3) sometimes	4) seldom	5) almost never
1 2 3 4 5	1 2 3 4 5	1 2 3 4 5	1 2 3 4 5

1.	26.	51. 1 2 3 4 5	76 1 2 3 4 5
2.	27.	52.	77. 1 2 3 4 5
3. 1 2 3 4 5	28.	53.	78.
4.	29.	54.	79.
5.	30. 1 2 3 4 5	55.	80. 1 2 3 4 5
6.	31.	56.	81.
7.	32.	57. 5 4 3 2 1	82. 1 2 3 4 5
8.	33.	58.	83.
9.	34.	59. 1 2 3 4 5	84.
10. 5 4 3 2 1	35.	60.	85.
11.	36.	61.	86. 1 2 3 4 5
12. 5 4 3 2 1	37.	63.	87.
13.	38.	62.	88.
14.	39.	64. 1 2 3 4 5	89.
15.	40.	65.	90.
16.	41. 1 2 3 4 5	66. 1 2 3 4 5	91. 5 4 3 2 1
17. 1 2 3 4 5	42.	67.	92.
18.	43. 5 4 3 2 1	68.	93.
19.	44.	69.	94.
20.	45.	70.	95.
21.	46.	71. 1 2 3 4 5	96.
22.	47.	72.	97.
23.	48.	73.	98.
24.	49. 1 2 3 4 5	74.	99. 1 2 3 4 5
25. 1 2 3 4 5	50.	75.	100.

Fisher Divorce Adjustment Scale
Scoring Transparency

Scoring Transparency #3 is Feelings of Anger

Make a transparency of this sheet making sure it is exactly the same size betweeo numbers as this sheet. Place the transparency over the completed answer sheet. Give each mark on the answer sheet the number value just to the right of the mark. Add the total value of the marks on this sheet, and write the total points on the profile and summary sheets in either the pre or post-test squares.

The maximum score is 60, and the minimum score is 12 for this anger subtest.

1) almost always	2) usually	3) sometimes	4) seldom	5) almost never
1 2 3 4 5	1 2 3 4 5	1 2 3 4 5	1 2 3 4 5

1.	26.	51.	76.
2.	27. 1 2 3 4 5	52.	77.
3.	28.	53. 1 2 3 4 5	78.
4.	29.	54.	79.
5. 1 2 3 4 5	30.	55.	80.
6.	31.	56.	81.
7.	32. 1 2 3 4 5	57.	82.
8. 5 4 3 2 1	33.	58.	83.
9.	34. 1 2 3 4 5	59.	84. 1 2 3 4 5
10.	35.	60.	85.
11.	36.	61. 1 2 3 4 5	86.
12.	37. 1 2 3 4 5	62.	87.
13.	38.	63.	88.
14. 5 4 3 2 1	39.	64.	89.
15.	40.	65.	90.
16.	41.	66.	91.
17.	42.	67.	92.
18.	43.	68.	93. 1 2 3 4 5
19.	44.	69.	94.
20.	45. 1 2 3 4 5	70.	95.
21.	46.	71.	96.
22.	47.	72.	97.
23.	48.	73.	98.
24.	49.	74.	99.
25.	50.	75.	100.

Fisher Divorce Adjustment Scale
Scoring Transparency

Scoring Transparency #4 is Symptoms of Grief

Make a transparency of this sheet making sure it is exactly the same size between numbers as this sheet. Place the transparency over the completed answer sheet. Give each mark on the answer sheet the number value just to the right of the mark. Add the total value of the marks on this sheet, and write the total points on the profile and summary sheets in either the pre or post-test squares.

The maximum score is 120, and the minimum score is 24 for this grief subtest.

1) almost always	2) usually	3) sometimes	4) seldom	5) almost never

	1 2 3 4 5		1 2 3 4 5		1 2 3 4 5		1 2 3 4 5
1.		26.		51.		76.	
2.	1 2 3 4 5	27.		52.		77.	
3.		28.		53.		78.	
4.		29.	1 2 3 4 5	54.		79.	
5.		30.		55.		80.	
6.		31.		56.	1 2 3 4 5	81.	1 2 3 4 5
7.	1 2 3 4 5	32.		57.		82.	
8.		33.		58.	1 2 3 4 5	83.	
9.		34.		59.		84.	
10.		35.		60.		85.	
11.	1 2 3 4 5	36.	1 2 3 4 5	61.		86.	
12.		37.		62.		87.	1 2 3 4 5
13.		38.		63.		88.	
14.		39.		64.		89.	1 2 3 4 5
15.		40.	1 2 3 4 5	65.	1 2 3 4 5	90.	1 2 3 4 5
16.	1 2 3 4 5	41.		66.		91.	
17.		42.	1 2 3 4 5	67.		92.	
18.	1 2 3 4 5	43.		68.		93.	
19.		44.	1 2 3 4 5	69.		94.	1 2 3 4 5
20.		45.		70.		95.	
21.		46.		71.		96.	1 2 3 4 5
22.		47.		72.		97.	
23.		48.	1 2 3 4 5	73.		98.	1 2 3 4 5
24.	5 4 3 2 1	49.		74.		99.	
25.		50.	1 2 3 4 5	75.	1 2 3 4 5	100.	

Fisher Divorce Adjustment Scale
Scoring Transparency

Scoring Transparency #5 is Rebuilding Social Trust

Make a transparency of this sheet making sure it is exactly the same size between numbers as this sheet. Place the transparency over the completed answer sheet. Give each mark on the answer sheet the number value just to the right of the mark. Add the total value of the marks on this sheet, and write the total points on the profile and summary sheets in either the pre or post test squares.

The maximum score is 40, and the minimum score is 8 for this trust subtest.

1) almost always	2) usually	3) sometimes	4) seldom	5) almost never

1 2 3 4 5	1 2 3 4 5	1 2 3 4 5	1 2 3 4 5
1.	26.	51.	76.
2.	27.	52.	77.
3.	28.	53.	78.
4.	29.	54.	79.
5.	30.	55.	80.
6.	31.	56.	81.
7.	32.	57.	82.
8.	33.	58.	83. 5 4 3 2 1
9.	34.	59.	84.
10.	35.	60.	85.
11.	36.	61.	86.
12.	37.	62. 1 2 3 4 5	87.
13.	38. 1 2 3 4 5	63. 5 4 3 2 1	88. 1 2 3 4 5
14.	39.	64.	89.
15.	40.	65.	90.
16.	41.	66.	91.
17.	42.	67.	92.
18.	43.	68.	93.
19.	44.	69.	94.
20.	45.	70.	95. 1 2 3 4 5
21.	46. 1 2 3 4 5	71.	96.
22.	47.	72.	97.
23.	48.	73.	98.
24.	49.	74. 1 2 3 4 5	99.
25.	50.	75.	100.

Scoring Transparency

Scoring Transparency #6 is Social Self-Worth

Make a transparency of this sheet making sure it is exactly the same size between numbers as this sheet. Place the transparency over the completed answer sheet. Give each mark on the answer sheet the number value just to the right of the mark. Add the total value of the marks on this sheet, and write the total points on the profile and summary sheets in either the pre or post test squares.

The maximum score is 45, and the minimum score is 9 for this social self worth subtest.

1) almost always	2) usually	3) sometimes	4) seldom	5) almost never
1 2 3 4 5	1 2 3 4 5	1 2 3 4 5	1 2 3 4 5	
1. 5 4 3 2 1	26.	51.	76.	
2.	27.	52.	77.	
3.	28.	53.	78.	
4. 1 2 3 4 5	29.	54. 1 2 3 4 5	79.	
5.	30.	55.	80.	
6.	31.	56.	81.	
7.	32.	57.	82.	
8.	33.	58.	83.	
9.	34.	59.	84.	
10.	35.	60.	85. 5 4 3 2 1	
11.	36.	61.	86.	
12.	37.	62.	87.	
13.	38.	63.	88.	
14.	39.	64.	89.	
15.	40.	65.	90.	
16.	41.	66.	91.	
17.	42.	67.	92. 5 4 3 2 1	
18.	43.	68.	93.	
19. 1 2 3 4 5	44.	69.	94.	
20.	45.	70.	95.	
21.	46.	71.	96.	
22. 5 4 3 2 1	47.	72.	97. 5 4 3 2 1	
23. 1 2 3 4 5	48.	73.	98.	
24.	49.	74.	99.	
25.	50.	75.	100.	

Fisher Divorce Adjustment Scale Interpretations

The following comments are designed to help you interpret the FDAS Profile Sheet Scores. There are interpretative comments on the back of the Profile sheets designed to help the person interpret their own scores. The following comments will help you make better interpretations than what is possible from the comments on the back of the profile sheets.

As I make these interpretations I will refer to the FDAS Research Data on the following pages. I will be writing to those of you who are facilitating the "Rebuilding When Your Relationship Ends" educational seminars. If you are working only with individuals and not facilitating the educational seminar I suggest you think about offering the educational seminar. I have found people adjust more rapidly by taking the seminar than they do in individual therapy.

Demographic Data.

A typical seminar will have 1/2 dumpees, 1/3 dumpers, and 1/6 mutuals. The dumpees will tend to take the class to survive emotionally and usually have been separated less than six months. The dumpers tend to take the class after they have been separated for a longer period of time. There is dumper euphoria that is verified by the profiles in the Research Data. The dumpers may not take the class until they are through the dumper euphoria period. I think the profiles on the last page of the Research Data are important. I would suggest you become familiar with them.

The male-female ratio in the class is typically 1/3 males and 2/3 females. If you check into population statistics you will find this ratio to be representative of the general population of formerly married people. There may be many reasons for this but two reasons help explain the unusual ratio. Females live longer and the older the age you are looking at, the larger the percent of females. Secondly, males remarry quicker after divorce and often remarry someone younger who has not been married before.

Most of the people in the class will be from 30 to 50 years of age. As you can see by the profiles in the Research Data, people in their twenties score much lower than the participants in their fifties on the pre-test but their gain scores are higher and there is not much difference on the post-test scores.

The length of separation will vary with the class but typically there might be 30% separated less than six months, 30% separated six to twelve months, 30% separated one to three years, and 10% separated more than three years. The 10% separated more than three years indicates two things. First, many people enroll in the class because they are stuck in the adjustment process. They have not adjusted even though they have been separated more than three years. Secondly, there is a great deal of personal growth taking place during the class. Many people take the class for personal growth rather than for adjusting to their divorce. In addition, many people have not been successful in relationships. They take the divorce class after a relationship has ended even though they were not married again after their divorce.

Testing Disclaimer.

Please be skeptical of any test scores concerning personality. The statistics on the Fisher Divorce Adjustment Scale are very good. However, any test has a Standard Error of Measurement and various other flaws which make me skeptical of personality test scores. I suggest to people that if the personality test scores agree with their perceptions of themselves, accept the scores. On the other hand, they may learn something about themselves if the test scores disagree with how they perceive themselves. The personality test may be wrong or inaccurate, consequently the feedback is less helpful. I emphasize again that the FDAS is designed to measure the adjustment to the ending of a love relationship. It is not designed to measure mental illness. However, there have been hundreds of Doctoral Dissertations using the FDAS and it appears there is a high correlation between the FDAS scores and scores on other personality instruments such as the Minnesota Multiphasic Personality Inventory.

The Importance of the Total Score

Always pay more attention to the total score than to the subtest scores. The total score has better statistics partly because the number of questions in the total score is higher than in the subtest scores. The subtest scores in the FDAS highly correlate with each other which minimizes the differences between the meaning of the various subtest scores. I have found it easy to pay more attention to the subtest scores than the total score. Keep in mind that the total score is more meaningful and important than the subtest scores.

Typical Class Average Profile Scores.

The Research Data shows typical class pre-test and post-test profiles. If your class pre-test average is low some of the following statements might be true.

1) You have a large number of recently separated participants which may lower the class average.

2) You have a large number of dumpees which may lower the class average.

3) You have a large number of males which may lower your class average.

4) You may have an unusual population, such as people who are in therapy or in a personal growth process of emotional pain.

5) You may have people that are having more difficulty in adjusting for various reasons.

If your class average profile is low, you may want to recruit more volunteers and give more support to the class. You may want to take more time to talk about suicide because the lower the total score on the FDAS profile, the more the person is likely to think about or attempt suicide. Many people in the class will be barely surviving emotionally. The class with low scores will be more difficult to teach but the potential change, healing, and transformation is much greater. Personal growth might be measured in feelings of surviving rather than growing.

If your class average is higher than the typical one in the Research Data you may have the opposite ratios of those mentioned above. You may have participants who have been in therapy or a growth group before attending this class. For example, in the Beginning Experience Program participants have been in the Ten-week Level One support group before enrolling in the Level Two Divorce class. They score much higher on the pre-test class average profile. You may have a class of people who are better able to adjust to a crisis for many and various reasons.

Typical Sub-test Class Average Profile Scores.

As you can see in the Research Data, the average pre-test profile score is relatively flat with anger, social intimacy. Social self-worth sub-test scores are somewhat higher. There will be some differences from class to class in the various subtest scores. You may have an angry class that will score lower on the anger subtest. You may have a class with low self-worth scores. You may find it helpful to look at the class average pre-test scores as soon as possible in order to better understand the needs of your class. The FDAS subtest scores will give you feedback and compliment what your personal perceptions are about the special needs of each class.

Denial and the Anger Subtest Score

This is a subjective interpretation not backed by research or statistics. I have observed two kinds of denial concerning anger. Some participants have denied anger but the FDAS picks it up and they become more aware of their anger from observing

their FDAS scoring results. They say, "I didn't know I was that angry until I got my test results back." The FDAS test results are very helpful in working with these people. On the other hand, some people are obviously very angry but the FDAS results don't show it. They seem to have denied their anger to the point that even the FDAS doesn't pick it up. These people will be more difficult to work with.

There is a small minority of people who are in so much denial that the FDAS scores are less meaningful. It is obvious to everyone around the person that they are not adjusted but their FDAS scores are high. My observation is that this is more likely to be a male person than a female person but I have observed both sexes in this kind of denial.

Taking the FDAS for Each Relationship Ending

The instructions for the FDAS suggest people think about a specific relationship when they are taking the test. It may be hard for some people to separate the different relationships. Their scores are contaminated by the old unfinished emotional work from relationships that have ended in the past. One thing that may help these people is to have them take the FDAS more than once. They may take it for each relationship that has ended. The FDAS scores can be entirely different for each one. Almost every person who does take the FDAS for each relationship reports it to be useful feedback and a worthwhile experience.

Inter-Related Subtest Scores

Some subtest scores must go up or down before other subtest scores can go up or down just as the pistons of an internal combustion engine must go up and down in order for the engine to work. I think during the adjustment process the various subtest scores are inter related just as the pistons of an internal combustion engine are interrelated.

For example, a person with a low self-worth may not feel confident or secure enough to access and express their anger. Their self-worth score is low and their anger score is low because they can't express anger. As they improve their self-worth and their self-worth score goes up they feel strong enough to access and express their anger. As they deal with their anger it helps them to feel better about themselves which allows their self-worth score to improve. Result: both subtest scores go up. Conclusion: There can be a high correlation between feelings of self-worth and being able to work through anger.

Another example: A person has a high score on disentanglement but their anger score is very low. They may say something like, "I'm disentangled. I never think about that SOB anymore." When you are angry at the other person you are still entangled. There also is a connection between disentanglement and grief in that grieving helps you disentangle. You may have used anger to emotionally distance the other person so you don't grieve and haven't disentangled. The process might be like this. 1) You are aware first of your anger. As you get in touch with your anger and start to dissipate that energy your anger score goes up. 2) As you let go of being angry you are able to feel the sadness that you had covered up with anger and you start grieving then your grief score goes down. 3) As you grieve you are able to realize that you have not disentangled. Your anger has diminished which allows you to feel your love feelings for the other person. Your disentanglement score goes down (still entangled) as a result of being able to feel the love feelings. You had used anger as a way of distancing the other person. 4) The end result of the piston interactions is that subtest scores of anger, disentanglement, and grief scores going up and down results in higher scores on all three subtests. Conclusion: There is a high correlation between anger and disentanglement. It is hard to be disentangled if you are still angry at your former love partner.

Another example: You have an emotional love-wound and your score on the social intimacy subtest is low. Remember there are questions on sexuality and friends in the intimacy subtest scores. You may have a great deal of anger which results in you being non-sexual. You are lonely which increases your anger (lonely people may be unconsciously angry). Being non-sexual and lonely causes your intimacy score to be lower. The loneliness makes your self-worth scores lower. As you improve your feelings of self-worth you are able to express your anger. As you dissipate your anger you eventually begin to feel emotionally closer to another. As you experience more intimacy your love-wound begins healing and your intimacy score goes up. Conclusion: Having a love-wound results in your intimacy score being low. In order to improve your intimacy score and heal your love-wound you may need to grieve and dissipate anger.

Does this make sense to you? Can you think of some ways the various piston subtest scores go up and down as you work through the adjustment process?

Gain Scores

Notice the bottom row on the profile sheet for the gain scores. This is the difference between the pre-test and post-test scores. It is an indication of the amount of adjustment and growth the participant experienced during the ten-week class. Looking at the class profile gain scores may be helpful feedback for you as a facilitator in order to determine the effectiveness of the class. It is a mistake to evaluate teaching on the basis of personality tests but it can be feedback to help you determine the progress of the participants during the ten-weeks.

The lower the person's pre-test score the more the potential for a high gain score. The person who has a very low pre-test score will most likely have the highest gain score of anyone in the class.

Almost all of the forty facilitator's who are represented in the class averages in the Research Data had participated in the FRLC Training Workshop for Facilitator's. I measured another set of classes where the facilitator's had not attended the Training Workshop. The gain scores in these classes were only 43 points. Does attending the Training Workshop help the facilitator's do a better job of teaching as evidenced by the participants showing more adjustment during the ten weeks? It appears so. The staff at the Learning Center have been teaching the Divorce Class for many years. We expect to have class average gain scores of 100 points in our classes.

There is a high correlation between the subtest score on self-worth and the gain score. A person with good feelings of self worth will be better able to adjust to a crisis such as the ending of a love-relationship.

Giving Back FDAS Scoring Results to Those with Low Scores

We need to be sensitive to how it feels to a person who is in emotional pain to get back scoring results that are at the bottom of the profile sheet. They are already hurting emotionally and looking at low scores does not make them feel any better.

I emphasize that the test does not measure mental illness but gives feedback about how much emotional pain the people are feeling. I believe they already know they are hurting and the test scores reinforce what they already know. Also, those with a low score will probably have the highest gain scores when they take the post test at the end of the ten weeks.

People Showing Little or no Gain Scores

Almost every class I taught had a person whose post-test score was the same or lower than their pre-test score. I ask them if they were denying some of their feelings at the beginning of the class and they usually say yes. I ask them if the class helped them access and express their feelings. Again they say yes. I ask them if they felt badly about not having any improvement in their test scores. They say no. I then joke and state that maybe they aren't going to ask for their money back that they paid for the class. Of course the answer is no!

Some Generalizations Based Upon Research Using the FDAS

The following generalizations are based upon the Research Data. The statements are in the same order as the various graphs on the following pages.

1. Participants in the Ten Week Seminar show higher gain scores on the self-worth, grief, social intimacy, and social self-worth subtests. They show lower gain scores on anger and disentanglement. (See the profile for the recent class taught here at the Learning Center.)

2. Males score lower than females on disentanglement which indicates they have more trouble disentangling. (Males often have no other close friends and confidants other than the female love partner.)

3. Females score lower than males on social intimacy. (Symbolically it is harder for a female than a male to visit a bar by herself.)

4. Males have a higher gain score during the ten-week class than do females. I compiled research indicating males had half again higher gain scores than females.

5. Dumpees hurt more than dumpers and their scores on the FDAS are lower. It is appropriate and normal for a recently separated dumpee to score below the sixteenth percentile.

6. Dumpees score lower on the anger and disentanglement subtests. There is more difference between a dumper and dumpee profile in the disentanglement subtest than in any other subtest score. (The dumper has been disentangling before the separation.)

7. There is little difference between a dumper and a dumpee profile in the self-worth subtest. (It is hard to be a dumper. Many friends and family members are critical of the dumper.)

8. There is also little difference between a dumper and dumpee profile in the social intimacy pre-test scores. (Everyone is afraid of intimacy after a relationship ends.)

9. People in their twenties score lower on the pre-test than people in their fifties. However, the people in the twenties have higher gain scores during the class and their post-test scores are similar to those in their fifties.

10. Mutual profiles are more similar to dumper profiles than to dumpee profiles.

11. Female mutuals have an easier time adjusting than female dumpers.

12. Male mutuals have a more difficult time adjusting than male dumpers.

13. The person's FDAS scores go down after the people file and start the legal court process.

14. The higher the person's financial income, the lower the FDAS scores.

15. People with two or more children score lower on the FDAS.

16. The more education a person has attained, the higher the scores on the FDAS.

17. Dumpees score the lowest immediately after separation but their scores continue to improve with the passage of time. Dumpers score lower after seven months separation than they do the first six months after separation.

18. A person adjusts as much during the ten-week class as they might adjust in ten months without taking the class. (Subjective interpretation, not statistical.)

19. There are exceptions to all generalizations. (I learned that back on the Fisher Farm in Iowa.)

Research Data
Fisher Divorce Adjustment Scale

History of the FDAS

The FDAS was developed as part of Dr. Bruce Fisher's Dissertation in 1976. It was revised and statistically improved in 1978. There have been hundreds of Doctoral Dissertations which have used the FDAS. A partial list of these Dissertations is available from the Learning Center.

Purpose of the FDAS

The Scale is designed to measure a person's adjustment to the ending of a love relationship. It is not designed to measure a person's mental or emotional illness although researchers have found a high correlation between the FDAS and other Personality Instruments such as the Minnesota Multiphasic Personality Inventory.

Widowed people may want to take the FDAS. The Disentanglement Sub-Test does not work well for them so it has been modified to make it more applicable to them. The scores have not been normed and standardized for widowed people so the Disentanglement Subtest scores, and thus the total score, are not as meaningful.

We recommend the FDAS be administered at the beginning of the Ten Week Seminar, and again at the end. The pre-test score gives the participant feedback concerning their adjustment to the ending of their Relationship. The post-test score gives feedback concerning the progress of adjustment made during the ten weeks. The FDAS also works as a pre-test, post-test instrument for individual therapy or other kinds of intervention programs.

Description and Statistics

The scoring includes a total score and six subtest scores of self-worth, disentanglement, anger, grief, trust-intimacy-sexuality, and a subtest which is not homogeneous titled social self-worth. The total score is the most important score but the sub-test scores are helpful and interesting.

The Alpha Internal Reliability for the total score is .985 which is high for a personality test. The subtest scores reliability range from .87 to .95. (A statistical packet is available) Face validity is good as evidenced by test takers reactions when they relate to the hundred items. Validity is indicated by the fact that scores improve with time just as divorce adjustment improves with time. Validity was also verified by a high correlation between votes by the seminar participants on who adjusted the most during the seminar and the pre-test, post-test gain scores on the FDAS. This voting was not recorded and is not available.

Discussion of the Research Data Concerning Longevity of Sub-Test Scores.

The following graphs are concerned with the question, "Does it take the same amount of time to adjust for each subtest?" These results are from the 1976 Dissertation version of the FDAS rather than the 1978 revised version. The Self-Acceptance Subtest has lower statistical meaning, and the Tennessee Self-Concept Scale was used instead of the Self-Worth subtest found in the revised FDAS. The numbers are percentile rank order scores. A 32 percentile score means that out of every hundred people taking the FDAS, 32 scored lower and 68 scored higher. The months at the bottom of the graph indicate how many months the person has been physically separated.

Self-Acceptance of Divorce

Symptoms of Grief

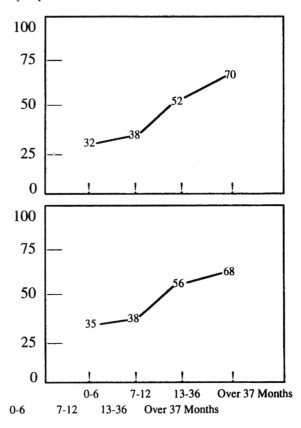

Disentanglement of Love Relationship

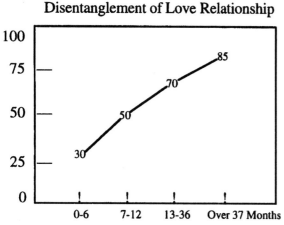

Rebuilding Social Relationships

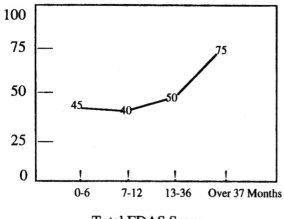

Total FDAS Score

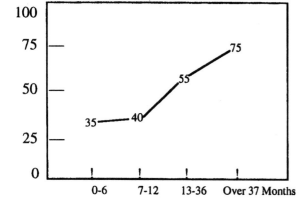

Feelings of Self-Worth
(Tennessee Self-Concept Scale)

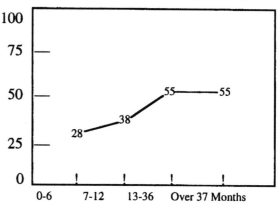

Feelings of Anger

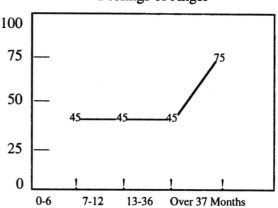

Conclusions

There were 100 white middle seminar people from Colorado taking part in the above research. There were about equal numbers in each of the four different lengths of separation. Even though the sample was not obtained statistically, it appears to be a good representative sample of the total population.

The total scores on the FDAS increase after one year but the scores increase even more after three years. The results indicate that divorce adjustment is partially completed after one year,

but more divorce adjustment takes place for three years after the physical separation. Participation in the Rebuilding Educational Seminar speeds up divorce adjustment, and the scores after the ten week seminar appear to improve about the same as one year of adjustment without participation in the seminar.

The scores on the Anger and Rebuilding Social Relationships subtests show very little change until after three years. We can conclude that on the average people stay angry and lonely for three years after the physical separation.

The scores on the Tennessee Self-Concept Scale are standardized and normed on a non-divorced population—not a formerly married population. The scores level off at the fifty-five percentile instead of reaching higher percentile scores. The problem of not having a self-worth subtest was corrected when I added a self-worth subtest to the FDAS in 1978.

164

Scoring Profiles For The *Fisher Divorce Adjustment Scale*

Population Data for the Profiles on the Following Pages
1978 Revised Version of FDAS
497 Total Population, 371 Female (75%), 126 Male (25%)
Includes Forty Different Seminars In Eight Different States
Pre-Test and Post-Test Averages for Various Sub-groups
Research Compiled in 1980

Explanation of FDAS Scoring Results
On the following two pages are copies of the Fisher Divorce Adjustment Scale Profile. The six sub-test vertical lines range from the more adjusted values listed at the top of the graph to the less adjusted values listed at the bottom of the graph. The total score vertical line is at the right side of the graph. People looking at this profile the first time will often ask if a high score on anger means more anger or less anger. It means less anger. The four values in the box at the top of the graph are sex, age, separation length in months, and separation type meaning dumper, dumpee, or a mutual decision to end the relationship. The method of deciding the separation type for the person taking the test is done simply by asking who decided to end the relationship. This question seems to discover in most cases who was the dumper or dumpee. About ten percent of the people change their answer to that question on the post-test answer sheet compared to their answer on the pre-test answer sheet. I believe the post-test answer to be more valid.

On the bottom of the graph are the scores for the various subtests and total score for the pre-test and for the post-test. These raw scores were arrived at by counting the marks on the answer sheet with values of one through five for the seventy forward scored items, or five through one for the thirty reversed scored items. The graph has built in standardization and norming so the person's individual score is compared to the standardized population scores. For example, a score of 280 points for the total score comes out to be at the 10 percentile.

Total pre and post averages for the Ten-Week Seminar
The following two pages show profile graphs for pre- and post-test scores of participants in the ten week seminars. The first page shows the average scores for the 497 population of people taking the Ten Week Seminar. The difference between the two lines is the amount of adjustment they experienced during the seminar. Note the greater difference in the self-worth, grief sub-tests, and the good social self-worth subtest. At the lower right side of the profile is the total raw points for the pre-test and post-test scores. 405 minus 339 equals a gain score of 66 points. This represents the average gain for these forty classes.

The second page shows a pre-test, post-test class average for a seminar taught here at the Learning Center by Jere Bierhaus. We expect to have about one hundred points of total gain scores. We have observed that the lower pre-test scores show more gain during the ten weeks. This seminar taught by Jere started with lower pre-test scores than the research sample classes illustrated in the previous graph. Lower pre-test scores will tend to have higher gain scores while participating in the Ten-Week Seminar.

Fisher Divorce Adjustment Scale Profile
Pre- and Post-Test Average Scores for Forty Classes in Eight States

Name: _____ Identification Number: _____ Sex: _____

Age: _____ Months Separated: _____ Dumper, Dumpee, Mutual (Circle one)

> The higher your score, the more you approach the values at the top of the profile graph.
> The lower your score, the more you approach the values at the bottom of the profile graph.
> Further explanations of your scoring results are given on the reverse side of this page.

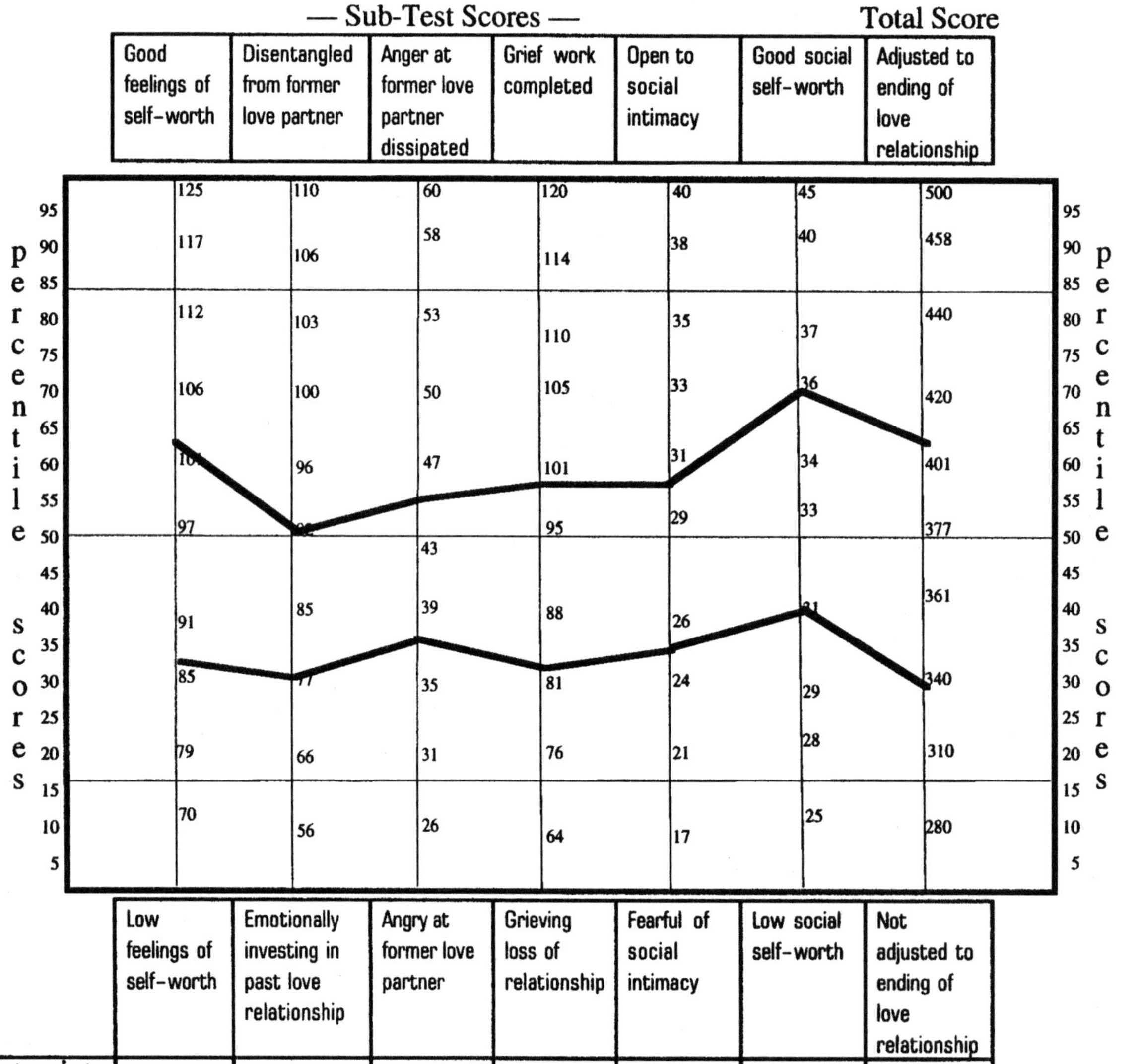

— Sub-Test Scores —   Total Score

	Good feelings of self-worth	Disentangled from former love partner	Anger at former love partner dissipated	Grief work completed	Open to social intimacy	Good social self-worth	Adjusted to ending of love relationship
95	125	110	60	120	40	45	500
90	117	106	58	114	38	40	458
80	112	103	53	110	35	37	440
70	106	100	50	105	33	36	420
60	10_	96	47	101	31	34	401
50	97	9_	43	95	29	33	377
45							361
40	91	85	39	88	26	31	
30	85	77	35	81	24	29	340
20	79	66	31	76	21	28	310
10	70	56	26	64	17	25	280

	Low feelings of self-worth	Emotionally investing in past love relationship	Angry at former love partner	Grieving loss of relationship	Fearful of social intimacy	Low social self-worth	Not adjusted to ending of love relationship
Post-Test points	102	92	45	100	30	36	405
Pre-Test points	87	77	37	82	25	31	339
Pre to post gain	15	15	8	18	5	5	66

The pre- and post-test point scores are obtained by counting the one through five marks on your FDAS answer sheet. These point scores are compared to a sample population group giving a percentile comparison score. The percentile scores listed on the sides of the above graph are rank order scores. If you scored 280 points on the total score, your percentile score would be 10. This means that out of every hundred people who took the FDAS, 10 would score lower than you and 80 would score higher than you. The total score is the most important score. The sub-test scores are interesting but not as significant statistically.

Fisher Divorce Adjustment Scale Profile
One Class Taught by Jere Bierhaus Showing Learning Center Seminar Gain Scores

Name: _____ Identification Number: _____ Sex: _____

Age: _____ Months Separated: _____ Dumper, Dumpee, Mutual (Circle one)

> The higher your score, the more you approach the values at the top of the profile graph.
> The lower your score, the more you approach the values at the bottom of the profile graph.
> Further explanations of your scoring results are given on the reverse side of this page.

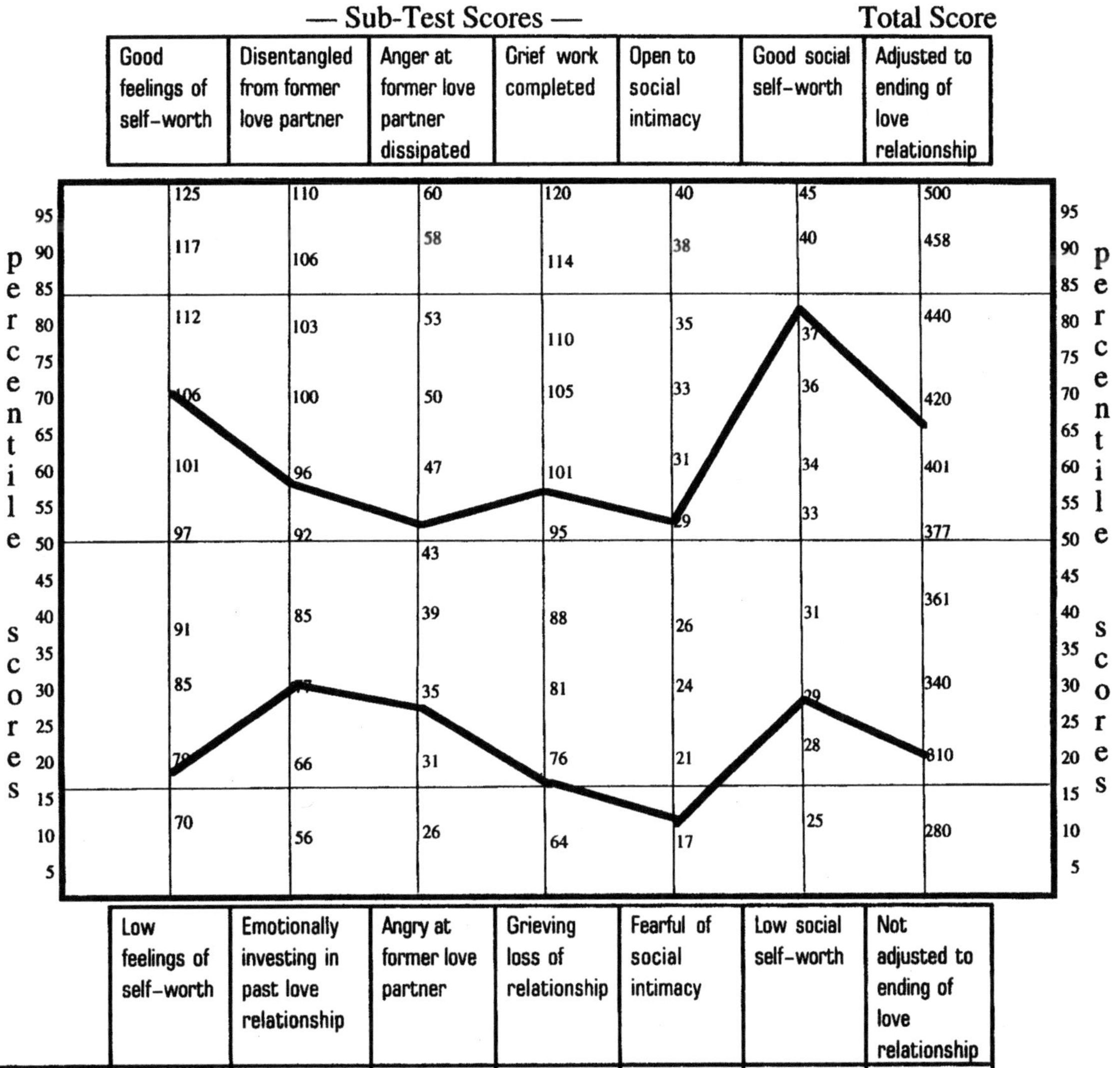

— Sub-Test Scores —   Total Score

	Good feelings of self-worth	Disentangled from former love partner	Anger at former love partner dissipated	Grief work completed	Open to social intimacy	Good social self-worth	Adjusted to ending of love relationship
95	125	110	60	120	40	45	500
90	117	106	58	114	38	40	458
85							
80	112	103	53	110	35	37	440
75							
70	106	100	50	105	33	36	420
65							
60	101	96	47	101	31	34	401
55						33	377
50	97	92		95	29		
45			43				
40	91	85	39	88	26	31	361
35							
30	85		35	81	24	29	340
25						28	
20	78	66	31	76	21		310
15							
10	70	56	26	64	17	25	280
5							

(percentile scores)

	Low feelings of self-worth	Emotionally investing in past love relationship	Angry at former love partner	Grieving loss of relationship	Fearful of social intimacy	Low social self-worth	Not adjusted to ending of love relationship
Post-Test points	106	95	44	99	29	38	411
Pre-Test points	78	77	34	74	18	29	310
Pre to post gain	28	22	10	25	11	9	101

The pre- and post-test point scores are obtained by counting the one through five marks on your FDAS answer sheet. These point scores are compared to a sample population group giving a percentile comparison score. The percentile scores listed on the sides of the above graph are rank order scores. If you scored 280 points on the total score, your percentile score would be 10. This means that out of every hundred people who took the FDAS, 10 would score lower than you and 80 would score higher than you. The total score is the most important score. The sub-test scores are interesting but not as significant statistically.

167

Female and Male Pre- and Post-Test Scoring Averages

Is there a difference between male and female scores for participants in the ten-week Seminars? Yes, there is. Males in this sample have lower pre-test scores but their gain score average in this graph is about one-third higher than females. In another research sample I completed, the male gain scores are one-half more than the female gain scores. The reasons for this are conjecture. 1) The lower the pre-test score, the more room there is to grow. 2) Many males may not have had an experience in a growth group situation before taking the Seminar and they respond by growing and adjusting a great deal.

Male scores are lower than females in disentanglement. Note in this graph they are lower both on the pre-test and the post-test. Again the reason for this is conjecture. Usually the male does not have another confidant person besides the love partner. They have lost both their lover and their confidant which makes their letting go of that person more difficult.

On the other hand, females score lower on the intimacy sub-test than males. Remember this subtest includes the new friends, trust, and sexuality blocks. Conjecture is that females are more cautious in becoming emotionally involved again after the relationship has ended.

Males are the darker lines in this graph.

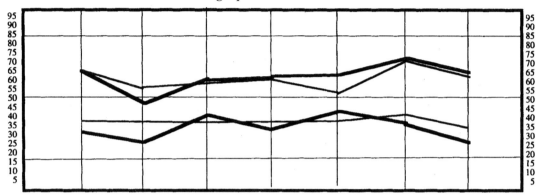

	Self–worth	Disentangled	Anger	Grief	Intimacy	Social	Total Score
Females post	102	93	45	100	29	36	405
Females pre	88	80	36	83	25	31	342
Pre to post gain	14	13	9	17	4	5	63

	Self–worth	Disentangled	Anger	Grief	Intimacy	Social	Total Score
Males post	102	88	46	101	31	36	405
Males pre	84	69	38	79	26	30	326
Pre to post gain	18	19	8	22	5	6	79

Dumper and Dumpee Average Profiles

Dumpers typically score higher than dumpees on personality tests. This indicates better emotional and psychological adjustment. However the differences in scores between the two groups become less after a longer period of separation. Dumpees have more difficulty disentangling and have more anger than dumpers. Those ending a relationship mutually tend to have scores like the dumpers. The darker line is for female dumpers, and the lighter line is for female dumpees.

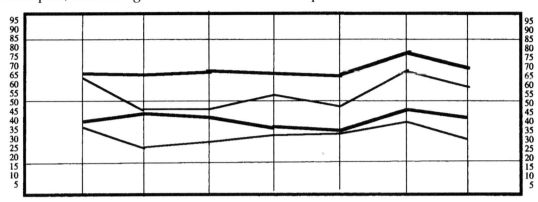

Dumpers	Self-worth	Disentangled	Anger	Grief	Intimacy	Social	Total Score
Females post	103	97	48	102	30	36	416
Females pre	90	88	39	87	25	32	362
Pre to post gain	13	9	9	15	5	4	54

Dumpees	Self-worth	Disentangled	Anger	Grief	Intimacy	Social	Total Score
Females post	102	88	46	101	31	36	405
Females pre	84	69	38	79	26	30	326
Pre to post gain	18	19	8	22	5	6	79

Different Age Groups Profile Scores

The participants in their fifties score much higher on the pre-test than those in their twenties. However, the twenty-year-olds have higher gain scores which makes their post-test scores about the same as the participants in their fifties. The darker line is for participants in their fifties, and the lighter is for participants in their twenties.

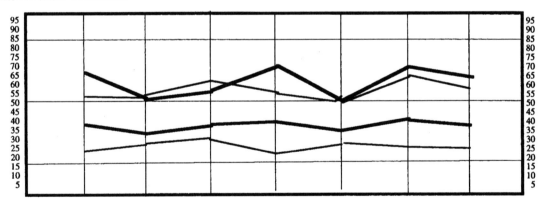

	Self-worth	Disentangled	Anger	Grief	Intimacy	Social	Total Score
Fifties post-test	104	92	45	104	28	36	409
Fifties pre-test	91	78	38	88	25	31	351
Pre to post gain	13	14	7	16	3	5	58

	Self-worth	Disentangled	Anger	Grief	Intimacy	Social	Total Score
Twenties post	98	92	46	97	28	35	395
Twenties pre	81	76	36	76	23	29	322
Pre to post gain	17	16	10	11	5	6	73

Separated Over Three Years vs. Separated Less than Six Months Profile Scores
Ten percent of the participants of the Seminar have been separated more than three years. They have a higher pre-test profile but the recently separated have higher gain scores so their post-test scores are almost as high as the longer separated group. The separated over three years are the darker line, and the lighter line is for those separated less than six months.

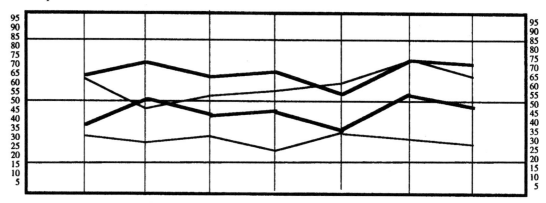

	Self-worth	Disentangled	Anger	Grief	Intimacy	Social	Total Score
3 years sep post	102	101	47	103	29	36	419
3 years sep pre	90	92	40	91	23	33	371
Pre to post gain	12	11	7	12	4	3	48

	Self-worth	Disentangled	Anger	Grief	Intimacy	Social	Total Score
0-6 Months post	102	89	44	99	30	36	400
0-6 Months pre	85	71	35	77	25	30	323
Pre to post gain	17	18	9	22	5	6	77

Representative Sample for Population Not Taking Seminar
The following profiles are for 474 people who have not participated in the Ten-Week Seminar, or in any other type of therapy or treatment. Sixteen percent of the scores are pre-test scores for Seminar Participants. There are 325 female (69%) and 149 male (31%).

Males score lower on disentanglement and social self-worth, and females score lower on intimacy. Male profile is the darker line, and female is the lighter line. The total profile line is not shown.

	Self-worth	Disentangled	Anger	Grief	Intimacy	Social	Total Score
Total Average	92	83	41	89	27	32	364
Female Average	92	84	40	89	26	32	363
Males Average	91	80	42	90	29	31	365

Female Dumpers, Dumpees, and Mutuals

The biggest difference between dumpers and dumpees is in the disentanglement sub-test. Dumpers have done more disentangling before they separated than dumpees. Note the female mutuals score much higher than female dumpers. Dumpers are the dark line, dumpees the medium line, and mutuals the lightest line.

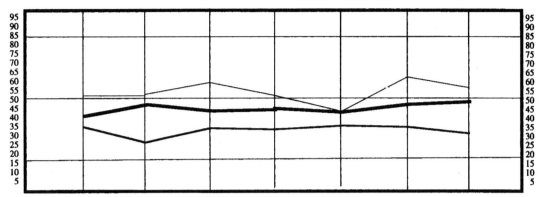

	Self-worth	Disentangled	Anger	Grief	Intimacy	Social	Total Score
Female mutuals	97	92	46	95	27	34	390
Female dumpers	93	91	40	91	27	32	375
Female dumpee	88	71	36	82	25	30	331

Male Dumpers, Dumpees, and Mutuals

The most obvious difference between this male profile and the previous female profile graph is that male mutuals score lower than male dumpers which is in contrast to female mutuals which score higher than dumpers. Male dumpers score higher than female dumpers. The difference between dumpers and dumpees on the male disentanglement subtest continues. Males continue to score higher on the intimacy subtest than females. The dark line is dumpers, the medium line is dumpees, and the lightest line is mutuals.

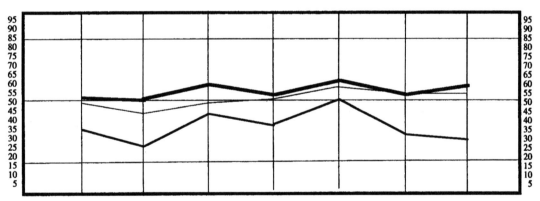

	Self-worth	Disentangled	Anger	Grief	Intimacy	Social	Total Score
Male mutuals	96	87	43	94	30	33	384
Male dumpers	97	91	46	97	31	33	394
Male dumpees	86	71	40	84	28	30	339

Separated 37+ and 0-6 Months
The conclusion might be made that scores on the FDAS correlate positively with length of separation. The dark line is for those separated more than 37 months, and the light line is for those separated less than six months. The profile for those separated more than three years is still at about the fifty percentile. We can conclude that many people in the general population have not adjusted to the ending of their love relationship even though they have been separated more than three years.

	Self-worth	Disentangled	Anger	Grief	Intimacy	Social	Total Score
Separated 37+	87	94	46	99	27	34	385
Separated 0-6	83	79	40	88	25	32	346

Profiles for Ending Marriage and Ending Living Together Love Relationships.
Those ending a living together love relationship scored lower than those ending a marriage. The sample number for living together is small with only 20 compared to 324 for ending a marriage. There is not much difference between the two profiles but it appears those ending a living together relationship are in more emotional pain than those ending a marriage. It is unknown whether those ending a living together relationship have already been divorced. Often the relationship after divorce is more painful when it ends than is the divorce. The dark line is for ending a marriage, and the light line is for ending a living together love relationship.

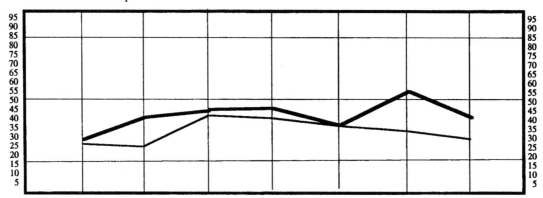

	Self-worth	Disentangled	Anger	Grief	Intimacy	Social	Total Score
Marriage	84	85	41	91	25	33	359
Living Together	83	70	38	86	25	31	331

Divorce Adjustment Goes Down After One or Both File for Divorce

The FDAS scores go down after one or both of the parties file for divorce, although the difference in scores is small. This is in spite of the fact that those filing have probably been separated longer which should increase their divorce adjustment scores. It is interesting that after filing the people score higher on disentanglement and lower on anger. Filing increases entanglement and decreases anger. The adversarial court process allows people to dissipate anger by attacking the other person. The dark line is for those who have filed, and the light line is for those who have not filed.

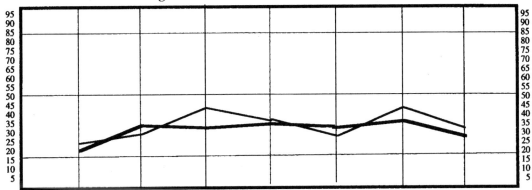

	Self-worth	Disentangled	Anger	Grief	Intimacy	Social	Total Score
Filed	79	79	36	85	24	31	335
Not filed	81	75	41	86	23	31	338

Net Income and Divorce Adjustment

Those with higher incomes score lower on the FDAS. Remember this research was done in 1980 when annual incomes were much lower. We can speculate those with more money have more to fight over, and have more money for the adversarial court process. There is probably a high correlation between the size of the divorce court file and the amount of annual income. The dark line is for those with more than $25,000 annual income, and the light line is for those with less than $5,000 annual income.

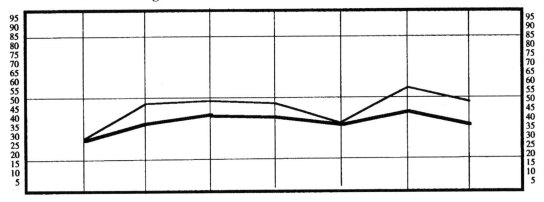

	Self-worth	Disentangled	Anger	Grief	Intimacy	Social	Total Score
Over $25,000	83	81	40	89	25	32	350
Less $5,000	85	88	43	92	25	33	366

Profiles for No Children and Two or More Children

Those with two or more children score lower on the FDAS than those with no children. It appears to make sense that divorce is more painful when there are children involved. The dark line is for those with no children, and the light line is for those with two or more children.

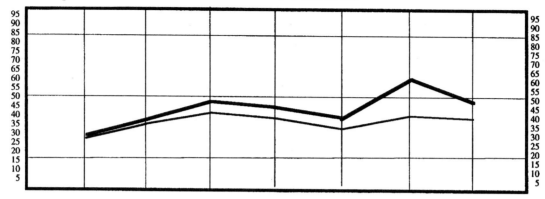

	Self-worth	Disentangled	Anger	Grief	Intimacy	Social	Total Score
No children	84	82	43	92	26	34	360
Two or more	83	82	40	88	25	31	349

Remarried vs Not in Relationship Profiles

The people who have remarried have higher adjustment scores than those who are not in a love relationship. The problem is I don't know how long they have been separated. We have to assume those not in relationship have been separated a much shorter period of time. The difference in these profiles probably has more to do with length of separation than whether the person is remarried. The dark line is for those remarried, and the light line is for those not in relationship.

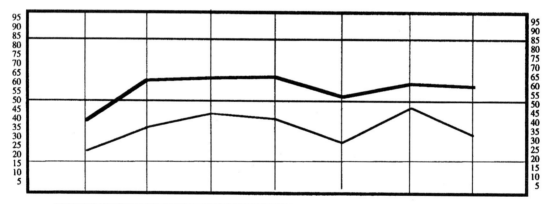

	Self-worth	Disentangled	Anger	Grief	Intimacy	Social	Total Score
Remarried	92	95	46	101	28	34	395
No relationship	81	80	40	87	24	32	345

Level of Education and FDAS Scores

Those with a graduate college degree have much higher FDAS scores than those with a high school education. Perhaps we should send our kids to Graduate School so they will have a less painful divorce! The dark line is for those with a graduate degree, and the light line is for those who are high school graduates.

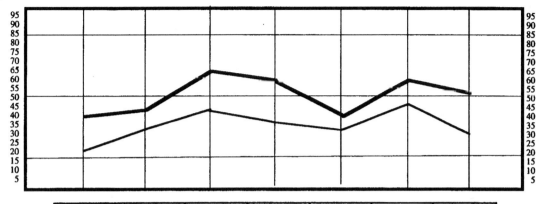

	Self-worth	Disentangled	Anger	Grief	Intimacy	Social	Total Score
Graduate	90	86	46	97	26	34	379
High school	79	79	39	85	24	32	337

Length of Time and Divorce Adjustment

Remember the profiles showing the adjustment for the various Rebuilding Blocks? Following are profiles for the various sub-tests showing scores for dumpers, dumpees, and mutuals. In this sample the mutuals have higher scores. Perhaps it is easier to divorce when the two people are working together at ending the relationship.

There is such a concept as dumper euphoria! Dumper's scores go down in the second period of six to twelve months separation. Dumpers are more unhappy in the marriage and often feel a sense of relief at the point of separation. However the grass may not be greener in the "Singles pasture," and after the original feelings of relief, which may include some denial of feelings, the hard reality of living as a single person sets in. Sometimes the dumper may have had another relationship at the point of separation, and these relationships usually are stressful and often end after a short period of time. The dark line is dumpers, the medium line is dumpees, and the light line is mutuals.

Self-Worth

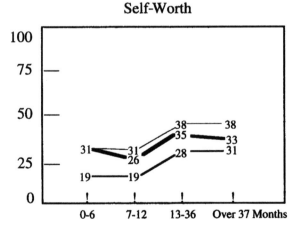

Dumper	85	83	88	86
Dumpee	78	78	83	85
Mutual	85	85	91	91

Disentanglement

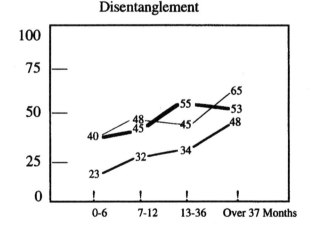

Dumper	86	89	94	93
Dumpee	69	78	80	90
Mutual	86	90	89	98

175

Anger

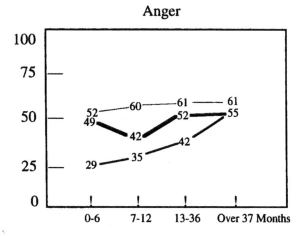

	0-6	7-12	13-36	Over 37
Dumper	43	40	44	45
Dumpee	35	37	40	45
Mutual	44	47	48	47

Grief

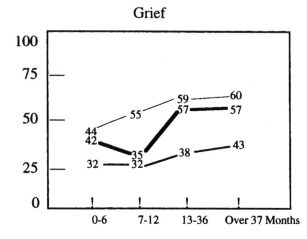

	0-6	7-12	13-36	Over 37
Dumper	91	86	99	99
Dumpee	82	82	88	92
Mutual	92	98	100	101

Intimacy

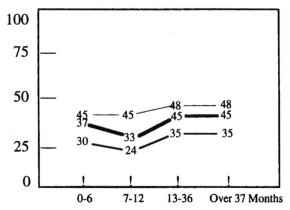

	0-6	7-12	13-36	Over 37
Dumper	26	25	28	28
Dumpee	24	22	25	25
Mutual	27	27	27	27

Social Self-Worth

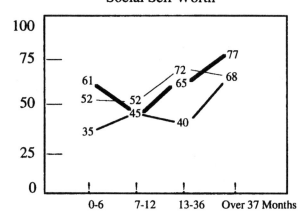

	0-6	7-12	13-36	Over 37
Dumper	34	32	35	37
Dumpee	30	32	31	35
Mutual	33	33	36	35

Total FDAS Score

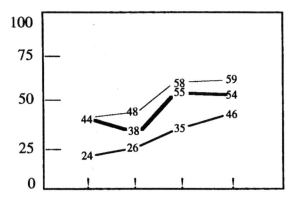

	0-6	7-12	13-36	Over 37
Dumper	365	355	380	379
Dumpee	320	328	350	370
Mutual	365	375	390	400

Rebuilding Blocks for Widows and Widowers

The following pages are a substitution for Chapter One in the *Rebuilding* textbook.

The purpose of this section is to provide some understanding into the unique issues affecting the widowed. The rebuilding concepts are translated into a language that fits better for widowed people.

Dumper and Dumpee for the Widowed

You may be saying or at least thinking, "What does dumper or dumpee have to do with me? I am widowed."

At first glance these terms do not seem to apply. The person you loved did not leave the relationship to continue with his or her life. Your love-partner left the relationship in one of two ways: Through sudden death or lingering illness. Remember that dumpers are those who begin to grieve before the end of the relationship. Dumpees begin the grieving when the relationship ends. Using these definitions it is possible to apply the terms to yourself.

A widow or widower whose spouse died quickly is forced to begin the grieving process and can feel emotionally numb at first. The full impact of what has happened is often not felt until after the funeral. In one sense, the widowed have been dumped on. That person did not choose the relationship's end. Therefore, the surviving spouse is similar to the dumpee in a divorce, experiencing many of the same thoughts and feelings, because the death occurred suddenly.

However, when the death is slow, its course over a period of time, the surviving spouse may experience more thoughts and feelings parallel to the dumper. Widows whose spouses die after a prolonged illness will be more likely to start the grieving process before the death of their loved one. They may react to the death of their spouse with relief. They will often appear to be coping well, but also have had more time to react to the situation because they started grieving at a different point in the relationship.

It is also possible you will have some combination of dumper and dumpee thoughts and feelings. You may not precisely fit into one of the categories. What is important is that you become aware of, and acknowledge, how you are experiencing your spouse's death. You may have conflicting feelings regarding how being widowed will impact your life. You may have some underlying judgments regarding those feelings which hinder you from fully embracing what you are experiencing.

The following is an attempt to translate the rebuilding blocks into a more meaningful exploration of the issues directly impacting your life.

Denial

Denial is an emotional safety valve. When faced with something physically painful the body will try to compensate, and in severe pain, will cause unconsciousness. Emotions can respond to pain in a similar way.

For dumpees, denial is reflected in statements like: "This can't be happening to me," "This is a sick joke, it can't be true." In extreme cases denial may include clinging to the delusion that the spouse will return. You may have said to yourself, "When I go home today my wife will be in the kitchen like she always is cooking dinner", or "If I just wait long enough he'll be back."

Dumpers also experience denial, but usually before the actual death. Denial for you occurs when you first hear the news that your spouse is dying. "He isn't really dying," or "Medicine will find a cure," are statements which may indicate denial. It may be difficult to distinguish between denial and hope. However, an unwillingness to even acknowledge the possibility of death is a strong sign you may be struggling with denial. The important thing to remember about this stage is that it occurs very strongly at first and does not fade entirely until the grieving process is well underway.

Fear

This may be your most predominant emotion. It is one of the reasons for denial; facing the fears seems like too much to bear. There are two primary categories of fears you may experience: 1) Fear of dying, and 2) Fear of living. When your spouse died you came closer than ever to your own mortality. Many people avoid facing the prospect that death is inevitable. When your spouse died your own underlying fear that you too will die may have surfaced. This is especially true if your spouse died suddenly. You may also fear dying because your spouse is no longer available to meet your needs or take care of you. Many were totally dependent in some way upon their spouses. "What's going to happen to me now?" is a common fear.

The fear of living may take on any of a number of faces. You may fear all the lifestyle adjustments and new choices. You may fear your own feelings and thoughts related to your spouse's death, especially if you experienced some relief- which is likely to be true when death occurs over a period of time.

Adaptation

We live in a couple's world. None of us planned that when we pledged, "till death do us part," we would actually see the end of our marriage. Oh, we knew that we would not live forever, but we never consciously thought that our spouse would die. Well, yours did, and here you are, still alive, left to make a thousand adjustments. The first one being dealing with the fact you are single.

You may resist accepting the fact that you are single. What if someone asks you out on a date. That would be absolutely terrifying. All the dynamics of potentially starting a new relationship may seem so complicated. Stepping into the unknown of meeting another person is one of the major adjustments of being widowed. The longer the marriage the more difficult this prospect may be. You may cling to an image of your love-partner, and may have an even more idealized image now that your partner is dead.

It may sound cruel, but the death of your spouse is an opportunity for self-examination. How do you view yourself, life, and others? In which areas have you fallen into a rut or become stagnant? The death of your spouse is a way for you to examine any places where you have taken life for granted.

This time is also an opportunity to consider why you got married in the first place. Did you experience a successful, full, interactive relationship? Were you satisfied with the nature and dynamics of the relationship. As you adjust to singleness, introspection is an option for increasing present awareness, and future freedom.

Loneliness

You may be feeling the loneliest you've ever felt. It's painful to live with the knowledge that our spouse is not going to laugh at our jokes, or be there for us when we cry. You may have had a time apart before, such as a vacation, business trip, or hospitalization, but not have experienced this depth of loneliness. Now that the relationship has permanently ended, the other person is no longer there, and you feel totally alone.

That loneliness is magnified by the question, "Am I going to be lonely like this forever?" You begin to wonder if you'll ever have the companionship of a love-relationship again. Even with the comfort and encouragement of children or friends, this feeling can be overwhelming.

You may have felt lonely while in the relationship, especially if your spouse was in the hospital or diagnosed with a terminal illness. That form of loneliness is a special kind of pain, and the death of your spouse may actually ease some of that burden.

Socially, you might isolate yourself. You feel like the third wheel on a bicycle — not really fitting in— not needed. You can imagine that everyone is talking about you, while privately you wonder who really cares about your pain. When someone asks you about your dead spouse you don't know whether to be offended, cry, or just walk away.

You may even try to escape the feelings of loneliness by being in a crowd or constantly having people around you, while still feeling lonely. You may seek relief by becoming super busy, doing anything to escape being home alone. You may find people to go out with just to keep from being alone, even if you don't enjoy the other person's company. Sometimes anything is better than being home alone with all those feelings and memories.

As time goes on you will move beyond loneliness into accepting your *aloneness.* Aloneness is the process of becoming comfortable with yourself. It involves a willingness to stop running from the pain, and accepting all aspects of who you are during this time. It also means realizing there is a uniqueness to your experience that others may not be able to share in or fully understand.

To reach this point we have to realize that the fear of being alone is much worse than actually being alone. When we experience being alone we discover resources we never knew we had. We also learn to gather the resources we need but don't have. We then are able to accept that aloneness is part of the human condition.

Being alone can become a way of healing ourselves. You need time to be introspective and reflective, to reconnect with disowned thoughts and feelings. Through reclaiming feelings and thoughts you come to realize that you are not empty, but rather full, when alone. This inner fullness comes when you allow yourself to grow and develop, reaching a point of comfort when not in the company of others. Eventually, you will reach the point of understanding that being with another person to escape aloneness is destructive and painful. Learning what you need for healing- so that you can choose to enter into relationships rather than needing one to escape loneliness- is one of your greatest challenges.

Friendship

When we experience pain, especially emotional pain, it is often helpful to share that pain with friends. It is not that they can remedy our pain, but the act of sharing seems to lessen the burden. Unfortunately, many of the friends we had while married will no longer be with us now that we are single. There are three reasons why you may experience the loss of friends. The first is, as a single, you may be seen as a threat to your married friends, as you are now an eligible love-object. If their relationship is not secure, you may pose a threat. It is also threatening to others to acknowledge that one's partner is mortal. Since your partner has died you are a reminder of this fact. Another reason is that since you are now single you have become, regardless of your willingness to accept it, a member of a different subculture— that of being a single adult. It may be more difficult for you to relate to your married friends. If you want to keep your friends you must remember that the similarities of your past are now differences. Other similarities will have to be strengthened. Also, you may want to reach out to others who are in a similar situation, that of being singled again, as they have similar circumstances you can relate to.

Rejection and Guilt

It may not sound rational, but you can feel rejection because you are still alive. We may feel that our spouse chose death, rather than to live with us. This is a normal thought, and part of the grieving process. However, rejection implies there is something wrong with you. You may begin searching for some imagined defect in your personality. What is so terrible about you that your partner would choose death rather than life with you? Perhaps you feel guilty because you did not express your feelings of love often enough. Another cause for guilt is surviving, or moving on with your life. You can feel guilty because you did not want to be left alone; even if it meant your spouse suffered. If your spouse was experiencing pain, you may feel guilty because of your relief from the stress of watching a loved one suffer.

This is not all negative. If, when looking at your own behavior, you find that it causes difficulty in your interactions with others, you can change that. The goal of working through this process is to be able to see yourself as a loving and beautiful person, and to come to appreciate yourself as if you are your own best friend.

Guilt is not entirely useless. It helps us realize we have not lived up to our own standards. However, excessive guilt is destructive. When we live our lives as "ought to's," "should haves," or "could have been," we are not able to live life fully. We end up becoming inhibited and controlled. If you have not lived up to realistic expectations, you may need to make amends (if possible), and change the behavior in the future. If the guilt you feel is based on an unrealistic expectation you need to remind yourself that you did the best with what you had at the time. The goal here is to be able to look rationally at your guilt and see if it is appropriate. To feel guilty because we want to go on with our lives, or that we prayed for the suffering of our loved one to end, is normal. However, to feel guilty because you didn't prevent your spouse's death is being unfair to yourself.

Grief

People experience the stages of grieving in many different ways. However, some patterns do emerge, regardless of whether one is a dumper or dumpee. You will most likely experience denial, bargaining, anger, depression, and eventually acceptance.

Grief is an important part of the healing process once your partner has died. The death of your spouse included a funeral, burial, and the surrounding of friends and relatives. However, the grief process is not something that has a time limit. People, who are well intentioned, will say, "Isn't it time for you to move on with your life? It has been X number of months." What they don't realize is that we need to grieve in order to say good-bye to the relationship and that we have to say good-bye not only to our spouse, but also our way of life. We often limit ourselves by not allowing ourselves to cry and feel the pain. Unfortunately, this only forestalls the grieving process, it doesn't put it aside. We need to acknowledge the pain and the loss of control in our lives. Only then are we able to move on with our lives.

There are two different faces to the bargaining phase of the grief process. For dumpers, it often takes the form of, "I'd do anything to prevent this from happening to my love partner." For dumpees, it may mean attending church to guarantee safe passage for your loved one or a willingness to give anything to ensure that the pain will be less. Bargaining can be helpful. Many people come to support groups in an effort to bargain away their grief. In these cases, the person grieving will try to get into another relationship to shortcut the pain and insecurity of being alone. It should be stressed that if you are hurting from a past relationship you will not be able to dedicate the needed time and energy to create an authentic intimate relationship..

The depression stage usually lasts one day longer than we thought we could stand. We spend so much of our energy being concerned with our love partner that when we do not have access to that partner it hurts. You may have the sensation that everything you touch dies. This is not the case, but the feelings of depression still need to be examined and dealt with. Some people argue that depression is anger that has no external outlet. Whatever the cause, it is important to realize that others have, or are experiencing, the same emotion.

When you finally stop asking the question, "Why did my spouse have to die?" the process of acceptance is well underway. The emotional pain of separation does lessen over time. Hopefully, the pain you are experiencing will enable you to learn who you are and to reach out toward a full and enriching experience. Acceptance is funny because we don't know we have it until we are confronted by either our past or someone else's pain. Acceptance can be achieved partially and can slip away when we have uncovered some painful feelings from our past. When acceptance does slip from us it is often an indicator that we are needing more self-discovery and personal growth.

Anger

Anger is a natural part of the grieving and therefore, healing, process. You may have many targets for your anger. God is often a good target, because He took your love partner away. You might feel angry with your dead spouse for leaving you, or friends and clergy for not realizing your emotional pain. Even those who understand, or are willing to help, may become targets of your anger. You may also feel angry at yourself because your emotional upheaval makes it difficult to go on with life.

Anger is a feeling, and feelings are a part of life. You may be tempted to deny or suppress your anger. However, anger can be very constructive as a positive energy force because it leads you to acknowledge your humanness and the humanness of others. As you work through your anger you begin to experience feelings of peace, and of letting go of what you could not, and cannot, control.

Letting Go

This difficult and painful process is about releasing our emotional ties with our former spouse. At some point your heart releases all the rights and privileges of being married to your spouse. Your mind declares that it is time to go on with what you still do have, as your focus moves away from what was, toward what can be.

An example of someone who has not disentangled from her past is a widow who still wears her wedding band or refers to herself as Mrs. John Doe, where John is the name of her dead spouse. A part of you may resist the disentanglement process. You may experience anger or guilt as you attempt to let go.

This final stage of the grieving process can be much easier if you have, or develop, other interests such as a job or hobby, and you maintain a good support system. To help you disentangle it is suggested you move the bedroom furniture, put away personal belongings of your dead spouse, and experiment with some small changes in your life. Later, when you have fewer emotional ties to your past you can revisit those items you have put away. However, you may want to have a friend nearby when you journey back into those memories.

Self-Worth

Your self-concept may be at an all-time low when your love-relationship ends. So much of your personality was invested into the relationship it is devastating to face the empty place in your identity. All too often we thought of ourselves only in terms of the relationship. When we used to introduce ourselves to others we often referred to ourselves as the spouse of... When we weren't with our mates others would jokingly ask, "Where's your better half?"

Dr. Fisher found that it's common for people to have a low self-image immediately following the loss of a love relationship. He argues that our self-image is a learned attitude. The way we refer to ourselves as spouse of, children of, or parents of, gives us a sense of identity. When you are widowed you lose that identification. If your self-esteem has dropped, and remains low, the grieving process can become even more difficult.

Transition

You are in the midst of perhaps the greatest transition of your life. What makes it even more difficult is that it wasn't one that you chose. In all aspects of your life you are moving from a lifestyle of marriage toward becoming single.

Beneath this surface transition may be an even larger one — a transition from unconscious influences over your life into a new freedom. With your spouse no longer a part of your life, you may begin to evaluate many of the choices you made in your marriage, including the motivations behind those choices. You may experience a new awareness of how leftovers from your past may be still influencing your life.

Openness

This refers to your willingness to drop your guard, a willingness to pursue intimacy with another person. The thought of becoming vulnerable to another may stir up feelings of fear and guilt. You may have created masks to keep people from knowing your pain in the grieving process. Perhaps you have hidden behind masks your entire life. Taking the chance to let someone "in" may seem too risky.

There are many masks you might take on to protect yourself during this time. One common one is the "Merry Widowed." Everything is seen in a positive light, all pain is covered up. Another mask is the "Busy Beaver," which refers to the widowed who preoccupies themselves with only logistical details. This mask means keeping conversations on the surface. There are many different masks. Have you adopted a mask to help cope with the pain and uncertainty of this time?

Masks are not always bad. They are often necessary for surviving difficult circumstances, such as losing a spouse to death. However, there comes a time when the energy required to maintain the mask hinders personal growth and the potential for intimacy. At that point the mask is a burden. You will need to decide when the time is right to begin letting others see beyond your mask. Try writing down the masks you use to protect yourself. Which, if any, developed as a result of your spouse's death? What feelings does each mask hide or protect? Which would you like to let go of?

Love

Typically we define love only in terms of some external object, usually a person. However, the beginning point of true love is with yourself. You may discover some parts of yourself you consider unacceptable; grieving has a way of exposing deeper parts of our being. Learning to embrace those parts is the beginning point of loving others. How can you love others if you don't love yourself?

You have lost the one person toward whom you directed your love. Now you may feel lost trying to direct that same love inward. Perhaps you have not experienced the beauty of that type of acceptance from another person, making it even more difficult to give it to yourself. Yet, this time can become an opportunity to appreciate the unique person you are. In the midst of caring for yourself, you may begin to discover the desire to experience love again with another. You may find it difficult to avoid comparing potential future partners to your former spouse. You may wish to find someone to replace your spouse. While the desire is understandable, it is not possible. However, experiencing intimacy is.

Trust

You may be thinking to yourself, "Don't love others; they can die on you." Then you get past this thought and those who may be available just don't measure up. What's happening is you might be making yourself unavailable so you don't have to be hurt. Being with others requires that we share ourselves. When we trust, we expose ourselves to pain. However, if we don't trust, we merely exist and fail to live life. We lived, our spouses died, and yet if we fail to get involved in life we are the one who is acting emotionally dead. The lack of trust is not necessarily a bad thing, but failure to trust anyone including ourselves, causes pain, doubt, and fear that only we can feel.

Relatedness

As you continue along the "climb," as Dr. Fisher refers to the healing process you are in, you may find others to connect with along the way. It is not uncommon for the widowed to seek out someone else from whom they can receive comfort, support, and encouragement. These "growing" relationships are not necessarily romantic, and often are not permanent.

Sexuality

When you were married you knew what to expect sexually from your love-partner. You may not have always had your needs met or felt satisfied in this area of the relationship, but what you did have was familiar. For some, the thought of entering a sexual relationship may be exciting. For many however, the unknown variables make this stressful.

You are also faced with a new set of choices. What are your values around sex? Losing our love-partner creates the need for sexual fulfillment and exposes the fears we have in becoming intimate with another person. You may even feel guilty for being sexually attracted to someone new.

Singleness

Earlier in the grieving process you may have felt you could not live without another love relationship. When you get to the point of saying, "I am content being single," then you reach a stage of personal satisfaction. This doesn't mean you will be single for the rest of your life, but it does mean you have accepted your aloneness.

If most of your identity revolved around being related to your former spouse, singleness may at first feel like failure. Something inside you may say, "I'm only OK if I'm married." Although this is a difficult belief to change, it is possible for you to renew your view of yourself. This renewal is an awakening, or an understanding that your value as a human being does not come from being related to another person. You are valuable even if you are alone. In your marriage or family of origin you may either have not felt valued, or somehow along the way of bonding, given up your value. Now you have an opportunity to reclaim what is rightfully yours.

Purpose

This exciting time signals that you are nearing the end of the grieving process. You begin to feel alive as if for the first time. You may be opening up to experiences which before were taken for granted or simply neglected, because you were immersed in the pain of losing your spouse.

During this period you stop defining your life in the context of your former marriage. Purpose begins to develop based upon your needs, perceptions, and goals. This may be a time to evaluate the direction your life has been going and decide if its the path you really want. You also begin living more in the present, letting go of the past, while planning ahead for the future.

Freedom

Freedom is about fully being yourself. It is accepting, and acting upon, an integration of your various personality parts. You are free to feel, to think, and to relate. Assuming you are successful in resolving the former building blocks, you are now free to become the person you want to be. You realize that relationships can be your teachers, and that connecting to others means reconnecting with yourself. You have climbed the mountain and are now ready to move on with your life. You have grieved the loss of your former love partner, and are now open to experiencing intimacy with others. Congratulations

This section for the widowed was written and compiled by Nelse Grundvig from Bismark, North Dakota, and Robert Stewart from Denver, Colorado. Thank you Nelse and Robert for an important contribution which allows widowed people to participate and have a more positive experience in the Rebuilding class.

Fisher Widowed and Widowers Adjustment Scale

The following statements are feelings and attitudes that people frequently experience after a love-relationship has ended. Read each statement. Decide how frequently the statement applies to your present feelings and attitudes. Mark your response on your answer sheet. If a statement is not appropriate, try to imagine how you would respond if the statement was appropriate.

The five responses to choose from on the answer sheet are:
(1) almost always **(2)** usually **(3)** sometimes **(4)** seldom **(5)** almost never

1. I am comfortable telling people my love-partner (spouse) has died.

2. I am physically and emotionally exhausted from morning until night.

3. I am constantly thinking of my former love-partner.

4. I feel rejected by many of the friends I had when I was in the love-relationship.

5. I become upset when I think about my former love-partner.

6. I like being the person I am.

7. I feel like crying because I feel so sad.

8. I can calmly talk to God about being alone.

9. There are many things about my personality I would like to change.

10. It is easy for me to accept my becoming a single person.

11. I feel depressed.

12. I feel emotionally separated from my former love-partner.

13. People would not like me if you got to know me.

14. I feel comfortable visiting my former love-partner's gravesite.

15. I feel like I am an attractive person.

16. I feel as though I am in a daze and the world doesn't seem real.

17. I find myself doing things just because my former love-partner would have liked my doing those things.

18. I feel lonely.

19. There are many things about my body I would like to change.

20. I have many plans and goals for the future.

21. I feel I don't have much sex appeal.

22. I am relating and interacting in many new ways with people since my partner's death.

23. Joining a singles' group would make me feel I was a loser like them.

24. It is easy for me to organize my daily routine of living.

25. I find myself talking about my former love-partner all the time.

26. Because my love-partner is dead, I must not enjoy life.

27. I wish I could unload my feelings of anger and pain on my former love-partner.

28. I feel comfortable being with people.

29. I have trouble concentrating.

30. I think of my former love-partner as a part of me rather than as a separate person.

31. I feel like an okay person.

32. I wish my former love-partner could feel the emotional pain I'm feeling.

33. I have close friends who know and understand me.

34. I am unable to control my emotions.

35. I feel capable of building a deep and meaningful love-relationship.

36. I have trouble sleeping.

37. I easily become angry at my former love-partner.

38. I am afraid to trust people who might become love-partners.

39. Because my love-partner died, I feel I am being punished.

40. I either have no appetite or eat continuously, which is unusual for me.

41. I don't want to accept that my love-partner has died.

42. I force myself to eat even though I'm not hungry.

43. I've decided to join the living; my dead love-partner can no longer satisfy my needs.

44. I feel very frightened inside.

45. It is important that my family, friends, and associates share my feelings about my former love-partner.

46. I feel uncomfortable even thinking about dating.

47. I feel capable of living the kind of life I would like to live.

48. I have noticed my body weight is changing a great deal.

49. I often feel that if I had prayed harder or done things right, my love-partner wouldn't have died.

50. My abdomen feels empty and hollow.

51. I have feelings of romantic love for my deceased love-partner.

52. I can make the decisions I need to because I know and trust my feelings.

53. I sometimes wish my dead partner was alive and I were dead so that he/she could know what it is like to hurt this way.

54. I avoid people even though I want and need friends.

55. I have really made a mess of my life.

56. I sigh a lot.

57. I believe I have accepted the death of my spouse.

58. I perform daily activities in a mechanical and unfeeling manner.

59. I become upset when I think of my dead spouse having a peace I cannot share.

60. I feel capable of dealing with my problems.

61. I blame my former love-partner for dying on me.

62. I am afraid of becoming sexually involved with another person.

63. I feel adequate as a love-partner.

64. I often think about the day I will be able to join my dead partner.

65. I feel detached and removed from activities around me as though I were watching a movie screen.

66. I often imagine having sex with my former love-partner.

67. Life is somehow passing me by.

68. I feel comfortable going by myself to public places such as a movie.

69. It is good to feel alive again after having felt numb and emotionally dead.

70. I feel I know and understand myself.

71. I still feel emotionally committed to my former love-partner.

72. I want to be with people but I feel emotionally distant.

73. I am the type of person I would like to have for a friend.

74. I am afraid of becoming emotionally close to another love-partner.

75. Even on the days when I am feeling good I may suddenly become sad and start crying.

76. I can't believe my partner has died.

77. I become upset when I think my dead partner can no longer share my feelings or my life.

78. I feel I have a normal amount of self-confidence.

79. People seem to enjoy being with me.

80. I feel I can never again give myself permission to be in love.

81. I wake up in the morning feeling there is no good reason for me to get out of bed.

82. I find myself daydreaming about all the good times I had with my love-partner.

83. People want to have a love-relationship with me because I feel like a lovable person.

84. If it were possible, I'd get satisfaction out of letting my dead partner know how much I'm hurting.

85. I feel comfortable going to social events even though I'm single.

86. I feel guilty about my being alive when my love-partner is dead.

87. I feel emotionally insecure.

88. I feel uncomfortable even thinking about having a sexual relationship.

89. I feel emotionally weak and helpless.

90. I think about ending my life with suicide.

91. I no longer feel the need to understand why my partner died.

92. I feel comfortable that my friends know my partner died.

93. I am angry at my former partner because I am left alone.

94. I feel like I am going crazy.

95. I am unable to perform sexually.

96. I feel as though I am the only single person in a couple's society.

97. I feel like a single person rather than a married wo/man.

98. I feel my friends look at me as unstable now that I'm single.

99. I daydream about being with and talking to my former love-partner.

100. I need to improve my feelings of self-worth about being a wo/man.

Note: The scoring results of this questionnaire are not statistically accurate. This scale has not been normed and standardized.

This adjustment Scale for the widowed and widowers was done in part by Nelse Grundvig of Bismark, North Dakota.
Thank you Nelse for an important contribution which allows widowed people to assess their process.

Fisher Widowed and Widowers Adjustment Scale **Answer Sheet**

First name   Last name

Address   City   State   Zip

Home phone   Work phone   Date

I am ___ male ___ female.   I am _____ years old   I have been separated _____ months

Who decided to end my relationship? ___ I did ___ my spouse did ___ both of us did ___ widowed

Please fill in the following circles to answer the questions on the *Fisher Divorce Adjustment Scale.*
The five responses to choose from are:

1) almost always	2) usually	3) sometimes	4) seldom	5) almost never
1 2 3 4 5	1 2 3 4 5	1 2 3 4 5	1 2 3 4 5

	1 2 3 4 5		1 2 3 4 5		1 2 3 4 5		1 2 3 4 5
1.	O O O O O	26.	O O O O O	51.	O O O O O	76.	O O O O O
2.	O O O O O	27.	O O O O O	52.	O O O O O	77.	O O O O O
3.	O O O O O	28.	O O O O O	53.	O O O O O	78.	O O O O O
4.	O O O O O	29.	O O O O O	54.	O O O O O	79.	O O O O O
5	O O O O O	30.	O O O O O	55.	O O O O O	80.	O O O O O
6.	O O O O O	31.	O O O O O	56.	O O O O O	81.	O O O O O
7.	O O O O O	32.	O O O O O	57.	O O O O O	82.	O O O O O
8.	O O O O O	33.	O O O O O	58.	O O O O O	83.	O O O O O
9.	O O O O O	34.	O O O O O	59.	O O O O O	84.	O O O O O
10.	O O O O O	35.	O O O O O	60.	O O O O O	85.	O O O O O
11.	O O O O O	36.	O O O O O	61.	O O O O O	86.	O O O O O
12.	O O O O O	37.	O O O O O	62.	O O O O O	87.	O O O O O
13.	O O O O O	38.	O O O O O	63.	O O O O O	88.	O O O O O
14.	O O O O O	39.	O O O O O	64.	O O O O O	89.	O O O O O
15.	O O O O O	40.	O O O O O	65.	O O O O O	90.	O O O O O
16.	O O O O O	41.	O O O O O	66.	O O O O O	91.	O O O O O
17.	O O O O O	42.	O O O O O	67.	O O O O O	92.	O O O O O
18.	O O O O O	43.	O O O O O	68.	O O O O O	93.	O O O O O
19.	O O O O O	44.	O O O O O	69.	O O O O O	94.	O O O O O
20.	O O O O O	45.	O O O O O	70	O O O O O	95.	O O O O O
21.	O O O O O	46.	O O O O O	71.	O O O O O	96.	O O O O O
22.	O O O O O	47.	O O O O O	72.	O O O O O	97.	O O O O O
23.	O O O O O	48.	O O O O O	73.	O O O O O	98.	O O O O O
24.	O O O O O	49.	O O O O O	74.	O O O O O	99.	O O O O O
25.	O O O O O	50.	O O O O O	75.	O O O O O	100.	O O O O O

Note: If you copy this answer sheet on a copy machine, make sure the copy is exactly the same
spacing as the original if you want to hand score the answers using the transparencies.

Appendix A
Rebuilding for Kids Seminar

Purpose:
This seminar is designed to help parents and children begin talking together about issues the children are experiencing related to separation or divorce. It's is an opportunity for children and parents to bond in a new way, taking their mutual crisis and turning it into something that brings them closer together. The unique focus of this seminar is in bringing the parents and children together so rather than being an endpoint for the children, the seminar becomes a new beginning for the children to work with their parents through the rebuilding process.

Children's healing process is intricately woven into the fabric of their parent's healing process. The children can be helped, but what they receive will be impacted by their parent's level of understanding, awareness, and ability to meet their needs. Rebuilding for Kids is designed to encourage the parents to grow along with their children.

The educational model is a new paradigm of help for adults. Now it's time to use this model in our work with children. Parents are wanting information, guidance, and support so they can learn to make loving choices for themselves and their children.

Goals for Parents:
1. To gain an understanding of the "Rebuilding" issues for children.
2. To develop active listening skills.
3. To learn to facilitate discussions with their children related to the rebuilding issues.
4. To make a commitment to listen to their children without trying to change or control what they are experiencing.

Goals for Children:
1. To understand what they are experiencing related to the divorce or separation.
2. To feel safe discussing issues and feelings.
3. To have an opportunity to share what is happening for them.
4. To learn about changing stumbling blocks into rebuilding blocks.
5. To make a commitment to continue talking with their parents about what they are experiencing.

Stumbling blocks children need to work through:
1. It's my fault my parents got divorced.
2. I wish my parents would get back together.
3. I have all these different feelings stuck inside me.
4. I don't understand all the changes happening around me.
5. I don't have a family anymore.
6. I don't want my mom or dad to meet anyone else.

Stumbling blocks transformed into Rebuilding blocks:
1. My parents' divorce is their responsibility.
2. I'm accepting my parents won't get back together.
3. I'm aware of my feelings and can talk about them.
4. I'm learning how to handle the changes I'm experiencing.
5. I still have a mom and dad who care about me.
6. I can be a part of two families.

Appendix B
National Support Organizations

Rebuilding Seminars
For a list of Rebuilding Seminars online, go to rebuilding.org

American Fathers Coalition
2000 Pennsylvania Ave. NW, Ste. 148
Washington, DC. 20002
1-800-787-kids

Fathers Without Custody
PO Box 3075
Santa Monica, CA 90403

Grief Education Institute
1780 South Bellair Street, Suite 132
Denver, CO 80222
303-758-6048
　　　Since 1976 this agency has been providing help for both lay people and professionals in dealing with grief. Resources include Leadership Manual for Bereavement Support Groups.

National Organization for Single Mothers
Andrea Engber, Director
PO Box 68
Midland, NC 28107
704-888-2337 fax 704-888-1752
　　　The National Organization of Single Mothers is a non-profit corporation committed to helping single mothers meet the challenge of daily life with wisdom, dignity, and courage, and humor through its bi-monthly publication Single MOTHER, and by helping to establish nationwide self-help groups.

Parents Without Partners Inc.
1650 South Dixie Highway, Ste. 510
Boca Raton, FL 33432
561-391-8833
　　　This group is international with an emphasis upon emotional support. The National Magazine is excellent.

Beginning Experience International Ministry Center
1657 Commerce Drive, Ste. 2B
South Bend, IN 46628
866-810-8877 or 574-283-0279
Fax 574-283-0287
imc@beginningexperience.org
　　　This group was started in October of 1974. The local chapters need to be sponsored by a Christian Church. The local chapters offer growth groups in addition to support. BE has Chapters all over the United States and in many foreign countries.

Fathers For Equal Rights
1210 East Colfax Avenue
Denver, CO
831-7853

Single Mothers by Choice
212-988-0993

Mothers Without Custody
PO Box 56762
Houston, TX 77227-7418
1-800457-MWOC
　　　Purpose statement: To enhance the quality of life for our children by strengthening the role of the non-custodial parent in regard to custody, child support, visitation, and parenting.

North American Conference Separated and Divorced Catholics, Central Office
P.O. Box 360
Richland, OR 97870
541-893-6089
www.NACSDC.org
　　　This group offers emotional support with some growth groups. The local chapters are usually in a Roman Catholic Church.

Stepfamily Association of America, Inc.
650 J Street, Ste. 205
Lincoln, NE 68508
1-800-736-0329
www.saafamilies.org
　　　SAA was started in 1979 to meet the special needs of Stepfamilies. They provide manuals for starting local Stepfamily chapters, and a catalogue of excellent books available.

Bibliography

The Divorce Process

**Bloomfield, H. Colgrove, M. & McWilliams, P. (1993) *How to Survive the Loss of a Love.*
Los Angeles, CA: Prelude Press.
This book is easy to read early in the process. It is comforting and very helpful.

Larson, S. & Larson, H. (1993) *Suddenly Single: A Lifeline For Anyone Who Has Lost a Love.* San Francisco, CA:
Halo Books.
Focuses on the trauma of losing a loved one from death, separation, or break-up.

*Powell, J. (1996) *Why Am I Afraid to Tell You Who I Am ?* Allen, TX: Thomas Moore.
The divorce process encourages us to become open and vulnerable as part of our healing.

Wegscheider-Cruse, S. (1994) *Life After Divorce.* Deerfield Beach, FL: Health Communications.
Shows how the trauma of divorce can lead to growth and the promise of a new life.

Wilson, C.A. & Schilling, E. (1995) *Survival Manual for Men in Divorce: Straight-forward Answers About Your
Rights.* Kendall/Hunt Publishing Company.
Helpful financial help for men divorcing.

Adaptation

Abrams, J. (1990) *Reclaiming the Inner Child.* Los Angeles, CA: The Putnam Publishing Group.
A compilation of many different writers on the concept of the inner-child.

Bradshaw, J. (1990) *Homecoming: Reclaiming and Championing Your Inner Child.* New York: Bantam Books.
Bradshaw has been a leader in finding and nurturing your inner child.

Ferrucci, Piero. (1983) *What We May Be.* Los Angeles, CA: Putnam Publishing Group.
Techniques for psychological and spiritual growth through psycho-synthesis developed by the
Italian psychiatrist Roberto Assagioli.

James, M. & Jongeward. (1978) *Born to Win.* New York: Dutton.
The authors take Eric Berne's concept of ego-states, add some Gestalt theories, and the result is a
very readable book.

Kellogg, T. (1990) *Broken Toys, Broken Dreams: Understanding & Healing Boundaries, Codependence, Compulsion
& Family Relationships.* Amherst, MA: Brat Publishing.

*Paul, M. & Chopich, E. (1990) *Healing Your Aloneness: Finding Love and Wholeness Through Your Inner Child.*
San Francisco, CA: Harper.
Highly recommended as a way of getting acquainted with, and healing your inner child.

Satir, V. (1978) *Your Many Faces: The First Step to Being Loved.* Berkeley, CA: Celestial Arts.
A good book that helps us accept our own uniqueness and to recognize our potential.

*Stone, H. & Stone, S. (1993) *Embracing Our Selves.* San Rafael, CA: New World Library.
This is a helpful book about learning to identify and embrace your many sub-personalities.

Stone, H. & Stone, S. (1989) *Embracing Each Other.* San Rafael, CA: New World Library.
Using the theory of sub-personalities to understand problems in relationships.

Stone, H.& Stone, S. (1993) *Embracing Your Inner Critic.* San Francisco: Harper & Row.
Turning Self-Criticism into a Creative Asset.

Whitfield, C. (1989) *Healing The Child Within.* Deerfield Beach, FL: Health Communications.

Grief

Fintushel, N. & Hillard, N. (1991) *A Grief Out of Season.* New York: Little Brown.
    For adult children whose parents divorce.

Tatelbaum, J. (1984) *The Courage to Grieve: Creative Living, Recovery, & Growth Through Grief.* New York:
    Harper Collins.
    It is okay, even healthy, to grieve.

*Westberg, G. (1962) *Good Grief.* Philadelphia, PA: Fortress Press.
    Small but useful book to help you with grief of all kinds.

Anger

Alberti, R. & Emmons, M. (2001) *Your Perfect Right: Assertiveness and Equality in Your Life and Relationships.*
    Atascadero CA: Impact Publishers.
    Learn to be assertive and minimize the chances of feeling angry.

Frankel, L. (1992). *Women, Anger & Depression: Strategies fore Self-Empowerment.* Deerfield Beach, Florida.
    Health Communications Inc.
    How to become self-empowered instead of depressed.

Leaner, H. G. (1997) *The Dance of Anger.* New York: Harper Collins.
    A careful and compassionate exploration of women's anger.

Mace, David. (1982) *Love and Anger.* Zondervan.
    The grandfather of family therapy shares how to manage anger in a love relationship so that it helps
    both partners to grow.

Smedes, Lewis B. (1996) *Forgive and Forget.* New York: Harper Collins.
    Healing the hurts we don't deserve.

*Warren, N. (1999) *Make Anger Your Ally.* Colorado Springs, CO: Tyndale House Publishers.
    Anger can be a friend and an ally of love.

Self-Worth

Borysenko, J. (1991) *Guilt is the Teacher, Love is the Lesson.* New York: Warner Books.
    If knowledgeable words can help people get the most out of being human, this book is full of them.

Briggs, D.(1975) *Your Child's Self-Esteem.* New York: Doubleday.
    Step by step guidelines for raising responsible, productive, happy children.

Briggs, D. (1986) *Celebrate Your Self: Enhancing Your Own Self-Esteem.* New York: Doubleday.
    Your most important characteristic is how you feel about yourself.

Branden, N. (1985) *Honoring The Self.* Toronto: Bantam Books.
    The psychology of confidence and respect.

Hendricks, G. (1982) *Learning To Love Yourself.* New York: Simon & Schuster.
    A Guide to Becoming Centered.

Hendricks, G. (1990) *Learning To Love Yourself Workbook.* New York: Simon & Schuster.
    Companion to *Learning To Love Yourself* book.

*Newman, M. & Berkowitz, B. (1974) *How to Be Your Own Best Friend.* New York. Random House.
    Simple and easy to read, highly effective in building self-worth. Start with this book first.

Palmer, P. & Froehner, M. (2000) *Teen Esteem: A Self-Direction Manual for Young Adults.* Atascadero, CA: Impact Publishers.

Powell, J. (1976) *Fully Human, Fully Alive.* Allen, TX: Tabor Publications. A new life through a new vision.

Powell, J. (1996) *Why Am I Afraid To Tell You Who l Am?* Allen, TX: Thomas Moore. Insights into personal growth.

Robbins, A. (1992) *Awaken The Giant Within.* New York: Simon & Schuster. How to take control of your mental, emotional, physical & financial destiny.

Satir, V. (1988) *The New Peoplemaking.* Palo Alto, CA: Science & Behavior Books.

Wegsscheider-Cruse, S. (1987) *Learning To Love Yourself: Finding Your Self-Worth.* Deerfield Beech, FL: Health Communications, Inc. Self-worth is a choice, not a birthright.

Books on Family of Origin

*Bloomfield, H. (1996) *Making Peace With Your Parents.* New York: Random House. Explains how to make peace with your internalized parent. An excellent book.

Leman, K. (1998) *The Birth Order Book.* New York: Fleming H. Revell Company. Why Are You The Way You Are?

Toman, W. (1995) *Family Constellation.* New York: Jason Aronson Publishers. A classic dealing with birth order and it's affect upon personality.

Books on Childhood

Abrams, Jeremiah. (1990) *Reclaiming the Inner Child.* Los Angeles, CA: Jeremy P. Tarcher. A very comprehensive and informative reader by the various authors who have written about the inner child.

Erikson, E. (1993) *Childhood and Society.* W.W. Norton & Co. Erikson is noted for his theories on the developmental stages and the development of feelings of trust in the early years of childhood.

Erikson, Erik (1994) *Identity: Youth and Crisis.* W. W. Norton & CO. How children gain an identity in their developmental years.

*Hansen. Paul. (1991) *Survivors & Partners: Healing the Relationships of Sexual Abuse Survivors.* Longmont, CO: Heron Hill Publishing. An excellent book for adult survivors of abuse and their partners.

*Karen, Robert. (*Atlantic Monthly.* February, 1990) "Becoming Attached." A discussion on the research concerning emotional attachment conducted by Dr. Mary Ainsworth who is continuing the work done by John Bowlby. An excellent article!

Liedloff, Jean (1986) *The Continuum Concept.* Reading, MA: Perseus Publishing. Describes the advantages of children emotionally attaching by being continually touched physically the first three years of life.

Palmer, P. & Froehner, M. (2000) *Teen Esteem.* Atascadero, CA: Impact Publishers. A self-direction manual for young adults.

*Paul, M. & Chopich, E. (1990) *Healing Your Aloneness: Finding Love and Wholeness Through Your Inner Child.* San Francisco, CA: Harper & Row.

An excellent book on the inner child healing. Has specific exercises designed to help you access and heal your inner child.

Piaget, J. (1972) *The Psychology of the Child.* Basic Books Inc.
Traces the stages of cognitive development from infancy to adolescence.

White, B. (1995) *The First Three Years of Life (Revised).* Simon & Schuster.
"The most important book on child rearing to be published in a generation."

*Woititz, Janet. (1990) Adult *Children of Alcoholics.* Deerfiel Beach, Fl.: Health Communications, Inc.
Help for children who grew up in dysfunctional families.

Books on Societal Expectations

Ferguson, M. (1980) *Acquarian Conspiracy: Personal and Social Transformation in the 1980s.* Los Angeles, CA: Jeremy P. Tarcher.
An exiting vision of a truly man-made future.

Harmon, Willis. (1990) *Global Mind Change.* Warner Books, Inc..
The change taking place today on the planet is powerful because, "by deliberately changing their internal image of reality, people are changing the world."

Books on Rebellion

*Bach, R. (1973) *Jonathan Livingston Seagull.* New York: Avon.
A poetic description of the rebellion transition process.

*Pirsig, R. (2000) *Zen and Art of Motorcycle Maintenance.* New York: Harper Collins.
A father and son's journey on a motorcyle. It brings about understanding of each other and life.

Books on Transition

Brennan, B. (1987) *Hands of Light.* Toronto: Bantam Books.
A bio-energetics book on the importance of the electromagnetic field around our bodies.

Brennan, B. (1993) *Light Emerging.* New York: Bantam Books.
The Journey of Personal Healing. Filled with wisdom and knowledge that bridges the gap between science and the healing arts.

*Bridges, W. (1980) *Transitions: Making Sense of Life's Changes.* Reading, MA: Addison-Wesley Publishing Co.
Strategies for coping with the difficult, painful and confusing times in our lives.

*Buscaglia, L. (1982) *Living, Loving, and Learning.* New York: Fawcett Columbine.
Once you are involved in the process of becoming, there is no stopping. What a fantastic journey!

*Gawain, S. (2002) *Creative Visualizations.* New York: New World Library.
Visualizing what we can be will help us to become what we are capable of being.

*Gawain, S. (1993) *Living in the Light.* Bantam Doubleday Dell.
This book will help you to learn how to access and trust your intuition.

Gerber, R. (2001) *Vibrational Medicine: New Choices for Healing Ourselves.* Inner Traditions International, Limited.
A physician explains how energetic healing, which may include using the power of the mind, can lead to many new choices in healing yourself

Grof & Grof. (1989) *Spiritual Emergency.* Los Angeles, CA: Jeremy P. Tarcher.
   Excellent for helping understand several different kinds of major transitions.

*Jampolsky, G. (1982) *Love is Letting Go of Fear.* Ten Speed Press.
   To experience love, we must let go of our obsession with the past and with the future.

Jung, C. (1976) *Modern Man In Search of a Soul.* San Diego: Harcourt, Brace, & World.
   Jung connects the fields of psychology and spirituality.

*Keyes, K. (1975) *Handbook to Higher Consciousness.* Coos Bay, OR: Love Line Books.
   A classic on motivating us to pursue higher consciousness.

*Keyes, K. (1981) *Prescriptions for Happiness.* Coos Bay, OR: Love Line Books.
   A simple and easy to read book with good prescriptions for happiness.

*Satir, V. (1976) *Making Contact.* Berkeley, CA: Celestrial Arts.
   Techniques to help you make intimate contacts with others.

*Wanderer, Z. (1987) *Letting Go.* New York: Dell Publishing Company.
   An excellent book to help you disentangle from a former love partner.

Welwood, J. Ed. (1985) *Challenge of the Heart: Love, Sex and Intimacy in Changing Times.* Boston, MA:
   Shambhala Publications.
   This book discusses he challenges of love between men and women. It addresses the difficulties
   people face in relationships today.

Self-Disclosure

*Powell, J. (1996) *Why Am l Afraid to Tell You Who l Am?* Allen, TX: Thomas Moore.
   The divorce process encourages us to become open and vulnerable as part of our healing.

Powell, J. (1995) *Why Am l Afraid to Love ?* Allen, TX: RCL Company.
   How to overcome rejection and indifference.

Satir, V. (1976) *Making Contact.* Berkeley. Berkeley, CA: Celestial Arts.
   A helpful book in learning how to make communicating with another person.

Overcoming Male Roles and Masks

Bly, R. (1992) *Iron John: A Book About Men.* New York: Random House.
   Important, timely, powerful.

Keen, S. (1992) *Fire In The Belly: On Being A Man.* New York: Bantam Books.
   How does one become a real man?

*Goldberg, H. (2000) *The Hazards of Being Male.* New York: Wellness Institute.
   Helps males to acknowledge the many expectations society places upon them.

Goldberg, H. (2001) *The New Male.* New York. Wellness Institute.
   What is it like to be a male in today's society?

Kundtz, D. (1991) *Men And Feelings.* Deerfield Beach, FL: Health Communications, Inc. Understanding the
   Male Experience.

Lee, J. (1989) *The Flying Boy.* Deerfield Beach, FL: Health Communications, Inc.
   "Why Men Run From Relationships."

194

Wetcher, McCaughtry, & Barker. (1991) *Save The Males: Why Men Are Mistreated, Misdiagnosed and Misunderstood.* Washington, DC. The PIA Press.
A quiet but powerful book based upon the male groups held at the Wetcher Clinic.

Overcoming Female Roles and Masks

Austin & Phelps. (2002) *The Assertive Woman,* 4th Edition. Atascadero, CA: Impact Publishers.
Learning to overcome stereotypical female roles by being more assertive.

Bolen, J. (1984) *Goddesses in Every Woman.* New York: Harper. A new psychology of women.

Hayes, C. Anderson, D. Blau, M. (1993) *Our Turn.* New York: Simon & Schuster.
Women who triumph in the face of divorce.

Sanford, L. & Donovan, M. (1985) *Women & Self-Esteem. New* York: Penguin Books.
Understanding and improving the way we think and feel about ourselves.

Schaef-Wilson, A. (1985) *Women's Reality.* New York: Harper Collins.
How women can survive in a male dominated world.

Thoele, S. (2001) *The Courage to Be Yourself.* Red Wheel/Weiser.
A woman's guide to growing beyond emotional dependence.

Love

Hemfelt, R. Minirth, F. Meier, P. (1991) *Love Is A Choice.* Nashville, TN: Thomas Nelson Publisher
Recovery for codependent relationships.

Hendrix, H. (1992) *Keeping The Love You Find.* New York: Pocket Books.
A guide for singles.

James, L. (1994) *How To Really Love The One Your With.* Tulsa, OK: Career Assurance Press.
Affirmative guidelines for a healthy love relationship.

Keyes, K. (1990) *The Power of Unconditional Love.* Coos Bay, OR: Love Line Books.
The master of loving talks about unconditional love.

Powell, J. (1990) *Unconditional Love.* Allen, TX Thomas Moore.
Love without limits.

Ray, S. (1992) *Loving Relationships.* Berkeley, CA: Ten Speed Press.
Based on the spiritual truth that thoughts are creative.

Relationships

*Bloomfield, H.(1996) *Making Peace With Your Parents: The Key to Enriching Your Life and All Your Relationships.* New York: Random House.
An important book which addresses the child and parent in all of us.

Bloomfield, H.(1996) *Making Peace With Yourself: Turning Your Weaknesses Into Strengths.* New York: Ballantine Books
We need to make peace not only with our parents but with ourselves as well.

Driggs, J. & Finn, S. (1991) *Intimacy Between Men.* New York: Penguin Books.
How to find and keep gay love relationships.

*Fisher, B. & Fisher, N. (2000) *Loving Choices.* Atascadero, CA: Impact Publishers.
Awareness plus good communication skills helps us build healthy relationships.

*Hendrix, H. (2001) *Getting the Love You Want.* New York: Henry Holt & Company.
  A good book on specific ways to create healthy relationships.

Katherine, A. (1993) *Boundaries.* New York: Fireside/Parkside. Simon & Schuster.
  Where You End and I Begin.

*Smith, R. & Tessina, T. (2002) *How To Be A Couple & Still Be Free.* North Hollywood, CA: Career Press.
  The title says what the book is all about.

Whitfield, C. (1993) *Boundaries And Relationships.* Deerfield Beach, FL: Health Communications.
  Knowing, Protecting and Enjoying the Self.

Sexuality

Bass, E. & Davis, L. (1994) *The Courage to Heal.* New York: Harper Collins Publishers
  A guide for women survivors of child sexual abuse. Has companion workbook.

Blume, E. (1997) *Secret Survivors.* New York: Ballantine Books.
  Uncovering incest and its after effects in women.

Comfort, A. (1992) *The Joy Of Sex.* New York: Pocket Books.
  Deals with a new and healthy awareness of sexuality.

Ledray, L.(1995) *Recovering From Rape.* New York: Henry Holt & Co.
  Practical advice on overcoming the trauma for survivors, their families, lovers, and friends.

Lew, M. (1990) Victims *No Longer.* New York: Harper Collins Publishers.
  Men recovering from incest and other sexual child abuse.

Russell, D. (1999) *The Secret Trauma.* New York: Basic Books, Inc. Publishers.
  Incest in the lives of girls and women.

Children of Divorce

*Brown, L.& Brown, M. (1988) *Dinosaurs Divorce: A Guide for Changing Families.* Boston, MA: Little Brown & Company.
  A great book on divorce for children eight and under.

Brissett, M. & Burns, R. (1991) *The Adult Child of Divorce.* Nashville, TN: Oliver Nelson.
  How to overcome the effects of your parent's divorce when you were a child.

Lansky, V. (1989) *Vicki Lansky's Divorce Book for Parents.* New York: Book Pedlers
  Helping your children cope with divorce and its aftermath.

*Newman, G. (2003) *101 Ways To Be A Long Distance Super-Dad…or Mom Too!* Saratoga, CA: Blossom Valley Press.
  Some wonderful suggestions on how to be a successful long distance parent.

*Ricci, I. (1997) *Mom's House, Dad's House: A Complete Guide for Parents Who Are Separated, Divorced, orRemarried.* New York: Simon & Schuster
  Very helpful book on visitation and custody issues.

Healing and Healthy Relationships

Frankel, L. (1992) *Women, Anger & Depression: Strategies for Self Empowerment.* Deerfield Beach, Florida.
  Health Communications Inc.
  How to become self empowered instead of depressed.

Rodegast & Stanton. (1989) *Emmanuals Book II: The Choice for Love.* New York. Bantam. Choosing love helps us overcome our fears.

*Hendricks, G. (1982) *Learning to Love Yourself.* New York: Simon & Schuster. Practical exercises to help you learn to love yourself.

Powell, J. (1990) *Unconditional Love.* Allen, TX Thomas Moore Library. Love without limits.

RebuildingBooks
Relationships – Divorce – and Beyond

Loving Choices
An Experience in Growing Relationships (Second Edition)

Bruce Fisher, Ed.D. and Nina Hart
Softcover: $15.95   256 pages   ISBN: 978-1-886230-30-9
Also available: *Loving Choices Workbook* $15.95 128 pages ISBN: 978-0-9607250-4-5

Ever wanted to be better at building or maintaining romantic attachments friendships or family connections? Here's help! *Loving Choices* offers a powerful model for communication with yourself and others. Packed with insights examples and self-help exercises to help you understand yourself better and develop healing and healthy relationships with the significant others in your life.

Rebuilding: **When Your Relationship Ends** (Third Edition)

Bruce Fisher, Ed.D., and Robert E. Alberti, Ph.D.
Softcover: $17.95   304 pages   ISBN: 978-1-886230-69-9

Popular guide to divorce recovery. The "divorce process rebuilding blocks" format offers a nineteen-step process for putting life back together after divorce. Built on decades of research and practice, *Rebuilding* reflects feedback from, and the experiences of hundreds of thousands of divorced men and women. Clearly the most widely used approach to divorce recovery, Fisher's Rebuilding Model has made the divorce process less traumatic, even healthier, for his readers. One million in print!

Also available: *Rebuilding: When Your Relationship Ends Workbook* (Second Edition)
Softcover: $15.95   128 pages   ISBN: 978-1-886230-20-0

Take Control of Your Divorce
Strategies to Stop Fighting & Start Co-Parenting

Judith Margerum, Ph.D., Jerome A. Price, M.A., and James Windell, M.A.
Softcover: $18.95   168 pages   ISBN: 978-1-886230-97-2

This guide will help you save your children — and yourself — from the ravages of anger, hostility, and conflict. Includes strategies to resolve, overlook, or put aside the conflicts with your co-parent and get to the crucial task of being good parents.

Jigsaw Puzzle Family
The Stepkids' Guide to Fitting It Together

Cynthia MacGregor
Softcover: $12.95   120 pages   ISBN: 978-1-886230-63-7

"For all the kids who wonder how the jigsaw puzzle pieces of their newly combined family will ever fit together," MacGregor has created a warm and understanding resource for children of divorce. Helps guide kids through the challenges of dealing with a new stepparent... new rules in the house... new stepbrothers and/or stepsisters... living somewhere new. Dozens of practical and helpful suggestions for making stepfamily life better, lots of reassurance that time will help.

Crazy Love
Dealing With Your Partner's Problem Personality

W. Brad Johnson, Ph.D. and Kelly Murray, Ph.D.
Softcover: $17.95   248 pages   ISBN: 978-1-886230-80-4

Enlightening guide to the odd but common disorders of personality, and insight as to why so many of us are attracted to personality disordered partners. Provides strategies for detecting and avoiding such potential disasters and helps those in committed relationships to make the union more livable.

Ask your local or online bookseller, or write for our free catalog. Prices effective January 2012 and subject to change without notice.

Impact Publishers®

POST OFFICE BOX 6016, ATASCADERO, CALIFORNIA 93423-6016
Orders: 800-246-7228 • E-mail info@impactpublishers.com • Web at www.impactpublishers.com

Since 1970 — Psychology you can use, from professionals you can trust.

Parenting After Divorce
Resolving Conflicts and Meeting Your Children's Needs (Second Edition)
Philip M. Stahl, Ph.D.
Softcover: $17.95   208 pages   ISBN: 978-1-886230-84-2

"Your divorce doesn't have to damage your children," Stahl assures. This realistic perspective featuring knowledgeable advice from an expert custody evaluator, is packed with real-world examples, avoids idealistic assumptions, and offers practical help for divorcing parents, custody evaluators, family court counselors, marriage and family therapists, and others interested in the well-being of children.

After Your Divorce
Creating the Good Life on Your Own
Cynthia MacGregor and Robert E. Alberti, Ph.D.
Softcover: $16.95   256 pages   ISBN: 978-1-886230-77-4

It's over. The divorce is final, he's out of your house and – mostly – out of your life. Now what? Are you ready to get on with your life? Do you have dreams, plans, skills, energy for what comes next? And will you be *making* it happen, or *letting* it happen? This friendly, straightforward manual of advice and suggestions assumes every woman is capable of handling life on her own. Provides help for emotional recovery, practical matters, dealing with your ex, helping your children to cope, and much more.

Your Child's Divorce
What to Expect — What You Can Do
Marsha Temlock, M.A.
Softcover: $17.95   ISBN: 978-1-886230-66-8   272 pages

A friendly guidebook packed with helpful information and suggestions from parents of divorcees who've "been there." Helps readers stay grounded through the emotional upheavals they'll share with their children and grandchildren. This practical manual puts an arm around the shoulder of parents of divorcing adults and supports them through the difficult days of the divorce process and its aftermath.

The Divorce Helpbook for Teens
Cynthia MacGregor
Softcover: $13.95 144 pages   ISBN: 978-1-886230-57-6

A special book for teenagers in divorced and divorcing families. This friendly guide offers a helping hand to teens struggling to answer the tough questions when their parents divorce: Why do parents get divorced? How will the divorce change our lives? Who can I talk to about my problems? What's going to happen next? How do you say "no" to parents who want you to carry messages to, or spy on, the other parent? What is there to talk about when you visit a parent who's moved away?

The Divorce Helpbook for Kids
Cynthia MacGregor
Softcover: $13.95 144 pages   ISBN: 978-1-886230-39-2

Down-to-earth guide addressing many topics troubling kids when their parents divorce: reasons parents get divorced, ways the divorce will change kids' lives; kids' feelings about divorce, things kids can do to help themselves feel better (and reassurance that they are not to blame); who to talk to; and what's likely to happen next; life after divorce, visitation, custody, straddling two households, and making it all work.

Ask your local or online bookseller, or write for our free catalog. Prices effective January 2012 and subject to change without notice.

Impact Publishers®
POST OFFICE BOX 6016, ATASCADERO, CALIFORNIA 93423-6016
Orders: 800-246-7228 • E-mail info@impactpublishers.com • Web at www.impactpublishers.com

Since 1970 — Psychology you can use, from professionals you can trust.